2008 SUPPLEMENT TO
CRIMINAL PROCEDURE

CASES, PROBLEMS & EXERCISES
Third Edition

By

Russell L. Weaver
Professor of Law & Distinguished University Scholar
University of Louisville, Louis D. Brandeis School of Law

Leslie W. Abramson
Frost Brown Todd Professor of Law
University of Louisville, Louis D. Brandeis School of Law

Ronald Bacigal
Professor of Law
University of Richmond, T.C. Williams School of Law

John M. Burkoff
Professor of Law
University of Pittsburgh School of Law

Catherine Hancock
Geoffrey C. Bible & Murray H. Bring Professor of Constitutional Law
Tulane University School of Law

Donald E. Lively
Vice President for Academic Programs, Infilaw

Janet C. Hoeffel
Associate Professor of Law
Tulane University School of Law

AMERICAN CASEBOOK SERIES®

THOMSON
™
WEST

Mat #40709800

American Casebook Series and West Group are trademarks registered in the U.S. Patent and Trademark Office.

© West, a Thomson business, 2001–2007
© 2008 Thomson/West
      610 Opperman Drive
      St. Paul, MN 55123
      1–800–313–9378

Printed in the United States of America

ISBN: 978–0–314–19063–5

TEXT IS PRINTED ON 10% POST CONSUMER RECYCLED PAPER

Table of Contents

Page

TABLE OF CASES -- v

PART I. INTRODUCTION

Chapter

2. **Fourteenth Amendment Due Process** ---------------------------- 2
   Whorton v. Bockting -- 2

3. **The Right to Counsel** -- 8
   Indiana v. Edwards --- 9
   Wright v. Van Patten -- 20

PART II. POLICE PRACTICES

4. **Arrest, Search & Seizure** --------------------------------------- **26**
   Scott v. Harris --- 29
   Virginia v. Moore --- 33
   Brendlin v. California --- 41
   Los Angeles County v. Rettele ------------------------------------ 46

6. **Police Interrogations & Confessions** ----------------------- **53**
9. **The Exclusionary Rule** --------------------------------------- **55**

PART III. THE ADVERSARY SYSTEM

13. **Preliminary Proceedings** ---------------------------------- **60**
14. **Grand Juries** --- **61**
19. **Jury Trials** --- **62**
21. **Sentencing** -- **63**
    Kennedy v. Louisiana --- 63

23. **Appeals** -- **83**
24. **Collateral Remedies** -------------------------------------- **84**
    Carey v. Musladin --- 85

Appendix A. Selected Provisions of the United States Constitution 89
Appendix B. Selected Federal Statutory Provisions ----------------- 93
Appendix C. Federal Rules of Criminal Procedure for the United
             States District Courts ------------------------------------ 165
Appendix D. Pending Amendments to Federal Rules of Criminal
             Procedure -- 230
Appendix E. Proposed Amendments to the Federal Rules of Crimi-
             nal Procedure -- 235

*

iii

Table of Cases

The principal cases are in bold type. Cases cited or discussed in the text are roman type. References are to pages. Cases cited in principal cases and within other quoted materials are not included.

Abdul–Kabir v. Quarterman, ___ U.S. ___, 127 S.Ct. 1654, 167 L.Ed.2d 585 (2007), 88

Alverez–Tejeda, United States v., 491 F.3d 1013 (9th Cir.2007), 39

Arnold, United States v., 523 F.3d 941 (9th Cir.2008), 50

Athan, State v., 160 Wash.2d 354, 158 P.3d 27 (Wash.2007), 27

Boumediene v. Bush, ___ U.S. ___, 128 S.Ct. 2229 (2008), 84

Bowles v. Russell, ___ U.S. ___, 127 S.Ct. 2360, 168 L.Ed.2d 96 (2007), 83

Brendlin v. California, ___ U.S. ___, 127 S.Ct. 2400, 168 L.Ed.2d 132 (2007), **41**

Brewer v. Quarterman, ___ U.S. ___, 127 S.Ct. 1706, 167 L.Ed.2d 622 (2007), 88

Brewer v. Williams, 430 U.S. 387, 97 S.Ct. 1232, 51 L.Ed.2d 424 (1977), 8

Bryant, State v., 2008 WL 820197 (Vt. 2008), 27

Burton v. Stewart, 549 U.S. 147, 127 S.Ct. 793, 166 L.Ed.2d 628 (2007), 88

Carey v. Musladin, 549 U.S. 70, 127 S.Ct. 649, 166 L.Ed.2d 482 (2006), **85**

Center for Bio–Ethical Reform, Inc. v. City of Springboro, 477 F.3d 807 (6th Cir. 2007), 52

Crapser, United States v., 472 F.3d 1141 (9th Cir.2007), 40

Cutler, United States v., 520 F.3d 136 (2nd Cir.2008), 82

Diemler, United States v., 498 F.2d 1070 (5th Cir.1974), 40

Estep v. Dallas County, Tex., 310 F.3d 353 (5th Cir.2002), 40

Fenner v. State, 381 Md. 1, 846 A.2d 1020 (Md.2004), 60

Fisher, State v., 283 Kan. 272, 154 P.3d 455 (Kan.2007), 28

Frazier, People v., 2008 WL 782593 (Mich. App.2008), 19

Fry v. Pliler, ___ U.S. ___, 127 S.Ct. 2321, 168 L.Ed.2d 16 (2007), 83

Gall v. United States, ___ U.S. ___, 128 S.Ct. 586, 169 L.Ed.2d 445 (2007), 81

Garry, People v., 67 Cal.Rptr.3d 849 (Cal. App. 1 Dist.2007), 41

Gomez, People v., 805 N.Y.S.2d 24, 838 N.E.2d 1271 (N.Y.2005), 39

Grigg, United States v., 498 F.3d 1070 (9th Cir.2007), 40

Harris, People v., 228 Ill.2d 222, 319 Ill.Dec. 823, 886 N.E.2d 947 (Ill.2008), 46

Humphress v. United States, 398 F.3d 855 (6th Cir.2005), 81

Indiana v. Edwards, ___ U.S. ___, 128 S.Ct. 2379 (2008), **9**

Jamison, United States v., 509 F.3d 623 (4th Cir.2007), 53

Johnson, State v., 68 N.J. 349, 346 A.2d 66 (N.J.1975), 39

Johnston v. Tampa Sports Authority, 442 F.Supp.2d 1257 (M.D.Fla.2006), 51

Keenom v. State, 349 Ark. 381, 80 S.W.3d 743 (Ark.2002), 28

Kennedy v. Louisiana, ___ U.S. ___, 128 S.Ct. 2641 (2008), **63**

Kimbrough v. United States, ___ U.S. ___, 128 S.Ct. 558, 169 L.Ed.2d 481 (2007), 81

Lafferty, United States v., 503 F.3d 293 (3rd Cir.2007), 53

Lanier v. City of Woodburn, 518 F.3d 1147 (9th Cir.2008), 52

Lawrence v. Florida, ___ U.S. ___, 127 S.Ct. 1079, 166 L.Ed.2d 924 (2007), 84

Los Angeles County, California v. Rettele, ___ U.S. ___, 127 S.Ct. 1989, 167 L.Ed.2d 974 (2007), 26, **46**

Louthan, State v., 275 Neb. 101, 744 N.W.2d 454 (Neb.2008), 46

MacWade v. Kelly, 460 F.3d 260 (2nd Cir. 2006), 51
Marchwinski v. Howard, 309 F.3d 330 (6th Cir.2002), 52
McClish v. Nugent, 483 F.3d 1231 (11th Cir.2007), 28, 29
McGinnis, United States v., 247 Fed.Appx. 589 (6th Cir.2007), 51
McGrane, State v., 733 N.W.2d 671 (Iowa 2007), 50
McNeil v. Wisconsin, 501 U.S. 171, 111 S.Ct. 2204, 115 L.Ed.2d 158 (1991), 8
Mendez, United States v., 467 F.3d 1162 (9th Cir.2006), 46
Michigan v. Jackson, 475 U.S. 625, 106 S.Ct. 1404, 89 L.Ed.2d 631 (1986), 8
Muehler v. Mena, 544 U.S. 93, 125 S.Ct. 1465, 161 L.Ed.2d 299 (2005), 46
Murphy v. Commonwealth, 37 Va.App. 556, 559 S.E.2d 890 (Va.App.2002), 28

Never Misses A Shot v. United States, 413 F.3d 781 (8th Cir.2005), 81
Nicholas v. Goord, 430 F.3d 652 (2nd Cir. 2005), 27

Padilla v. United States, 416 F.3d 424 (5th Cir.2005), 81
Penry v. Lynaugh, 492 U.S. 302, 109 S.Ct. 2934, 106 L.Ed.2d 256 (1989), 88
People v. _____ (see opposing party)
Phaneuf v. Fraikin, 448 F.3d 591 (2nd Cir. 2006), 51

Rincon, State v., 122 Nev. 1170, 147 P.3d 233 (Nev.2006), 50
Rita v. United States, ___ U.S. ___, 127 S.Ct. 2456, 168 L.Ed.2d 203 (2007), 81, 82
Rothgery v. Gillespie County, Tex., ___ U.S. ___, 128 S.Ct. 2578 (2008), 8

Sanchez–Llamas v. Oregon, 548 U.S. 331, 126 S.Ct. 2669, 165 L.Ed.2d 557 (2006), 53, 55
Santana, United States v., 427 U.S. 38, 96 S.Ct. 2406, 49 L.Ed.2d 300 (1976), 28
Schriro v. Landrigan, ___ U.S. ___, 127 S.Ct. 1933, 167 L.Ed.2d 836 (2007), 19, 87
Scott v. Harris, ___ U.S. ___, 127 S.Ct. 1769, 167 L.Ed.2d 686 (2007), **29**
Snyder v. Louisiana, ___ U.S. ___, 128 S.Ct. 1203, 170 L.Ed.2d 175 (2008), 62
State v. _____ (see opposing party)
Stewart, United States v., 473 F.3d 1265 (10th Cir.2007), 46

Turvin, United States v., 517 F.3d 1097 (9th Cir.2008), 46

United States v. _____ (see opposing party)
Uttecht v. Brown, ___ U.S. ___, 127 S.Ct. 2218, 167 L.Ed.2d 1014 (2007), 62, 87

Virginia v. Moore, ___ U.S. ___, 128 S.Ct. 1598, 170 L.Ed.2d 559 (2008), **33**

Warshak v. United States, 490 F.3d 455 (6th Cir.2007), 27
Washington, United States v., 490 F.3d 765 (9th Cir.2007), 41
Washington, United States v., 387 F.3d 1060 (9th Cir.2004), 40
Whorton v. Bockting, ___ U.S. ___, 127 S.Ct. 1173, 167 L.Ed.2d 1 (2007), **2**
Wilson v. United States, 414 F.3d 829 (7th Cir.2005), 81
Wright v. Van Patten, ___ U.S. ___, 128 S.Ct. 743, 169 L.Ed.2d 583 (2008), **20**

Ziegler, United States v., 474 F.3d 1184 (9th Cir.2007), 40

2008 SUPPLEMENT TO
CRIMINAL PROCEDURE

CASES, PROBLEMS & EXERCISES

Third Edition

*

Part I

INTRODUCTION

Chapter 2

FOURTEENTH AMENDMENT
DUE PROCESS

On p. 25, at the end of the material, add the following new case:

WHORTON v. BOCKTING

127 S.Ct. 1173 (2007).

Justice Alito delivered the opinion of the Court.

This case presents the question whether, under the rules set out in *Teague v. Lane,* 489 U.S. 288 (1989), our decision in *Crawford v. Washington,* 541 U.S. 36 (2004), is retroactive to cases already final on direct review. We hold that it is not.

Respondent Marvin Bockting lived in Las Vegas, Nevada, with his wife, Laura Bockting, their 3–year-old daughter Honesty, and Laura's 6–year-old daughter from a previous relationship, Autumn. One night, while respondent was at work, Autumn awoke from a dream crying, but she refused to tell her mother what was wrong, explaining: " '[D]addy said you would make him leave and that he would beat my butt if I told you.' " After her mother reassured her, Autumn said that respondent had frequently forced her to engage in numerous and varied sexual acts with him.

The next day, Laura Bockting confronted respondent and asked him to leave the house. He did so but denied any wrongdoing. Two days later, Laura called a rape crisis hotline and brought Autumn to the hospital for an examination. At the hospital, Detective Charles Zinovitch from the Las Vegas Metropolitan Police Department Sexual Assault Unit attempted to interview Autumn but found her too distressed to discuss the assaults. Detective Zinovitch then ordered a rape examination, which revealed strong physical evidence of sexual assaults.

Two days later, Detective Zinovitch interviewed Autumn in the presence of her mother, and at that time, Autumn provided a detailed description of acts of sexual assault carried out by respondent; Autumn also demonstrated those acts using anatomically correct dolls. Respon-

2

dent was then arrested, and a state grand jury indicted him on four counts of sexual assault on a minor under 14 years of age.

At respondent's preliminary hearing, Autumn testified that she understood the difference between a truth and a lie, but she became upset when asked about the assaults. Although she initially agreed that respondent had touched her in a way that "[she] didn't think he was supposed to touch [her]," she later stated that she could not remember how respondent had touched her or what she had told her mother or the detective. The trial court, however, found the testimony of Laura Bockting and Detective Zinovitch to be sufficient to hold respondent for trial.

At trial, the court held a hearing outside the presence of the jury to determine whether Autumn could testify. After it became apparent that Autumn was too distressed to be sworn in, the State moved under Nev.Rev.Stat. § 51.385 (2003) to allow Laura Bockting and Detective Zinovitch to recount Autumn's statements regarding the sexual assaults. Under the Nevada statute, out-of-court statements made by a child under 10 years of age describing acts of sexual assault or physical abuse of the child may be admitted if the court finds that the child is unavailable or unable to testify and that "the time, content and circumstances of the statement provide sufficient circumstantial guarantees of trustworthiness." Over defense counsel's objection that admission of this testimony would violate the Confrontation Clause, the trial court found sufficient evidence of reliability to satisfy § 51.385.

As a result of this ruling, Laura Bockting and Detective Zinovitch were permitted at trial to recount Autumn's out-of-court statements about the assaults. Laura Bockting also testified that respondent was the only male who had had the opportunity to assault Autumn. In addition, the prosecution introduced evidence regarding Autumn's medical exam. Respondent testified in his own defense and denied the assaults, and the defense brought out the fact that Autumn, unlike many children her age, had acquired some knowledge about sexual acts, since she had seen respondent and her mother engaging in sexual intercourse and had become familiar with sexual terms. The jury found respondent guilty of three counts of sexual assault on a minor under the age of 14, and the trial court imposed two consecutive life sentences and another concurrent life sentence.

Respondent took an appeal to the Nevada Supreme Court, which handed down its final decision in 1993, more than a decade before *Crawford*. In analyzing respondent's contention that the admission of Autumn's out-of-court statements had violated his Confrontation Clause rights, the Nevada Supreme Court looked to *Ohio v. Roberts,* 448 U.S. 56 (1980), which was then the governing precedent of this Court. *Roberts* had held that the Confrontation Clause permitted the admission of a hearsay statement made by a declarant who was unavailable to testify if the statement bore sufficient indicia of reliability, either because the statement fell within a firmly rooted hearsay exception or because there were "particularized guarantees of trustworthiness" relating to the statement in question. Applying *Roberts,* the Nevada Supreme Court held that the admission of Autumn's statements was constitutional because the circumstances surrounding the making of the statements provided particularized guarantees of trustworthiness. The Court cited the "natural spontaneity" of Autumn's initial statements to her mother, her reiteration of the same account to Detective Zinovitch several days later, her use of anatomically correct dolls to demonstrate the assaults, and her detailed descriptions of sexual acts with which a 6–year-old would generally not be familiar.

Respondent then filed a petition for a writ of habeas corpus with the United States District Court for the District of Nevada, arguing that the Nevada Supreme Court's decision violated his Confrontation Clause rights. The District Court denied the petition, holding that respondent was not entitled to relief under the habeas statute, because the Nevada Supreme Court's decision was not "contrary to" and did not "involv[e] an unreasonable application of, clearly established Federal law, as determined by the Supreme Court of the United States." Respondent then appealed to the United States Court of Appeals for the Ninth Circuit.

While this appeal was pending, we issued our opinion in *Crawford,* in which we overruled *Roberts* and held that "[t]estimonial statements of witnesses absent from trial" are admissible "only where the declarant is unavailable, and only where the defendant has had a prior opportunity to cross-examine [the witness]." We noted that the outcome in *Roberts*-as well as the outcome in all similar cases decided by this Court-was consistent with the rule announced in *Crawford,* but we concluded that the interpretation of the Confrontation Clause set out in *Roberts* was unsound in several respects. First, we observed that *Roberts* potentially excluded too much testimony because it imposed Confrontation Clause restrictions on nontestimonial hearsay not governed by that Clause. At the same time, we noted, the *Roberts* test was too "malleable" in permitting the admission of *ex parte* testimonial statements. . . .

On appeal from the denial of his petition for writ of habeas corpus, respondent contended that if the rule in *Crawford* had been applied to his case, Autumn's out-of-court statements could not have been admitted into evidence and the jury would not have convicted him. Respondent further argued that *Crawford* should have been applied to his case because the *Crawford* rule was either (1) an old rule in existence at the time of his conviction or (2) a " 'watershed' " rule that implicated "the fundamental fairness and accuracy of the criminal proceeding." *Saffle v. Parks,* 494 U.S. 484, 495 (1990) (quoting *Teague,* 489 U.S., at 311 (plurality opinion)).

A divided panel of the Ninth Circuit reversed the District Court, holding that *Crawford* applies retroactively to cases on collateral review. . . . The panel's decision . . . conflicts with the decision of every other Court of Appeals and State Supreme Court that has addressed this issue. We granted certiorari to resolve this conflict.

In *Teague* and subsequent cases, we have laid out the framework to be used in determining whether a rule announced in one of our opinions should be applied retroactively to judgments in criminal cases that are already final on direct review. Under the *Teague* framework, an old rule applies both on direct and collateral review, but a new rule is generally applicable only to cases that are still on direct review. A new rule applies retroactively in a collateral proceeding only if (1) the rule is substantive or (2) the rule is a " 'watershed rul[e] of criminal procedure' implicating the fundamental fairness and accuracy of the criminal proceeding." *Saffle, supra,* at 495 (quoting *Teague, supra,* at 311 (plurality opinion)).

In this case, it is undisputed that respondent's conviction became final on direct appeal well before *Crawford* was decided. We therefore turn to the question whether *Crawford* applied an old rule or announced a new one. A new rule is defined as "a rule that [was] not *'dictated* by precedent existing at the time the defendant's conviction became final.' " *Saffle, supra,* at 488 (quoting *Teague, supra,* at 301 (plurality opinion)) (emphasis in original).

Applying this definition, it is clear that *Crawford* announced a new rule. The *Crawford* rule was not "dictated" by prior precedent. Quite the opposite is true: The *Crawford* rule is flatly inconsistent with the prior governing precedent, *Roberts,* which *Crawford* overruled. "The explicit overruling of an earlier holding no doubt creates a new rule." *Saffle, supra,* at 488. [T]he *Crawford* Court was quick to note that "the rationales" of our prior decisions had been inconsistent with the *Crawford* rule. " The 'new rule' principle . . . validates reasonable, good-faith interpretations of existing precedents made by state courts even though they are shown to be contrary to later decisions.' " *Lockhart v. Fretwell,* 506 U.S. 364 (1993) (quoting *Butler v. McKellar,* 494 U.S. 407 (1990)). And it is stating the obvious to say that, prior to *Crawford,* "reasonable jurists" could have reached the conclusion that the *Roberts* rule was the rule that governed the admission of hearsay statements made by an unavailable declarant.

Because the *Crawford* rule was not dictated by the governing precedent existing at the time when respondent's conviction became final, the *Crawford* rule is a new rule.

Because *Crawford* announced a "new rule" and because it is clear and undisputed that the rule is procedural and not substantive, that rule cannot be applied in this collateral attack on respondent's conviction unless it is a " 'watershed rul[e] of criminal procedure' implicating the fundamental fairness and accuracy of the criminal proceeding." *Saffle,* 494 U.S., at 495 (quoting *Teague,* 489 U.S., at 311 (plurality opinion)). This exception is "extremely narrow." We have observed that it is " 'unlikely' "that any such rules " 'ha[ve] yet to emerge,' " *ibid.* (quoting *Tyler v. Cain,* 533 U.S. 656 (2001)). And in the years since *Teague,* we have rejected every claim that a new rule satisfied the requirements for watershed status. See, *e.g., Summerlin, supra* (rejecting retroactivity for *Ring v. Arizona,* 536 U.S. 584 (2002)); *Beard v. Banks,* 542 U.S. 406

(2004) (rejecting retroactivity for *Mills v. Maryland,* 486 U.S. 367 (1988)); *O'Dell, supra* (rejecting retroactivity for *Simmons v. South Carolina,* 512 U.S. 154 (1994)); *Gilmore v. Taylor,* 508 U.S. 333 (1993) (rejecting retroactivity for a new rule relating to jury instructions on homicide); *Sawyer v. Smith,* 497 U.S. 227 (1990) (rejecting retroactivity for *Caldwell v. Mississippi,* 472 U.S. 320 (1985)).

In order to qualify as watershed, a new rule must meet two requirements. First, the rule must be necessary to prevent "an 'impermissibly large risk' " of an inaccurate conviction. *Summerlin, supra,* at 356. Second, the rule must "alter our understanding of the bedrock procedural elements essential to the fairness of a proceeding." *Ibid.* (internal quotation marks and emphasis omitted). We consider each of these requirements in turn.

The *Crawford* rule does not satisfy the first requirement relating to an impermissibly large risk of an inaccurate conviction. To be sure, the *Crawford* rule reflects the Framers' preferred mechanism (cross-examination) for ensuring that inaccurate out-of-court testimonial statements are not used to convict an accused. But in order for a new rule to meet the accuracy requirement at issue here, "[i]t is . . . not enough . . . to say that [the] rule is aimed at improving the accuracy of trial," *Sawyer,* 497 U.S., at 242 or that the rule "is directed toward the enhancement of reliability and accuracy in some sense." Instead, the question is whether the new rule remedied "an 'impermissibly large risk' " of an inaccurate conviction.

Guidance in answering this question is provided by *Gideon v. Wainwright,* 372 U.S. 335 (1963), to which we have repeatedly referred in discussing the meaning of the *Teague* exception at issue here. In *Gideon,* the only case that we have identified as qualifying under this exception, the Court held that counsel must be appointed for any indigent defendant charged with a felony. When a defendant who wishes to be represented by counsel is denied representation, *Gideon* held, the risk of an unreliable verdict is intolerably high. See *Mickens v. Taylor,* 535 U.S. 162 (2002). The new rule announced in *Gideon* eliminated this risk.

The *Crawford* rule is in no way comparable to the *Gideon* rule. The *Crawford* rule is much more limited in scope, and the relationship of that rule to the accuracy of the factfinding process is far less direct and profound. *Crawford* overruled *Roberts* because *Roberts* was inconsistent with the original understanding of the meaning of the Confrontation Clause, not because the Court reached the conclusion that the overall effect of the *Crawford* rule would be to improve the accuracy of fact finding in criminal trials. Indeed, in *Crawford* we recognized that even under the *Roberts* rule, this Court had never specifically approved the introduction of testimonial hearsay statements. Accordingly, it is not surprising that the overall effect of *Crawford* with regard to the accuracy of fact-finding in criminal cases is not easy to assess.

With respect to *testimonial* out-of-court statements, *Crawford* is more restrictive than was *Roberts,* and this may improve the accuracy of fact-finding in some criminal cases. Specifically, under *Roberts,* there may have been cases in which courts erroneously determined that testimonial statements were reliable. But whatever improvement in reliability *Crawford* produced in this respect must be considered together with *Crawford's* elimination of Confrontation Clause protection against the admission of unreliable out-of-court nontestimonial statements. Under *Roberts,* an out-of-court nontestimonial statement not subject to prior cross-examination could not be admitted without a judicial determination regarding reliability. Under *Crawford,* on the other hand, the Confrontation Clause has no application to such statements and therefore permits their admission even if they lack indicia of reliability.

It is thus unclear whether *Crawford,* on the whole, decreased or increased the number of unreliable out-of-court statements that may be admitted in criminal trials. But the question here is not whether *Crawford* resulted in some net improvement in the accuracy of fact finding in criminal cases. Rather, "the question is whether testimony admissible under *Roberts* is so much more unreliable than that admissible under *Crawford* that the *Crawford* rule is 'one without which the likelihood of an accurate conviction is *seriously* diminished.'" *Crawford* did not effect a change of this magnitude.

The *Crawford* rule also did not "alter our understanding of the *bedrock procedural elements* essential to the fairness of a proceeding." Contrary to the suggestion of the Court of Appeals, this requirement cannot be met simply by showing that a new procedural rule is *based on* a "bedrock" right. We have frequently held that the *Teague* bar to retroactivity applies to new rules that are based on "bedrock" constitutional rights. Similarly, "[t]hat a new procedural rule is 'fundamental' in some abstract sense is not enough." *Summerlin,* 542 U.S., at 352.

Instead, in order to meet this requirement, a new rule must itself constitute a previously unrecognized bedrock procedural element that is essential to the fairness of a proceeding.... In this case, it is apparent that the rule announced in *Crawford,* while certainly important, is not in the same category with *Gideon. Gideon* effected a profound and " 'sweeping' " change. The *Crawford* rule simply lacks the "primacy" and "centrality" of the *Gideon* rule, and does not qualify as a rule that "alter[ed] our understanding of the bedrock procedural elements essential to the fairness of a proceeding," *Sawyer,* 497 U.S., at 242.

In sum, we hold that *Crawford* announced a "new rule" of criminal procedure and that this rule does not fall within the *Teague* exception for watershed rules. We therefore reverse the judgment of the Court of Appeals and remand the case for further proceedings consistent with this opinion.

It is so ordered.

Chapter 3

THE RIGHT TO COUNSEL

A. GENERALLY

On p. 37, add the following at the end of note 4:

Most recently, in *Rothgery v. Gillespie County*, 128 S.Ct. 2578 (2008), the Court relied on *Brewer v. Williams*, 430 U.S. 387 (1977) and *Michigan v. Jackson*, 475 U.S. 625 (1986) in holding that the Sixth Amendment right to counsel attaches at a defendant's "first appearance before a judicial officer at which a defendant is told of the formal accusation against him and restrictions are imposed on his liberty." The case involved Rothgery who had never been convicted of a felony (although he had been charged), but who was arrested for being a felon in possession of a firearm based on erroneous police records. After concluding that probable cause existed, Rothgery was required to post a bond to obtain release. Rothgery could not afford a lawyer, and his requests for appointed counsel were ignored. He was then indicted, and was jailed when he was unable to post bail. When counsel was finally appointed (six months after the first hearing), Rothgery was released on bail and the charges were ultimately dismissed. Rothgery then filed suit under 42 U.S.C. § 1983, claiming denial of his Sixth Amendment right to counsel.

Relying on *McNeil v. Wisconsin*, 501 U.S. 171, 175 (1991), the Court held that the Sixth Amendment right to counsel attaches when a prosecution is "commenced." The Court reiterated that commencement occurs with "the initiation of adversary judicial criminal proceedings-whether by way of formal charge, preliminary hearing, indictment, information, or arraignment." The Court added that the focus is on whether government has "committed itself to prosecute," whether "the adverse positions of government and defendant have solidified," and whether the accused "finds himself faced with the prosecutorial forces of organized society, and immersed in the intricacies of substantive and procedural criminal law." The Court held that the prosecution had commenced even though the Texas hearing did not involve a prosecutor.

C. INEFFECTIVE ASSISTANCE OF COUNSEL

On p. 47, add the following at the end of the note, before the problems:

INDIANA v. EDWARDS

128 S.Ct. 2379 (2008).

JUSTICE BREYER delivered the opinion of the Court.

This case focuses upon a criminal defendant whom a state court found mentally competent to stand trial if represented by counsel but not mentally competent to conduct that trial himself. We must decide whether in these circumstances the Constitution forbids a State from insisting that the defendant proceed to trial with counsel, the State thereby denying the defendant the right to represent himself. See U.S. Const., Amdt. 6; *Faretta v. California,* 422 U.S. 806 (1975). We conclude that the Constitution does not forbid a State so to insist.

I

In July 1999 Ahmad Edwards, the respondent, tried to steal a pair of shoes from an Indiana department store. After he was discovered, he drew a gun, fired at a store security officer, and wounded a bystander. He was caught and then charged with attempted murder, battery with a deadly weapon, criminal recklessness, and theft. His mental condition subsequently became the subject of three competency proceedings and two self-representation requests, mostly before the same trial judge:

1. *First Competency Hearing: August 2000.* Five months after Edwards' arrest, his court-appointed counsel asked for a psychiatric evaluation. After hearing psychiatrist and neuropsychologist witnesses (in February 2000 and again in August 2000), the court found Edwards incompetent to stand trial, and committed him to Logansport State Hospital for evaluation and treatment.

2. *Second Competency Hearing: March 2002.* Seven months after his commitment, doctors found that Edwards' condition had improved to the point where he could stand trial. Several months later, however, but still before trial, Edwards' counsel asked for another psychiatric evaluation. In March 2002, the judge held a competency hearing, considered additional psychiatric evidence, and (in April) found that Edwards, while "suffer[ing] from mental illness," was "competent to assist his attorneys in his defense and stand trial for the charged crimes."

3. *Third Competency Hearing: April 2003.* Seven months later but still before trial, Edwards' counsel sought yet another psychiatric evaluation of his client. And, in April 2003, the court held yet another competency hearing. Edwards' counsel presented further psychiatric and neuropsychological evidence showing that Edwards was suffering from serious thinking difficulties and delusions. A testifying psychiatrist reported that Edwards could understand the

charges against him, but he was "unable to cooperate with his attorney in his defense because of his schizophrenic illness"; "[h]is delusions and his marked difficulties in thinking make it impossible for him to cooperate with his attorney." In November 2003, the court concluded that Edwards was not then competent to stand trial and ordered his recommitment to the state hospital.

4. *First Self–Representation Request and First Trial: June 2005.* About eight months after his commitment, the hospital reported that Edwards' condition had again improved to the point that he had again become competent to stand trial. And almost one year after that Edwards' trial began. Just before trial, Edwards asked to represent himself. He also asked for a continuance, which, he said, he needed in order to proceed *pro se.* The court refused the continuance. Edwards then proceeded to trial represented by counsel. The jury convicted him of criminal recklessness and theft but failed to reach a verdict on the charges of attempted murder and battery.

5. *Second Self–Representation Request and Second Trial: December 2005.* The State decided to retry Edwards on the attempted murder and battery charges. Just before the retrial, Edwards again asked the court to permit him to represent himself. Referring to the lengthy record of psychiatric reports, the trial court noted that Edwards still suffered from schizophrenia and concluded that "[w]ith these findings, he's competent to stand trial but I'm not going to find he's competent to defend himself." The court denied Edwards' self-representation request. Edwards was represented by appointed counsel at his retrial. The jury convicted Edwards on both of the remaining counts.

Edwards subsequently appealed to Indiana's intermediate appellate court. He argued that the trial court's refusal to permit him to represent himself at his retrial deprived him of his constitutional right of self-representation. U.S. Const., Amdt. 6. The court agreed and ordered a new trial. The matter then went to the Indiana Supreme Court [which held that] this Court's precedents, namely, *Faretta* and *Godinez v. Moran,* 509 U.S. 389 (1993), required the State to allow Edwards to represent himself. At Indiana's request, we agreed to consider whether the Constitution required the trial court to allow Edwards to represent himself at trial.

II

Our examination of this Court's precedents convinces us that those precedents frame the question presented, but they do not answer it. The two cases that set forth the Constitution's mental competence standard, *Dusky v. United States,* 362 U.S. 402 (1960)*(per curiam),* and *Drope v. Missouri,* 420 U.S. 162 (1975), specify that the Constitution does not permit trial of an individual who lacks "mental competency." *Dusky* defines the competency standard as including both (1) "whether" the defendant has "a rational as well as factual understanding of the proceedings against him" and (2) whether the defendant "has sufficient present ability *to consult with his lawyer* with a reasonable degree of rational understanding." *Drope* repeats that standard, stating that it "has long been accepted that a person whose mental condition is such that he lacks the capacity to understand the nature and object of the proceedings against him, *to consult with counsel, and to assist in preparing his defense* may not be subjected to a trial." Neither case considered the mental competency issue presented here, namely, the relation of the mental competence standard to the right of self-representation.

The Court's foundational "self-representation" case, *Faretta,* held that the Sixth and Fourteenth Amendments include a "constitutional right to proceed *without* counsel when" a criminal defendant "voluntarily and intelligently elects to do so." The Court implied that right from: (1) a "nearly universal conviction," made manifest in state law, that "forcing a lawyer upon an unwilling defendant is contrary to his basic right to defend himself if he truly wants to do so," Sixth Amendment language granting rights to the "accused;" (3) Sixth Amendment structure indicating that the rights it sets forth, related to the "fair administration of American justice," are "persona[l]" to the accused; (4) the absence of historical examples of *forced* representation; and (5) "respect for the individual."

Faretta does not answer the question before us both because it did not consider the problem of mental competency, and because *Faretta* itself and later cases have made clear that the right of self-representation is not absolute. See *Martinez v. Court of Appeal of Cal., Fourth Appellate Dist.,* 528 U.S. 152 (2000) (no right of self-representation on direct appeal in a criminal case); *McKaskle v. Wiggins,* 465 U.S. 168 (1984) (appointment of standby counsel over self-represented defendant's objection is permissible); *Faretta,* 422 U.S., at 835, n. 46 (no right "to abuse the dignity of the courtroom"). The question here concerns a mental-illness-related limitation on the scope of the self-representation right.

The sole case in which this Court considered mental competence and self-representation together, *Godinez,* presents a question closer to that at issue here. The case focused upon a borderline-competent criminal defendant who had asked a state trial court to permit him to represent himself and to change his pleas from not guilty to guilty. The state trial court had found that the defendant met *Dusky*'s mental competence standard, that he "knowingly and intelligently" waived his right to assistance of counsel, and that he "freely and voluntarily" chose to plead guilty. And the state trial court had consequently granted the defendant's self-representation and change-of-plea requests. A federal appeals court, however, had vacated the defendant's guilty pleas on the ground that the Constitution required the trial court to ask a further question, namely, whether the defendant was competent to waive his constitutional right to counsel.... This Court, reversing the Court of Appeals, "reject[ed] the notion that competence to plead guilty or to waive the right to counsel must be measured by a standard that is higher than (or even different from) the *Dusky* standard.'' The decision to plead guilty, we said, ''is no more complicated than the sum total of decisions that a [represented] defendant may be called upon to make during the course of a trial.'' Hence ''there is no reason to believe that the decision to waive counsel requires an appreciably higher level of mental functioning than the decision to waive other constitutional rights.'' And even assuming that self-representation might pose special trial-related difficulties, ''the competence that is required of a defendant seeking to waive his right to counsel is the competence to *waive the right,* not the competence to represent himself.'' For this reason, we concluded, ''the defendant's 'technical legal knowledge' is 'not relevant' to the determination.''

We concede that *Godinez* bears certain similarities with the present case. Both involve mental competence and self-representation. Both involve a defendant who wants to represent himself. Both involve a mental condition that falls in a gray area between *Dusky*'s minimal constitutional requirement that measures a defendant's ability to stand trial and a somewhat higher standard that measures mental fitness for another legal purpose.

We nonetheless conclude that *Godinez* does not answer the question before us now. In part that is because the Court of Appeals higher standard at issue in *Godinez* differs in a critical way from the higher standard at issue here. In *Godinez,* the higher standard sought to measure the defendant's ability to proceed on his own to enter a guilty plea; here the higher standard seeks to measure the defendant's ability to conduct trial proceedings. To put the matter more specifically, the *Godinez* defendant sought only to change his pleas to guilty, he did not seek to conduct trial proceedings, and his ability to conduct a defense at trial was expressly not at issue. . . . In this case, the very matters that we did not consider in *Godinez* are directly before us. . . .

III

We now turn to the question presented. We assume that a criminal defendant has sufficient mental competence to stand trial (*i.e.*, the defendant meets *Dusky*'s standard) and that the defendant insists on representing himself during that trial. We ask whether the Constitution permits a State to limit that defendant's self-representation right by insisting upon representation by counsel at trial-on the ground that the defendant lacks the mental capacity to conduct his trial defense unless represented.

Several considerations taken together lead us to conclude that the answer to this question is yes. First, the Court's precedent, while not answering the question, points slightly in the direction of our affirmative answer. *Godinez,* as we have just said, simply leaves the question open. But the Court's ''mental competency'' cases set forth a standard that focuses directly upon a defendant's ''present ability to consult with his lawyer,'' a ''capacity . . . to consult with counsel,'' and an ability ''to assist [counsel] in preparing his defense,'' *Drope,* 420 U.S., at 171. These

standards assume representation by counsel and emphasize the importance of counsel. They thus suggest (though do not hold) that an
instance in which a defendant who would choose to forgo counsel at trial
presents a very different set of circumstances, which in our view, calls
for a different standard.

At the same time *Faretta,* the foundational self-representation case,
rested its conclusion in part upon pre-existing state law set forth in cases
all of which are consistent with, and at least two of which expressly
adopt, a competency limitation on the self-representation right.

Second, the nature of the problem before us cautions against the use
of a single mental competency standard for deciding both (1) whether a
defendant who is represented by counsel can proceed to trial and (2)
whether a defendant who goes to trial must be permitted to represent
himself. Mental illness itself is not a unitary concept. It varies in degree.
It can vary over time. It interferes with an individual's functioning at
different times in different ways. The history of this case illustrates the
complexity of the problem. In certain instances an individual may well be
able to satisfy *Dusky's* mental competence standard, for he will be able
to work with counsel at trial, yet at the same time he may be unable to
carry out the basic tasks needed to present his own defense without the
help of counsel.

The American Psychiatric Association (APA) tells us (without dispute) in its *amicus* brief [that] "[d]isorganized thinking, deficits in
sustaining attention and concentration, impaired expressive abilities,
anxiety, and other common symptoms of severe mental illnesses can
impair the defendant's ability to play the significantly expanded role
required for self-representation even if he can play the lesser role of
represented defendant." Motions and other documents that the defendant prepared in this case suggest to a layperson the common sense of
this general conclusion.

Third, in our view, a right of self-representation at trial will not
"affirm the dignity" of a defendant who lacks the mental capacity to
conduct his defense without the assistance of counsel. To the contrary,
given that defendant's uncertain mental state, the spectacle that could
well result from his self-representation at trial is at least as likely to
prove humiliating as ennobling. Moreover, insofar as a defendant's lack
of capacity threatens an improper conviction or sentence, self-representation in that exceptional context undercuts the most basic of the
Constitution's criminal law objectives, providing a fair trial. . . .

Further, proceedings must not only be fair, they must "appear fair
to all who observe them." *Wheat v. United States,* 486 U.S. 153 (1988).
An *amicus* brief reports one psychiatrist's reaction to having observed a
patient (a patient who had satisfied *Dusky*) try to conduct his own
defense: "[H]ow in the world can our legal system allow an insane man
to defend himself?" The application of *Dusky's* basic mental competence
standard can help in part to avoid this result. But given the different
capacities needed to proceed to trial without counsel, there is little

reason to believe that *Dusky* alone is sufficient. At the same time, the trial judge, particularly one such as the trial judge in this case, who presided over one of Edwards' competency hearings and his two trials, will often prove best able to make more fine-tuned mental capacity decisions, tailored to the individualized circumstances of a particular defendant.

We consequently conclude that the Constitution permits judges to take realistic account of the particular defendant's mental capacities by asking whether a defendant who seeks to conduct his own defense at trial is mentally competent to do so. That is to say, the Constitution permits States to insist upon representation by counsel for those competent enough to stand trial under *Dusky* but who still suffer from severe mental illness to the point where they are not competent to conduct trial proceedings by themselves.

IV

Indiana has also asked us to adopt, as a measure of a defendant's ability to conduct a trial, a more specific standard that would "deny a criminal defendant the right to represent himself at trial where the defendant cannot communicate coherently with the court or a jury." We are sufficiently uncertain, however, as to how that particular standard would work in practice to refrain from endorsing it as a federal constitutional standard here. . . .

Indiana has also asked us to overrule *Faretta*. We decline to do so. We recognize that judges have sometimes expressed concern that *Faretta*, contrary to its intent, has led to trials that are unfair. But recent empirical research suggests that such instances are not common. See, *e.g.*, Hashimoto, *Defending the Right of Self–Representation: An Empirical Look at the Pro Se Felony Defendant*, 85 N.C.L.REV. 423, 427, 447, 428 (2007) (noting that of the small number of defendants who chose to proceed *pro se*-"roughly 0.3% to 0.5%" of the total, state felony defendants in particular "appear to have achieved higher felony acquittal rates than their represented counterparts in that they were less likely to have been convicted of felonies"). At the same time, instances in which the trial's fairness is in doubt may well be concentrated in the 20 percent or so of self-representation cases where the mental competence of the defendant is also at issue. If so, today's opinion, assuring trial judges the authority to deal appropriately with cases in the latter category, may well alleviate those fair trial concerns.

For these reasons, the judgment of the Supreme Court of Indiana is vacated, and the case is remanded for further proceedings not inconsistent with this opinion.

So ordered.

APPENDIX

Excerpt from respondent's filing entitled "Defendant's Version of the Instant Offense," which he had attached to his presentence investigation report:

"The appointed motion of permissive intervention filed therein the court superior on, 6–26–01 caused a stay of action and apon it's expiration or thereafter three years the plan to establish a youth program to and for the coordination of aspects of law enforcement to prevent and reduce crime amoung young people in Indiana became a diplomatic act as under the Safe Streets Act of 1967, 'A omnibuc considerate agent: I membered clients within the public and others that at/production of the courts actions showcased causes. The costs of the stay (Trial Rule 60) has a derivative property that is: my knowledged events as not unexpended to contract the membered clients is the commission of finding a facilitie for this plan or project to become organization of administrative recommendations conditioned by governors.' "

JUSTICE SCALIA, with whom JUSTICE THOMAS joins, dissenting.

The Constitution guarantees a defendant who knowingly and voluntarily waives the right to counsel the right to proceed *pro se* at his trial. *Faretta v. California,* 422 U.S. 806 (1975). A mentally ill defendant who knowingly and voluntarily elects to proceed *pro se* instead of through counsel receives a fair trial that comports with the Fourteenth Amendment. *Godinez v. Moran,* 509 U.S. 389 (1993). The Court today concludes that a State may nonetheless strip a mentally ill defendant of the right to represent himself when that would be fairer. In my view the Constitution does not permit a State to substitute its own perception of fairness for the defendant's right to make his own case before the jury-a specific right long understood as essential to a fair trial. . . .

The Constitution guarantees to every criminal defendant the "right to proceed *without* counsel when he voluntarily and intelligently elects to do so." *Faretta,* 422 U.S., at 807.The right reflects "a nearly universal conviction, on the part of our people as well as our courts, that forcing a lawyer upon an unwilling defendant is contrary to his basic right to defend himself if he truly wants to do so." *Faretta*'s discussion of the history of the right includes the observation that "[i]n the long history of British criminal jurisprudence, there was only one tribunal that ever adopted a practice of forcing counsel upon an unwilling defendant in a criminal proceeding. The tribunal was the Star Chamber." *Faretta* described the right to proceed *pro se* as a premise of the Sixth Amendment, which confers the tools for a defense on the "accused," and describes the role of the attorney as one of "assistance." The right of self-representation could also be seen as a part of the traditional meaning of the Due Process Clause. See *Martinez v. Court of Appeal of Cal., Fourth Appellate Dist.,* 528 U.S. 152, 165 (2000) (SCALIA, J., concurring in judgment). Whichever provision provides its source, it means that a State simply may not force a lawyer upon a criminal defendant who wishes to conduct his own defense. *Faretta,* 422 U.S., at 807.

Exercising the right of self-representation requires waiving the right to counsel. A defendant may represent himself only when he "knowingly and intelligently" waives the lawyer's assistance that is guaranteed by the Sixth Amendment. He must "be made aware of the dangers and disadvantages of self-representation," and the record must "establish that 'he knows what he is doing and his choice is made with eyes open.'" *Ibid.* (quoting *Adams v. United States ex rel. McCann,* 317 U.S. 269, 279 (1942)). This limitation may be relevant to many mentally ill defendants, but there is no dispute that Edwards was not one of them. Edwards was warned extensively of the risks of proceeding *pro se.* The trial judge found that Edwards had "knowingly and voluntarily" waived his right to counsel at his first trial, and at his second trial the judge denied him the right to represent himself only by "carv[ing] out" a new "exception" to the right beyond the standard of knowing and voluntary waiver.

When a defendant appreciates the risks of forgoing counsel and chooses to do so voluntarily, the Constitution protects his ability to present his own defense even when that harms his case. In fact waiving counsel "usually" does so. *McKaskle v. Wiggins,* 465 U.S. 168, 177, n. 8 (1984). We have nonetheless said that the defendant's "choice must be honored out of 'that respect for the individual which is the lifeblood of the law.'" *Ibid.* What the Constitution requires is not that a State's case be subject to the most rigorous adversarial testing possible-after all, it permits a defendant to eliminate *all* adversarial testing by pleading guilty. What the Constitution requires is that a defendant be given the right to challenge the State's case against him using the arguments *he* sees fit.

In *Godinez,* 509 U.S. 389, we held that the Due Process Clause posed no barrier to permitting a defendant who suffered from mental illness both to waive his right to counsel and to plead guilty, so long as he was competent to stand trial and knowingly and voluntarily waived trial and the counsel right. It was "never the rule at common law" that a defendant could be competent to stand trial and yet incompetent to either exercise or give up some of the rights provided for his defense. We rejected the invitation to craft a higher competency standard for waiving counsel than for standing trial. That proposal, we said, was built on the "flawed premise" that a defendant's "competence to represent himself" was the relevant measure: "[T]he competence that is required of a defendant seeking to waive his right to counsel is the competence to *waive the right,* not the competence to represent himself." We grounded this on *Faretta*'s candid acknowledgment that the Sixth Amendment protected the defendant's right to conduct a defense to his disadvantage.

The Court is correct that this case presents a variation on *Godinez:* It presents the question not whether another constitutional requirement (in *Godinez,* the proposed higher degree of competence required for a waiver) limits a defendant's constitutional right to elect self-representation, but whether a State's view of fairness (or of other values) permits it to strip the defendant of this right. But that makes the question before us an easier one. While one constitutional requirement must yield to another in case of conflict, nothing permits a State, because of *its* view of what is fair, to deny a constitutional protection.... Until today, the right of self-representation has been accorded the same respect as other constitutional guarantees. The only circumstance in which we have permitted the State to deprive a defendant of this trial right is the one under which we have allowed the State to deny *other* such rights: when it is necessary to enable the trial to proceed in an orderly fashion. That overriding necessity, we have said, justifies forfeiture of even the Sixth Amendment right to be present at trial—if, after being threatened with removal, a defendant "insists on conducting himself in a manner so disorderly, disruptive, and disrespectful of the court that his trial cannot be carried on with him in the courtroom." *Illinois v. Allen,* 397 U.S. 337, 343 (1970). A *pro se* defendant may not "abuse the dignity of the courtroom," nor may he fail to "comply with relevant rules of procedural and substantive law," and a court may "terminate" the self-representation of a defendant who "deliberately engages in serious and obstructionist misconduct." *Faretta, supra,* at 834–835, n. 46. This ground for terminating self-representation is unavailable here, however, because Edwards was not even allowed to begin to represent himself, and because he was respectful and compliant and did not provide a basis to conclude a trial could not have gone forward had he been allowed to press his own claims.

Beyond this circumstance, we have never constrained the ability of a defendant to retain "actual control over the case he chooses to present to the jury"—what we have termed "the core of the *Faretta* right." *Wiggins, supra,* at 178. Thus, while *Faretta* recognized that the right of self-representation does not bar the court from appointing standby counsel, we explained in *Wiggins* that "[t]he *pro se* defendant must be allowed to control the organization and content of his own defense, to make motions, to argue points of law, to participate in *voir dire,* to question witnesses, and to address the court and the jury at appropriate points in the trial." Furthermore, because "multiple voices 'for the defense'" could "confuse the message the defendant wishes to convey," a standby attorney's participation would be barred when it would "destroy the jury's perception that the defendant is representing himself."

As I have explained, I would not adopt an approach to the right of self-representation that we have squarely rejected for other rights-allowing courts to disregard the right when doing so serves the purposes for which the right was intended. But if I were to adopt such an approach, I would remain in dissent, because I believe the Court's assessment of the purposes of the right of self-representation is inaccurate to boot. While there is little doubt that preserving individual "dignity" (to which the Court refers), is paramount among those purposes, there is equally little doubt that the loss of "dignity" the right is designed to prevent is *not* the defendant's making a fool of himself by presenting an amateurish or even incoherent defense. Rather, the dignity at issue is the supreme human dignity of being master of one's fate rather than a ward of the State-the dignity of individual choice. *Faretta* explained that the Sixth Amendment's counsel clause should not be invoked to impair "the exercise of [the defendant's] free choice" to dispense with the right, for "whatever else may be said of those who wrote the Bill of Rights, surely there can be no doubt that they understood the inestimable worth of free choice." Nine years later, when we wrote in *Wiggins* that the self-representation right served the "dignity and autonomy of the accused," we explained in no uncertain terms that this meant according every defendant the right to his say in court. In particular, we said that individual dignity and autonomy barred standby counsel from participating in a manner that would to "destroy the jury's perception that the defendant is representing himself," and meant that "the *pro se* defendant is entitled to preserve actual control over the case he chooses to present to the jury." In sum, if the Court is to honor the particular conception of "dignity" that underlies the self-representation right, it should respect the autonomy of the individual by honoring his choices knowingly and voluntarily made.

A further purpose that the Court finds is advanced by denial of the right of self-representation is the purpose of assuring that trials "appear fair to all who observe them." . . . When Edwards stood to say that "I have a defense that I would like to represent or present to the Judge," it seems to me the epitome of both actual and apparent unfairness for the judge to say, I have heard "your desire to proceed by yourself and I've denied your request, so your attorney will speak for you from now on." [I]n order for the defendant's right to call his own witnesses, to cross-examine witnesses, and to put on a defense to be anything more than "a tenuous and unacceptable legal fiction," a defendant must have consented to the representation of counsel. *Faretta, supra,* at 821. Otherwise, "the defense presented is not the defense guaranteed him by the Constitution, for in a very real sense, it is not *his* defense."

The facts of this case illustrate this point with the utmost clarity. Edwards wished to take a self-defense case to the jury. His counsel preferred a defense that focused on lack of intent. Having been denied the right to conduct his own defense, Edwards was convicted without having had the opportunity to present to the jury the grounds he believed supported his innocence. . . . In singling out mentally ill defendants for this treatment, the Court's opinion does not even have the questionable virtue of being politically correct. At a time when all society is trying to mainstream the mentally impaired, the Court permits them to be deprived of a basic constitutional right-for their own good.

Today's holding is extraordinarily vague. The Court does not accept Indiana's position that self-representation can be denied " 'where the defendant cannot communicate coherently with the court or a jury.' " It does not even hold that Edwards was properly denied his right to represent himself. It holds only that lack of mental competence can under some circumstances form a basis for denying the right to proceed *pro se* . . . . We will presumably give some meaning to this holding in the future, but the indeterminacy makes a bad holding worse. Once the right of self-representation for the mentally ill is a sometime thing, trial judges will have every incentive to make their lives easier—to avoid the painful necessity of deciphering occasional pleadings of the sort contained in the Appendix to today's opinion—by appointing knowledgeable and literate counsel.

Because I think a defendant who is competent to stand trial, and who is capable of knowing and voluntary waiver of assistance of counsel, has a constitutional right to conduct his own defense, I respectfully dissent.

On p. 47, add the following at the beginning of the problems:

0.1. Following the decision in this case, suppose that you are a trial court judge, and a defendant who suffers from mental illness demands the right to proceed *pro se*. How will you go about deciding whether to grant the request or deny it? Does this decision provide you with clear guidance regarding which defendants are *too* mentally ill to represent themselves, or how to make the decision regarding whether to permit *pro se* representation? Or, as Justice Scalia suggests, should you simply deny the right to proceed *pro se* because it is the easier course of action?

On p. 70, following the problems, add the following new problem:

5. *The Impact of Counsel's Conduct.* Suppose that a defendant's attorney recommends that he talk to police to explain his alibi to robbery/murder charges. However, counsel mistakenly believes that he cannot remain in the room during the questioning, and therefore leaves the room. Notwithstanding counsel's absence, defendant explains his alibi and it leads the police to two witnesses who testify against him. Defendant is ultimately convicted. Should defendant's conviction be reversed for ineffective assistance of counsel? *See People v. Frazier*, 2008 WL 782593.

On p. 85, at the end of Notes & Questions, add the following new note:

Notes & Questions

* * *

4. In its 2007 decision in *Schriro v. Landrigan*, 127 S.Ct. 1933 (2007), a 5–to–4 majority of the Court held that a federal district court did not abuse its discretion in declining to order a habeas corpus evidentiary hearing in a case where counsel failed to present significant mitigating evidence at a capital sentencing hearing where that failure was due to defendant's express request. As the majority pointed out, the Court's proper decisions did not "address[] a situation in which a client interferes with counsel's efforts to present mitigating evidence to a sentencing court ... [and] it was not objectively unreasonable for th[e district] court to conclude that a defendant who refused to allow the presentation of any mitigating evidence could not establish *Strickland* prejudice based on his counsel's failure to investigate further possible mitigating evidence." In dissent, Justice Stevens argued that

[s]ignificant mitigating evidence-evidence that may well have explained respondent's criminal conduct and unruly behavior at his capital sentencing hearing-was unknown at the time of sentencing. Only years later did respondent learn that he suffers from a serious psychological condition that sheds important light on his earlier actions. The reason why this and other mitigating evidence was unavailable is that respondent's counsel failed to conduct a constitutionally adequate investigation.... It may well be true that respondent would have completely waived his right to present mitigating evidence if that evidence had been adequately investigated at the time of sentencing. It may also be true that respondent's mitigating evidence could not outweigh his violent past. What is certainly true, however, is that an evidentiary hearing would provide answers to these questions.

What do you think? Should a mentally ill defendant's decisions against interest divest him of any opportunity to establish ineffective assistance after the fact?

On p. 89, after the problems but before the section on conflicts of interest, insert the following new case:

WRIGHT v. VAN PATTEN

128 S.Ct. 743 (2008).

PER CURIAM.

The Court of Appeals for the Seventh Circuit held that respondent Joseph Van Patten was entitled to relief under 28 U.S.C. § 2254, reasoning that his lawyer's assistance was presumptively ineffective owing to his participation in a plea hearing by speaker phone. We granted certiorari, vacated the judgment, and remanded the case for further consideration in light of *Carey v. Musladin,* 549 U.S. 70 (2006). On remand, the Seventh Circuit adhered to its original decision.... We grant the petition for certiorari now before us and this time reverse the judgment of the Seventh Circuit.

I

Van Patten was charged with first-degree intentional homicide and pleaded no contest to a reduced charge of first-degree reckless homicide. His counsel was not physically present at the plea hearing but was linked to the courtroom by speaker phone. After the state trial court imposed the maximum term of 25 years in prison, Van Patten retained different counsel and moved [to] withdraw his no-contest plea. The thrust of the motion was that Van Patten's Sixth Amendment right to counsel had been violated by his trial counsel's physical absence from the plea hearing. The Wisconsin Court of Appeals noted that, under state law, a postconviction motion to withdraw a no-contest plea will be granted only if a defendant establishes "manifest injustice" by clear and convincing evidence. While the court acknowledged that "the violation of the defendant's Sixth Amendment right to counsel may constitute a manifest injustice," it found that the absence of Van Patten's lawyer from the plea hearing did not violate his right to counsel:

"The plea hearing transcript neither indicates any deficiency in the plea colloquy, nor suggests that Van Patten's attorney's participation by telephone interfered in any way with [Van Patten's] ability to communicate with his attorney about his plea. Van Patten confirmed that he had thoroughly discussed his case and plea decision with his attorney and was satisfied with the legal representation he had received. The court gave Van Patten the opportunity to speak privately with his attorney over the phone if he had questions about the plea, but Van Patten declined. Further, when Van Patten exercised his right to allocution at sentencing, in the personal presence of his attorney, he raised no objection to his plea."

Applying *Strickland v. Washington,* 466 U.S. 668 (1984), the court concluded that "[t]he record does not support, nor does Van Patten's appellate brief include, any argument that counsel's performance was deficient or prejudicial," and denied Van Patten's motion.

After the Wisconsin Supreme Court declined further review, Van Patten petitioned for a writ of habeas corpus under 28 U.S.C. § 2254 in Federal District Court. The District Court denied relief, but the Court of Appeals for the Seventh Circuit reversed.... While the prison warden's petition for certiorari was pending, this Court decided *Musladin, supra.* Musladin had invoked this Court's cases recognizing "that certain courtroom practices are so inherently prejudicial that they deprive the defendant of a fair trial." The issue was the significance of these precedents in a case under § 2254, which bars relief on any claim "adjudicated on the merits" in state court, unless the state court's decision "was contrary to, or involved an unreasonable application of, clearly established Federal law, as determined by the Supreme Court of the United States." 28 U.S.C. § 2254(d)(1).

The prejudicial conduct involved in *Musladin* was courtroom conduct of private actors. We held that the "inheren[t] prejudic[e]" test, which we thus far have applied only in cases involving government-sponsored conduct, did not clearly extend to the conduct of independently acting courtroom spectators. See *Musladin, supra,* at ___, 127 S.Ct., at 654. For that reason, we reversed the Court of Appeals' grant of habeas relief.

Musladin's explanation of the "clearly established Federal law" requirement prompted us to remand Van Patten's case to the Seventh Circuit for further consideration. A majority of the panel reaffirmed its original judgment....

II

Strickland v. Washington, 466 U.S. 668 (1984) ordinarily applies to claims of ineffective assistance of counsel at the plea hearing stage. And it was in a different context that *Cronic* "recognized a narrow exception to *Strickland's* holding that a defendant who asserts ineffective assistance of counsel must demonstrate not only that his attorney's performance was deficient, but also that the deficiency prejudiced the defense." *Cronic* held that a Sixth Amendment violation may be found "without inquiring into counsel's actual performance or requiring the defendant to show the effect it had on the trial," when "circumstances [exist] that are so likely to prejudice the accused that the cost of litigating their effect in a particular case is unjustified," *Cronic, supra,* at 658. *Cronic,* not *Strickland,* applies "when . . . the likelihood that any lawyer, even a fully competent one, could provide effective assistance is so small that a presumption of prejudice is appropriate without inquiry into the actual conduct of the trial,"[1] and one circumstance warranting the presumption is the "complete denial of counsel," that is, when "counsel [is] either totally absent, or prevented from assisting the accused during a critical stage of the proceeding."

No decision of this Court, however, squarely addresses the issue in this case, or clearly establishes that *Cronic* should replace *Strickland* in this novel factual context. Our precedents do not clearly hold that counsel's participation by speaker phone should be treated as a "complete denial of counsel," on par with total absence. Even if we agree with Van Patten that a lawyer physically present will tend to perform better than one on the phone, it does not necessarily follow that mere telephone contact amounted to total absence or "prevented [counsel] from assisting the accused," so as to entail application of *Cronic.* The question is not whether counsel in those circumstances will perform less well than he otherwise would, but whether the circumstances are likely to result in such poor performance that an inquiry into its effects would not be worth the time. Our cases provide no categorical answer to this question, and for that matter the several proceedings in this case hardly point toward one. The Wisconsin Court of Appeals held counsel's performance by speaker phone to be constitutionally effective; neither the Magistrate Judge, the District Court, nor the Seventh Circuit disputed this conclusion; and the Seventh Circuit itself stated that "[u]nder *Strickland,* it seems clear Van Patten would have no viable claim."

Because our cases give no clear answer to the question presented, let alone one in Van Patten's favor, "it cannot be said that the state court 'unreasonabl[y] appli[ed] clearly established Federal law.'" *Musladin,* 549 U.S., at ___, 127 S.Ct. 649, 654 (quoting 28 U.S.C. § 2254(d)(1)). Under the explicit terms of § 2254(d)(1), therefore, relief is unauthorized.

Petitioner tells us that "[i]n urging review, [the State] does not condone, recommend, or encourage the practice of defense counsel assisting clients by telephone rather than in person at court proceedings, even

1. *Cronic* also applies when "there [is] a breakdown in the adversarial process," such that "counsel entirely fails to subject the prosecution's case to meaningful adversarial testing." We have made clear that "[w]hen we spoke in *Cronic* of the possibility of presuming prejudice based on an attorney's failure to test the prosecutor's case, we indicated that the attorney's failure must be complete." It is undisputed that this standard has not been met here.

in nonadversarial hearings such as the plea hearing in this case," and he acknowledges that "[p]erhaps, under similar facts in a direct federal appeal, the Seventh Circuit could have properly reached the same result it reached here." Our own consideration of the merits of telephone practice, however, is for another day, and this case turns on the recognition that no clearly established law contrary to the state court's conclusion justifies collateral relief.

The judgment is reversed, and the case is remanded for further proceedings consistent with this opinion.

It is so ordered.

JUSTICE STEVENS, concurring in the judgment.

An unfortunate drafting error in the Court's opinion in *United States v. Cronic,* 466 U.S. 648 (1984), makes it necessary to join the Court's judgment in this case.

In *Cronic,* this Court explained that some violations of the right to counsel arise in "circumstances that are so likely to prejudice the accused that the cost of litigating their effect in a particular case is unjustified." One such circumstance exists when the accused is "denied the presence of counsel at a critical stage of the prosecution." We noted that the "presence" of lawyers "is essential because they are the means through which the other rights of the person on trial are secured." Regrettably, *Cronic* did not "clearly establish" the full scope of the defendant's right to the presence of an attorney.

The Court of Appeals apparently read "the presence of counsel" in *Cronic* to mean "the presence of counsel *in open court.*" ... The fact that in 1984, when *Cronic* was decided, neither the parties nor the Court contemplated representation by attorneys who were not present in the flesh explains the author's failure to add the words "in open court" after the word "present."

"The Sixth Amendment's right-to-counsel guarantee recognizes 'the obvious truth that the average defendant does not have the professional legal skill to protect himself when brought before a tribunal with power to take his life or liberty.' *Johnson v. Zerbst,* 304 U.S. 458, 462–63 (1938).... Thus, a defendant requires an attorney's 'guiding hand' through every stage of the proceedings against him. *Powell v. Alabama,* 287 U.S. 45 (1932); *Cronic,* 466 U.S. at 658. It is well-settled that a court proceeding in which a defendant enters a plea (a guilty plea or, as here, a plea of no contest) is a 'critical stage' where an attorney's presence is crucial because 'defenses may be ... irretrievably lost, if not then and there asserted.' *Hamilton v. Alabama,* 368 U.S. 52 (1961). Indeed, with plea bargaining the norm and trial the exception, for most criminal defendants a change of plea hearing is *the* critical stage of their prosecution.

In deciding whether to dispense with the two-part *Strickland* inquiry, a court must evaluate whether the "surrounding circumstances make it unlikely that the defendant could have received the effective assistance of counsel," *Cronic,* 466 U.S. at 666, and thus "justify a presumption that [the] conviction was insufficiently reliable to satisfy the Constitution." In this case, although the transcript shows that the state trial judge did his best to conduct the plea colloquy with care, the arrangements made it impossible for Van Patten to have the "assistance of counsel" in anything but the most perfunctory sense. Van Patten stood alone before judge and prosecutor. Unlike the usual defendant in a criminal case, he could not turn to his lawyer for private legal advice, to clear up misunderstandings, to seek reassurance, or to discuss any last-minute misgivings. Listening over an audio connection, counsel could not detect and respond to cues from his client's demeanor that might have indicated he did not understand certain aspects of the proceeding, or that he was changing his mind. If Van Patten wished to converse with his attorney, anyone else in the courtroom could effectively eavesdrop.... In short, this was not an auspicious setting for someone about to waive very valuable constitutional rights." *Van Patten v. Deppisch,* 434 F.3d 1038, 1042–1043 (C.A.7 2006).... I acquiesce in this Court's conclusion that the state-court decision was not an unreasonable application of clearly established federal law. In doing so, however, I emphasize that today's opinion does not say that the state courts' interpretation of *Cronic* was correct, or that we would have accepted that reading if the case had come to us on direct review rather than by way of 28 U.S.C. § 2254.

Part II

POLICE PRACTICES

Chapter 4

ARREST, SEARCH & SEIZURE

A. SEARCH WARRANTS

6. *Warrant Execution*

On p. 133, at the end of Note 1, add the following:

In a per curiam decision handed down in 2007, *Los Angeles County v. Rettele*, 127 S.Ct. 1989 (2007), the Supreme Court upheld as reasonable the detention for a few minutes of occupants of a house being searched, although the occupants, who had been sleeping unclothed when the police entered were made to stand naked before they were allowed to dress:

> In executing a search warrant officers may take reasonable action to secure the premises and to ensure their own safety and the efficacy of the search. [Unreasonable] actions include the use of excessive force or restraints that cause unnecessary pain or are imposed for a prolonged and unnecessary period of time. [The] Fourth Amendment allows warrants to issue on probable cause, a standard well short of absolute certainty. Valid warrants will issue to search the innocent, and people like [the occupants here] unfortunately bear the cost. Officers executing search warrants on occasion enter a house when residents are engaged in private activity; and the resulting frustration, embarrassment, and humiliation may be real, as was true here. When officers execute a valid warrant and act in a reasonable manner to protect themselves from harm, however, the Fourth Amendment is not violated.

B. PROTECTED FOURTH AMENDMENT INTERESTS

On p. 151, after the note, add the following new problem:

Problems

1. *The Personal Computer.* A city employee (Bart) brings his personal computer to work, hooks it up to the office internet, and leaves it on all of the time (both day and night). There is no password protection on the computer and other city employees regularly enter the work area. However, Bart has never invited any other city employee to use his computer. When a

nearby employee has difficulty accessing the internet from her computer, she asks a police officer to check Bart's computer to see whether it's connection is working. The officer does so and finds child pornography on the computer. Did the officer violate Bart's "reasonable expectation of privacy" in the contents of his computer, and therefore did the office conduct a "search" of the computer within the meaning of the Fourth Amendment?

2. *Surreptitious DNA Collection.* When the police re-open a 20 year-old homicide investigation, they would like to obtain a DNA sample from the prime suspect, but fear that he will flee if it becomes clear that they are investigating him. As a result, the police decide to trick the suspect into voluntarily giving them a DNA sample by posing as "lawyers" who are planning to bring a class action lawsuit against the city relating to parking tickets. They send the suspect a letter informing him of the lawsuit, and asking him to return a form joining the class action. When the police receive the letter, they test the DNA of the saliva used to seal the envelope. In obtaining the DNA sample, did the police conduct a "search" within the meaning of the Fourth Amendment? *See Nicholas v. Goord*, 430 F.3d 652 (2d Cir. 2005); *State v. Athan*, 160 Wash.2d 354, 158 P.3d 27 (2007).

On p. 160, at the end of the problems, add the following new problems:

4. *Questioning Florida v. Riley.* In *State v. Bryant*, ___ A.2d ___, 2008 WL 820197 (Vt. 2008), in applying the Vermont Constitution, the Vermont Supreme Court declined to follow *Riley*. In its refusal, the Court emphasized the heightened privacy expectations associated with a home and its curtilage, and found the "air travel in this case—fifteen to thirty minutes of hovering over defendant's property at altitudes as low as 100 feet—to be distinctly unlike 'passing by a home on public thoroughfares.' " Do you agree with the reasoning in *Riley* or with the reasoning in *Bryant*?

5. *E-Mail Accounts.* Warshak maintains an e-mail account with an ISP (Internet service provider) which he protects through a used ID and password. Does Warshak have a "reasonable expectation of privacy" vis-a-vis the government in the contents of his e-mail account? Is your analysis affected by the fact that the ISP has a contractual right to access accounts, but rarely accesses in any way except to screen for viruses, spam or child pornography. *See Warshak v. United States*, 490 F.3d 455 (6th Cir. 2007).

6. *The Omnibus Camera System.* Britain has installed approximately 4.2 million cameras in public places to watch and monitor citizens. Louisville Courier–Journal, A–13 (Oct. 21, 2007). In other words, there is one camera for every 15 British citizens. *Id.* The system has produced enormous crime prevention and detection benefits. Following the London subway bombings, the camera system allowed the British police to locate the bombers. Suppose that a medium size U.S. city decides to install a comprehensive camera system that will allow it to monitor all public streets and detect crime. A citizen's group, concerned about a loss of privacy, sues the city claiming a violation of the Fourth Amendment. Assume that you are the judge assigned

to hear the case. Does the camera system run afoul of the Fourth Amendment?

On p. 169, problem #6, add the following language after the sentence that ends on the 3rd line of the problem:

For example, television advertisements tout a new device that will allow an individual to overhear conversations as far as a block away. The device sells for $14.99 plus $6.99 for shipping and handling.

D. WARRANTLESS SEARCHES AND SEIZURES

1. *Plain View Exception*

On p. 204, at the end of the problems, add the following new problems:

6. *The "Knock and Talk."* Suppose that the police believe that defendant (Fisher) is operating a meth lab out of his home. Lacking probable cause to obtain a warrant, the officers decide to go to Fisher's house and conduct a "knock and talk." In other words, they plan to knock on Fisher's door, talk to him a bit, and see if he will consent to a search. During the "knock and talk," the officer (who is standing at Fisher's front door) happens to see meth-related items (*e.g.*, pseudoephedrine) lying just inside the door on the coffee table. Does the "plain view" doctrine apply to the items? Do the police have the right to seize the items without a warrant? *See McClish v. Nugent*, 483 F.3d 1231 (11th Cir. 2007); *State v. Fisher*, 283 Kan. 272, 154 P.3d 455 (2007). Would the validity of a "knock and talk" be affected by the fact that a number of police officers come to defendant's door at the same time, and refuse to allow him to re-enter the house even though he is barefoot, bare chested, and the weather is cold and stormy. See Keenom v. State, 349 Ark. 381, 80 S.W.3d 743 (Ark. 2002).

7. *Immediate Apparency.* In conducting a pat down search (we will study "pat down" searches later, but (for now) assume that the officer can only "pat down" the suspect's outer clothing looking for a weapon), an officer feels a plastic baggie in a suspect's pocket. The officer is unable to precisely determine the contents of the baggie, but he knows from experience that plastic bags are often used to package marijuana. He removes the baggie from the pocket and realizes that his hunch was correct. Can the search be justified under the "plain view" doctrine? *See Murphy v. Commonwealth*, 37 Va.App. 556, 559 S.E.2d 890 (Va.Ct.App. 2002).

2. *Search Incident to Legal Arrest*

On p. 210, at the end of the first paragraph, add the following new problem and case:

Problem: The "Knock and Talk" Arrest

Under *Payton* (n. 3, *supra*), a police officer cannot arrest an individual at a private residence without a warrant. However, in *United States v. Santana*, 427 U.S. 38 (1976), the Court held that a suspect who was outside her home, and therefore knowingly exposed herself to "public view," could be arrested without a warrant. Suppose that the police decide to conduct a "knock and talk" at Jane's house. While the police have probable cause to believe that Jane is a drug dealer, they do not have a warrant for her arrest and do not have a warrant to search the house. In response to the police knock, Janes opens the door. Has Jane knowingly exposed herself to public view so that she can be arrested without a warrant? *See McClish v. Nugent*, 483 F.3d 1231 (11th Cir. 2007).

SCOTT v. HARRIS

127 S.Ct. 1769 (2007).

JUSTICE SCALIA delivered the opinion of the Court.

We consider whether a law enforcement official can, consistent with the Fourth Amendment, attempt to stop a fleeing motorist from continuing his public-endangering flight by ramming the motorist's car from behind. Put another way: Can an officer take actions that place a fleeing motorist at risk of serious injury or death in order to stop the motorist's flight from endangering the lives of innocent bystanders?

[After a police officer observed respondent speeding, he gave chase and radioed for help.] Petitioner, Deputy Timothy Scott, heard the radio communication and joined the pursuit along with other officers. In the midst of the chase, respondent pulled into the parking lot of a shopping center and was nearly boxed in by the various police vehicles. Respondent evaded the trap by making a sharp turn, colliding with Scott's police car, exiting the parking lot, and speeding off once again down a two-lane highway.... Six minutes and nearly 10 miles after the chase had begun, Scott decided to attempt to terminate the episode by employing a "Precision Intervention Technique ('PIT') maneuver, which causes the fleeing vehicle to spin to a stop." Having radioed his supervisor for permission, Scott was told to "[g]o ahead and take him out." Instead, Scott applied his push bumper to the rear of respondent's vehicle.[2] As a result, respondent lost control of his vehicle, which left the roadway, ran down an embankment, overturned, and crashed. Respondent was badly injured and was rendered a quadriplegic.

Respondent filed suit against Deputy Scott and others under 42 U.S.C. § 1983, alleging, *inter alia,* a violation of his federal constitutional rights, viz. use of excessive force resulting in an unreasonable seizure under the Fourth Amendment. In response, Scott filed a motion for summary judgment based on an assertion of qualified immunity. The District Court denied the motion.... Taking respondent's view of the facts[,] the Court of Appeals concluded that Scott's actions could constitute "deadly force" under *Tennessee v. Garner,* 471 U.S. 1 (1985), and that the use of such force in this context "would violate [respondent's] constitutional right to be free from excessive force during a seizure. Accordingly, a reasonable jury could find that Scott violated [respondent's] Fourth Amendment rights." [We] granted certiorari and now reverse.

2. Scott says he decided not to employ the PIT maneuver because he was "con-   cerned that the vehicles were moving too quickly to safely execute the maneuver."

In resolving questions of qualified immunity, courts are required to resolve a "threshold question: Taken in the light most favorable to the party asserting the injury, do the facts alleged show the officer's conduct violated a constitutional right? ..." *Saucier v. Katz,* 533 U.S. 194 (2001). If, and only if, the court finds a violation of a constitutional right, "the next, sequential step is to ask whether the right was clearly established ... in light of the specific context of the case." ... We therefore turn to the threshold inquiry: whether Deputy Scott's actions violated the Fourth Amendment....

III

A

[As] this case was decided on summary judgment, there have not yet been factual findings by a judge or jury, and respondent's version of events (unsurprisingly) differs substantially from Scott's version.... In qualified immunity cases, this usually means adopting [the] plaintiff's version of the facts.... [But the] videotape quite clearly contradicts the version of the story told by respondent.... There we see respondent's vehicle racing down narrow, two-lane roads in the dead of night at speeds that are shockingly fast. We see it swerve around more than a dozen other cars, cross the double-yellow line, and force cars traveling in both directions to their respective shoulders to avoid being hit. We see it run multiple red lights and travel for considerable periods of time in the occasional center left-turn-only lane, chased by numerous police cars forced to engage in the same hazardous maneuvers just to keep up. [W]hat we see on the video more closely resembles a Hollywood-style car chase of the most frightening sort, placing police officers and innocent bystanders alike at great risk of serious injury....

Judging the matter on that basis, we think it is quite clear that Deputy Scott did not violate the Fourth Amendment. Scott does not contest that his decision to terminate the car chase by ramming his bumper into respondent's vehicle constituted a "seizure." "[A] Fourth Amendment seizure [occurs] when there is a governmental termination of freedom of movement through means intentionally applied." *Brower v. County of Inyo,* 489 U.S. 593, 596–597. It is also conceded, by both sides, that a claim of "excessive force in the course of making [a] 'seizure' of [the] person [is] properly analyzed under the Fourth Amendment's 'objective reasonableness' standard." *Graham v. Connor,* 490 U.S. 386 (1989). The question we need to answer is whether Scott's actions were objectively reasonable.

Respondent urges us to analyze this case as we analyzed *Garner,* 471 U.S. 1. We must first decide, he says, whether the actions Scott took constituted "deadly force." (He defines "deadly force" as "any use of force which creates a substantial likelihood of causing death or serious bodily injury." If so, respondent claims that *Garner* prescribes certain preconditions that must be met before Scott's actions can survive Fourth Amendment scrutiny: (1) The suspect must have posed an immediate threat of serious physical harm to the officer or others; (2) deadly force must have been necessary to prevent escape; and (3) where feasible, the officer must have given the suspect some warning. . . .

Respondent's argument falters at its first step; *Garner* did not establish a magical on/off switch that triggers rigid preconditions whenever an officer's actions constitute "deadly force." *Garner* was simply an application of the Fourth Amendment's "reasonableness" test the use of a particular type of force in a particular situation. *Garner* held that it was unreasonable to kill a "young, slight, and unarmed" burglary suspect, by shooting him "in the back of the head" while he was running away on foot, and when the officer "could not reasonably have believed that [the suspect] posed any threat," and "never attempted to justify his actions on any basis other than the need to prevent an escape." . . . "*Garner* had nothing to do with one car striking another or even with car chases in general. . . . A police car's bumping a fleeing car is, in fact, not much like a policeman's shooting a gun so as to hit a person." *Adams v. St. Lucie County Sheriff's Dept.,* 962 F.2d 1563, 1577 (C.A.11 1992) (Edmondson, J., dissenting). Nor is the threat posed by the flight on foot of an unarmed suspect even remotely comparable to the extreme danger to human life posed by respondent in this case. . . . Whether or not Scott's actions constituted application of "deadly force," all that matters is whether Scott's actions were reasonable.

In determining the reasonableness of the manner in which a seizure is effected, "[w]e must balance the nature and quality of the intrusion on the individual's Fourth Amendment interests against the importance of the governmental interests alleged to justify the intrusion." *United States v. Place,* 462 U.S. 696 (1983). Scott defends his actions by pointing to the paramount governmental interest in ensuring public safety, and respondent nowhere suggests this was not the purpose motivating Scott's behavior. Thus, in judging whether Scott's actions were reasonable, we must consider the risk of bodily harm that Scott's actions posed to respondent in light of the threat to the public that Scott was trying to eliminate. Although there is no obvious way to quantify the risks on either side, it is clear from the videotape that respondent posed an actual and imminent threat to the lives of any pedestrians who might have been present, to other civilian motorists, and to the officers involved in the chase. It is equally clear that Scott's actions posed a high likelihood of serious injury or death to respondent-though not the near *certainty* of death posed by, say, shooting a fleeing felon in the back of the head, or pulling alongside a fleeing motorist's car and shooting the motorist. So how does a court go about weighing the perhaps lesser probability of injuring or killing numerous bystanders against the perhaps larger probability of injuring or killing a single person? We think it appropriate in this process to take into account not only the number of lives at risk, but also their relative culpability. It was respondent, after all, who intentionally placed himself and the public in danger by unlawfully engaging in the reckless, high-speed flight that ultimately produced the choice between two evils that Scott confronted. Multiple police cars, with blue lights flashing and sirens blaring, had been chasing respondent for nearly 10 miles, but he ignored their warning to stop. By contrast, those who might have been harmed had Scott not taken the action he did were entirely innocent. We have little difficulty in concluding it was reasonable for Scott to take the action that he did.

[Respondent argues that the public could have been protected by the cessation of police pursuit.] We think the police need not have taken that chance and hoped for the best. Whereas Scott's action—ramming respondent off the road—was *certain* to eliminate the risk that respondent posed to the public, ceasing pursuit was not. First of all, there would have been no way to convey convincingly to respondent that the chase was off, and that he was free to go. Had respondent looked in his rearview mirror and seen the police cars deactivate their flashing lights and turn around, he would have had no idea whether they were truly letting him get away, or simply devising a new strategy for capture. Perhaps the police knew a shortcut he didn't know, and would reappear down the road to intercept him; or perhaps they were setting up a roadblock in his path. Given such uncertainty, respondent might have been just as likely to respond by continuing to drive recklessly as by slowing down and wiping his brow.

Second, we are loath to lay down a rule requiring the police to allow fleeing suspects to get away whenever they drive *so recklessly* that they put other people's lives in danger. . . . Every fleeing motorist would know that escape is within his grasp, if only he accelerates to 90 miles per hour, crosses the double-yellow line a few times, and runs a few red lights. The Constitution assuredly does not impose this invitation to impunity-earned-by-recklessness. Instead, we lay down a more sensible rule: A police officer's attempt to terminate a dangerous high-speed car chase that threatens the lives of innocent bystanders does not violate the Fourth Amendment, even when it places the fleeing motorist at risk of serious injury or death. . . .

The car chase that respondent initiated in this case posed a substantial and immediate risk of serious physical injury to others; no reasonable jury could conclude otherwise. Scott's attempt to terminate the chase by forcing respondent off the road was reasonable, and Scott is entitled to summary judgment. The Court of Appeals' decision to the contrary is reversed.

It is so ordered.

JUSTICE STEVENS, dissenting.

[The] 13 cars that respondent passed on his side of the road before entering the shopping center, and both of the cars that he passed on the right after leaving the center, no doubt had already pulled to the side of the road or were driving along the shoulder because they heard the police sirens or saw the flashing lights before respondent or the police cruisers approached. A jury could certainly conclude that those motorists were exposed to no greater risk than persons who take the same action in response to a speeding ambulance, and that their reactions were fully consistent with the evidence that respondent, though speeding, retained full control of his vehicle. [R]espondent and his pursuers went through only two intersections with stop lights and in both cases all other vehicles in sight were stationary, presumably because they had been warned of the approaching speeders. [B]ecause the cameras were farther away when respondent [went through the lights,] it is not entirely clear that he ran either or both of the red lights. [P]assing a slower vehicle on a two-lane road always involves some degree of swerving and is not especially dangerous if there are no cars coming from the opposite direction. At no point during the chase did respondent pull into the opposite lane other than to pass a car in front of him; he did the latter no more than five times and, on most of those occasions, used his turn signal. On none of these occasions was there a car traveling in the opposite direction. [T]he video does not reveal any incidents that could even be remotely characterized as "close calls." . . . It is apparent from the record (including the videotape) that local police had blocked off intersections to keep respondent from entering residential neighborhoods and possibly endangering other motorists. [T]he videos also show that no pedestrians, parked cars, sidewalks, or residences. . . .

I recognize [that respondent's] refusal to stop and subsequent flight was a serious offense that merited severe punishment. It was not, however, a capital offense, or even an offense that justified the use of deadly force. . . . What would have happened if the police had decided to abandon the chase? We now know that they could have apprehended respondent later because they had his license plate number. Even if that were not true, and even if he would have escaped any punishment at all, the use of deadly force in this case was no more appropriate than the use of a deadly weapon against a fleeing felon in *Garner*. . . . There is no evidentiary basis for an assumption that dangers caused by flight from a police pursuit will continue after the pursuit ends. [U]nder the standard set forth in *Garner,* it is certainly possible that "a jury could conclude that Scott unreasonably used deadly force to seize Harris by ramming him off the road under the instant circumstances." . . . In my view, the risks inherent in justifying unwarranted police conduct on the basis of unfounded assumptions are unacceptable, particularly when less drastic measures-in this case, the use of stop sticks or a simple warning issued from a loudspeaker-could have avoided such a tragic result. In my judgment, jurors in Georgia should be allowed to evaluate the reasonableness of the decision to ram respondent's speeding vehicle in a manner that created an obvious risk of death and has in fact made him a quadriplegic at the age of 19.

On p. 216, after the problems, add the following new case:

VIRGINIA v. MOORE

128 S.Ct. 1598 (2008).

JUSTICE SCALIA delivered the opinion of the Court.

We consider whether a police officer violates the Fourth Amendment by making an arrest based on probable cause but prohibited by state law.

On February 20, 2003, two City of Portsmouth police officers stopped a car driven by David Lee Moore. They had heard over the police radio that a person known as "Chubs" was driving with a suspended license, and one of the officers knew Moore by that nickname. The officers determined that Moore's license was in fact suspended, and arrested him for the misdemeanor of driving on a suspended license, which is punishable under Virginia law by a year in jail and a $2,500 fine, Va.Code Ann. §§ 18.2–11, 18.2–272, 46.2–301(C). The officers subsequently searched Moore and found that he was carrying 16 grams of crack cocaine and $516 in cash.

Under state law, the officers should have issued Moore a summons instead of arresting him. Driving on a suspended license, like some other misdemeanors, is not an arrestable offense except as to those who "fail or refuse to discontinue" the violation, and those whom the officer reasonably believes to be likely to disregard a summons, or likely to harm themselves or others. Va.Code Ann. § 19.2–74.... Virginia also permits arrest for driving on a suspended license in jurisdictions where "prior general approval has been granted by order of the general district court," Va.Code Ann. § 46.2–936; Virginia has never claimed such approval was in effect in the county where Moore was arrested.

Moore was charged with possessing cocaine with the intent to distribute it in violation of Virginia law. He filed a pretrial motion to suppress the evidence from the arrest search. Virginia law does not, as a general matter, require suppression of evidence obtained in violation of state law. Moore argued, however, that suppression was required by the Fourth Amendment. The trial court denied the motion, and after a bench trial found Moore guilty of the drug charge and sentenced him to a 5–year prison term, with one year and six months of the sentence suspended. The conviction was reversed by a panel of Virginia's intermediate court on Fourth Amendment grounds, reinstated by the intermediate court sitting en banc, and finally reversed again by the Virginia Supreme Court. The Court reasoned that since the arresting officers should have issued Moore a citation under state law, and the Fourth Amendment does not permit search incident to citation, the arrest search violated the Fourth Amendment. We granted certiorari.

The Fourth Amendment protects "against unreasonable searches and seizures" of (among other things) the person. In determining whether a search or seizure is unreasonable, we ... look to the statutes and common law of the founding era to determine the norms that the Fourth Amendment was meant to preserve. See *Wyoming v. Houghton,* 526 U.S. 295 (1999).

We are aware of no historical indication that those who ratified the Fourth Amendment understood it as a redundant guarantee of whatever limits on search and seizure legislatures might have enacted. The immediate object of the Fourth Amendment was to prohibit the general warrants and writs of assistance that English judges had employed against the colonists, *Boyd v. United States,* 116 U.S. 616 (1886). That suggests, if anything, that founding-era citizens were skeptical of using the rules for search and seizure set by government actors as the index of reasonableness.

Joseph Story, among others, saw the Fourth Amendment as "little more than the affirmance of a great constitutional doctrine of the common law," 3 Commentaries on the Constitution of the United States § 1895, p. 748 (1833), which Story defined in opposition to statutes, *see* Codification of the Common Law in The Miscellaneous Writings of Joseph Story 698, 699, 701 (W. Story ed. 1852). No early case or commentary, to our knowledge, suggested the Amendment was intended to incorporate subsequently enacted statutes. None of the early Fourth Amendment cases that scholars have identified sought to base a constitutional claim on a violation of a state or federal statute concerning arrest.

Of course such a claim would not have been available against state officers, since the Fourth Amendment was a restriction only upon federal power. But early Congresses tied the arrest authority of federal officers to state laws of arrest. See *United States v. Di Re*, 332 U.S. 581 (1948); *United States v. Watson*, 423 U.S. 411 (1976). Moreover, even though several state constitutions also prohibited unreasonable searches and seizures, citizens who claimed officers had violated state restrictions on arrest did not claim that the violations also ran afoul of the state constitutions. The apparent absence of such litigation is particularly striking in light of the fact that searches incident to warrantless arrests (which is to say arrests in which the officer was not insulated from private suit) were, as one commentator has put it, "taken for granted" at the founding, as were warrantless arrests themselves, Amar, Fourth Amendment First Principles, 107 Harv. L.Rev. 757, 764 (1994)....

When history has not provided a conclusive answer, we have analyzed a search or seizure in light of traditional standards of reasonableness "by assessing, on the one hand, the degree to which it intrudes upon an individual's privacy and, on the other, the degree to which it is needed for the promotion of legitimate governmental interests." *Houghton*, 526 U.S., at 300. That methodology provides no support for Moore's Fourth Amendment claim. In a long line of cases, we have said that when an officer has probable cause to believe a person committed even a minor crime in his presence, the balancing of private and public interests is not in doubt. The arrest is constitutionally reasonable.

Our decisions counsel against changing this calculus when a State chooses to protect privacy beyond the level that the Fourth Amendment requires.... In *California v. Greenwood*, 486 U.S. 35 (1988), we held that search of an individual's garbage forbidden by California's Constitution was not forbidden by the Fourth Amendment. "[W]hether or not a search is reasonable within the meaning of the Fourth Amendment," we said, has never "depend[ed] on the law of the particular State in which the search occurs." While "[i]ndividual States may surely construe their own constitutions as imposing more stringent constraints on police conduct than does the Federal Constitution," state law did not alter the content of the Fourth Amendment.

We have applied the same principle in the seizure context. *Whren v. United States,* 517 U.S. 806 (1996), held that police officers had acted reasonably in stopping a car, even though their action violated regulations limiting the authority of plainclothes officers in unmarked vehicles. We thought it obvious that the Fourth Amendment's meaning did not change with local law enforcement practices-even practices set by rule. While those practices "vary from place to place and from time to time," Fourth Amendment protections are not "so variable" and cannot "be made to turn upon such trivialities."

Some decisions earlier than these excluded evidence obtained in violation of state law, but those decisions rested on our supervisory power over the federal courts, rather than the Constitution. In *Di Re,* 332 U.S. 581, federal and state officers collaborated in an investigation that led to an arrest for a federal crime. The Government argued that the legality of an arrest for a federal offense was a matter of federal law. We concluded, however, that since Congress had provided that arrests with warrants must be made in accordance with state law, the legality of arrests without warrants should also be judged according to state-law standards. This was plainly not a rule we derived from the Constitution, however, because we repeatedly invited Congress to change it by statute-saying that state law governs the validity of a warrantless arrest "in [the] absence of an applicable federal statute," and that the *Di Re* rule applies "except in those cases where Congress has enacted a federal rule." . . .

We are convinced that the approach of our prior cases is correct, because an arrest based on probable cause serves interests that have long been seen as sufficient to justify the seizure. Arrest ensures that a suspect appears to answer charges and does not continue a crime, and it safeguards evidence and enables officers to conduct an in-custody investigation. *See* W. LaFave, Arrest: The Decision to Take a Suspect into Custody 177–202 (1965).

Moore argues that a State has no interest in arrest when it has a policy against arresting for certain crimes. That is not so, because arrest will still ensure a suspect's appearance at trial, prevent him from continuing his offense, and enable officers to investigate the incident more thoroughly. State arrest restrictions are more accurately characterized as showing that the State values its interests in forgoing arrests more highly than its interests in making them, or as showing that the State places a higher premium on privacy than the Fourth Amendment requires. A State is free to prefer one search-and-seizure policy among the range of constitutionally permissible options, but its choice of a more restrictive option does not render the less restrictive ones unreasonable, and hence unconstitutional.

If we concluded otherwise, we would often frustrate rather than further state policy. Virginia chooses to protect individual privacy and dignity more than the Fourth Amendment requires, but it also chooses not to attach to violations of its arrest rules the potent remedies that federal courts have applied to Fourth Amendment violations. Virginia does not, for example, ordinarily exclude from criminal trials evidence obtained in violation of its statutes. Moore would allow Virginia to accord enhanced protection against arrest only on pain of accompanying that protection with federal remedies for Fourth Amendment violations, which often include the exclusionary rule. States unwilling to lose control over the remedy would have to abandon restrictions on arrest altogether. This is an odd consequence of a provision designed to protect against searches and seizures.

Even if we thought that state law changed the nature of the Commonwealth's interests for purposes of the Fourth Amendment, we would adhere to the probable-cause standard. In determining what is reasonable under the Fourth Amendment, we have given great weight to the "essential interest in readily administrable rules." *Atwater,* 532 U.S., at 347 .... Incorporating state-law arrest limitations into the Constitution would produce a constitutional regime no less vague and unpredictable than the one we rejected in *Atwater.* The constitutional standard would be only as easy to apply as the underlying state law, and state law can be complicated indeed. The Virginia statute in this case, for example, calls on law enforcement officers to weigh just the sort of case-specific factors that *Atwater* said would deter legitimate arrests if made part of the constitutional inquiry. It would authorize arrest if a misdemeanor suspect fails or refuses to discontinue the unlawful act, or if the officer believes the suspect to be likely to disregard a summons. Va.Code Ann. § 19.2–74.A.1. *Atwater* specifically noted the "extremely poor judgment" displayed in arresting a local resident who would "almost certainly" have discontinued the offense and who had "no place to hide and no incentive to flee." It nonetheless declined to make those considerations part of the constitutional calculus....

Finally, linking Fourth Amendment protections to state law would cause them to "vary from place to place and from time to time," *Whren,* 517 U.S., at 815. Even at the same place and time, the Fourth Amendment's protections might vary if federal officers were not subject to the same statutory constraints as state officers.... It would be strange to construe a constitutional provision that did not apply to the States at all when it was adopted to now restrict state officers more than federal officers, solely because the States have passed search-and-seizure laws that are the prerogative of independent sovereigns.

We conclude that warrantless arrests for crimes committed in the presence of an arresting officer are reasonable under the Constitution, and that while States are free to regulate such arrests however they desire, state restrictions do not alter the Fourth Amendment's protections.

Moore argues that even if the Constitution allowed his arrest, it did not allow the arresting officers to search him. We have recognized, however, that officers may perform searches incident to constitutionally permissible arrests in order to ensure their safety and safeguard evidence. *United States v. Robinson,* 414 U.S. 218 (1973).... The interests justifying search are present whenever an officer makes an arrest. A search enables officers to safeguard evidence, and, most critically, to ensure their safety during "the extended exposure which follows the taking of a suspect into custody and transporting him to the police station." *Robinson, supra,* at 234–235....

The Virginia Supreme Court may have concluded that *Knowles* required the exclusion of evidence seized from Moore because, under state law, the officers who arrested Moore should have issued him a citation instead.... But the arrest rules that the officers violated were those of state law alone, and ... it is not the province of the Fourth Amendment to enforce state law. That Amendment does not require the exclusion of evidence obtained from a constitutionally permissible arrest.

We reaffirm against a novel challenge what we have signaled for more than half a century. When officers have probable cause to believe that a person has committed a crime in their presence, the Fourth Amendment permits them to make an arrest, and to search the suspect in order to safeguard evidence and ensure their own safety. The judgment of the Supreme Court of Virginia is reversed, and the case is remanded for further proceedings not inconsistent with this opinion.

It is so ordered.

JUSTICE GINSBURG, concurring in the judgment.

I find in the historical record more support for Moore's position than the Court does. Further, our decision in *United States v. Di Re,* 332 U.S. 581 (1948), requiring suppression of evidence gained in a search incident to an unlawful arrest, seems to me pinned to the Fourth Amendment and not to our "supervisory power." And I am aware of no "long line of cases" holding that, regardless of state law, probable cause renders every warrantless arrest for crimes committed in the presence of an arresting officer "constitutionally reasonable." ... Because I agree that the arrest and search Moore challenges violated Virginia law, but did not violate the Fourth Amendment, I join the Court's judgment.

3. *Automobile Exception*

On p. 227, after the problem, add the following new problem:

2. *The Staged Accident.* The police have probable cause to make a warrantless search of an automobile for illegal drugs. However, because the owner is part of a drug ring, the police are reluctant to make an ordinary search and seizure for fear of tipping off other members of the drug ring. Instead, the police stage a phony automobile accident (that causes minor damage) using an undercover police officer who appears to be drunk (and who is purportedly "arrested" at the scene of the accident). The real suspects are told to leave their keys in their vehicle and sit in the back of a police cruiser. After the suspects are seated in the cruiser, a "thief" (really a

police operative) steals the vehicle. The police then search the vehicle and return it to the suspects. Did the police conduct a permissible automobile search? *See United States v. Alverez–Tejeda*, 491 F.3d 1013 (9th Cir. 2007).

5. *Consent*

On p. 252, following problem #1, insert the following new problem:

1a. In *State v. Johnson*, 68 N.J. 349, 346 A.2d 66 (1975), the New Jersey Supreme Court rejected *Schneckloth's* holding in its interpretation of the New Jersey Constitution. The Court reached that conclusion even though the New Jersey Constitution's language is taken almost verbatim from the Fourth Amendment ("'(T)he right of the people to be secure in their persons, houses, papers and effects, against unreasonable searches and seizures shall not be violated. . . .'"). The Court explained:

> We conclude that under Art. I, par. 7 of our State Constitution the validity of a consent to a search, even in a non-custodial situation, must be measured in terms of waiver; I.e., where the State seeks to justify a search on the basis of consent it has the burden of showing that the consent was voluntary, an essential element of which is knowledge of the right to refuse consent. Many persons, perhaps most, would view the request of a police officer to make a search as having the force of law. Unless it is shown by the State that the person involved knew that he had the right to refuse to accede to such a request, his assenting to the search is not meaningful. One cannot be held to have waived a right if he was unaware of its existence. . . . However, in a non-custodial situation, such as is here presented, the police would not necessarily be required to advise the person of his right to refuse to consent to the search. Our decision is only that in such a situation if the State seeks to rely on consent as the basis for a search, it has the burden of demonstrating knowledge on the part of the person involved that he had a choice in the matter. . . .

Does the New Jersey Supreme Court's holding in *Johnson* represent a preferable interpretation to the United States Supreme Court's holding in *Schneckloth*?

On p. 258, at the end of the problems, add the following new problem:

Problem: Causing Structural Damage

Police officers stopped a suspect's vehicle on the basis that it contained "excessively tinted windows." During the stop, one officer noticed that the vehicle had a fresh coat of undercoating, and requested consent to search the vehicle for weapons and drugs. During the subsequent search, the officer pulled up non-factory carpeting in the back seat of the car, noticed a small hole in the floor board, and proceeded to pry open the hole with a crowbar. Inside the hole, he found cocaine. Did the driver's consent authorize the officer to use a crowbar on his vehicle, thereby causing structural damage? When the suspect noticed that the officer intended to use the crowbar on his vehicle, could he have revoked his consent? *See People v. Gomez*, 5 N.Y.3d 416, 838 N.E.2d 1271, 805 N.Y.S.2d 24 (2005).

On p. 268, at the end of the problems, add the following new problem:

7. *The Executive's Computer.* The police have reason to believe that a corporation's high-level executive (the "Director of Operations") is accessing child pornography from his office computer. The computer is owned by the company, but is protected by an individual log-in and password. However, the company's IT department has complete administrative access to all computers, uses a firewall to monitor employee's internet activity, and makes employees aware of the monitoring. Under these circumstances, does the CFO have the authority to consent to a police search of the Director of Operations' computer? *See United States v. Ziegler*, 474 F.3d 1184 (9th Cir. 2007).

7. Stop and Frisk

On p. 295, following problem #8, insert the following new problems:

9. *Applying Terry at the Threshold of a Home.* Assume that police officers believe that Joe is manufacturing methamphetamine in his home, but that they do not have probable cause to search the defendant's home for drugs. They conduct a "knock and talk" at Joe's home in the hope of persuading him to consent to a search. When the officers knock on Joe's front door, a woman appears in the window next to the door. One officer asks her, through the glass, whether she will come out and speak to him and his partner. The woman nods her head, and moments later, the woman and Joe come out of the front door and shut it behind them. Assume that after conversing with the officers for ten minutes, Joe agrees to a search of his home, and the police discover an illegal firearm that leads to Joe's arrest for a firearm crime. If police had enough evidence to supply reasonable suspicion of methamphetamine manufacturing by Joe, was the police conduct lawful under *Terry*? If the police officers lacked such reasonable suspicion and conducted the knock and talk based only on a hunch, was their conduct lawful? Compare *United States v. Crapser*, 472 F.3d 1141 (9th Cir. 2007) with *United States v. Washington*, 387 F.3d 1060 (9th Cir. 2004).

10. *The NRA Sticker.* A police officer stops a pickup truck for speeding on a public highway. As the officer approaches the truck, he notices a "National Rifle Association" sticker on the back window. Even though the officer does not otherwise have a basis for concluding that the driver is "armed," can the officer conduct a stop and frisk on the basis of the sticker? *See Estep v. Dallas County*, 310 F.3d 353 (5th Cir. 2002).

On p. 302, after the problems, add the following new problem:

7. *Stops to Investigate Misdemeanors?* Based on *Mendenhall*, we know that the police can stop an individual to investigate a felony when sufficient justification exists. Does the same rule apply to misdemeanors? In other words, balancing the "need" versus the "intrusion," should the police be allowed to make investigative stops to ferret out misdemeanors. *See United States v. Grigg*, 498 F.3d 1070 (9th Cir. 2007).

a. Other Investigatory Searches and Seizures
On p. 307, after the problems, add the following new problems:

3. *The Searchlight and the Pedestrian.* A police officer is patrolling in a high-crime area when he sees an individual standing next to a parked car.

The officer shines the patrol car spotlight on the individual, exits his car, walks briskly towards the individual, and asks whether the individual is on probation or parole. The individual does not resist or attempt to run away. Was the individual "seized" when the officer exited the vehicle? *See People v. Garry*, 156 Cal.App.4th 1100, 67 Cal.Rptr.3d 849 (2007).

4. *Should Racial Identity be Relevant?* Suppose that there is a history of racial tension in a particular city, and that tension has been heightened by recent police shootings of African–American motorists. Around midnight, two white police officers approach an African–American man who was seated in his lawfully parked car in an effort to "find out what he is doing." Under the circumstances, has the man been seized? To what extent is the racial identity of the man, or the racial identity of the police officers, relevant to your answer? *See United States v. Washington*, 490 F.3d 765 (9th Cir. 2007).

On p. 307, after the problems, add the following new case and problems:

BRENDLIN v. CALIFORNIA

127 S.Ct. 2400 (2007).

JUSTICE SOUTER delivered the opinion of the Court.

When a police officer makes a traffic stop, the driver of the car is seized within the meaning of the Fourth Amendment. The question in this case is whether the same is true of a passenger. We hold that a passenger is seized as well and so may challenge the constitutionality of the stop.

Early in the morning of November 27, 2001, Deputy Sheriff Robert Brokenbrough and his partner saw a parked Buick with expired registration tags. In his ensuing conversation with the police dispatcher, Brokenbrough learned that an application for renewal of registration was being processed. The officers saw the car again on the road, and this time Brokenbrough noticed its display of a temporary operating permit with the number "indicating it was legal to drive the car through November." The officers decided to pull the Buick over to verify that the permit matched the vehicle, even though [there] was nothing unusual about the permit or the way it was affixed. Brokenbrough asked the driver, Karen Simeroth, for her license and saw a passenger in the front seat, petitioner Bruce Brendlin, whom he recognized as "one of the Brendlin brothers." He recalled that either Scott or Bruce Brendlin had dropped out of parole supervision and asked Brendlin to identify himself. Brokenbrough returned to his cruiser, called for backup, and verified that Brendlin was a parole violator with an outstanding no-bail warrant for his arrest. While he was in the patrol car, Brokenbrough saw Brendlin briefly open and then close the passenger door of the Buick. Once reinforcements arrived, Brokenbrough went to the passenger side of the Buick, ordered him out of the car at gunpoint, and declared him under arrest. When the police searched Brendlin incident to arrest, they found an orange syringe cap on his person. A patdown search of Simeroth revealed syringes and a plastic bag of a green leafy substance, and she was also formally arrested. Officers then searched the car and found tubing, a scale, and other things used to produce methamphetamine.

Brendlin was charged with possession and manufacture of methamphetamine, and he moved to suppress the evidence obtained in the searches of his person and the car as fruits of an unconstitutional seizure, arguing that the officers lacked probable cause or reasonable suspicion to make the traffic stop. He did not assert that his Fourth Amendment rights were violated by the search of Simeroth's vehicle, but claimed only that the traffic stop was an unlawful seizure of his person. The trial court denied the suppression motion.... Brendlin pleaded guilty, subject to appeal on the suppression issue, and was sentenced to four years in prison.... The California Court of Appeal reversed the denial of the suppression motion, holding that Brendlin was seized by the traffic stop, which they held unlawful. By a narrow majority, the Supreme Court of California reversed.... We granted certiorari to decide whether a traffic stop subjects a passenger, as well as the driver, to Fourth Amendment seizure. We now vacate.

A person is seized by the police and thus entitled to challenge the government's action under the Fourth Amendment when the officer, " 'by means of physical force or show of authority,' " terminates or restrains his freedom of movement, *through means intentionally applied," Brower v. County of Inyo,* 489 U.S. 593, 597 (1989) (emphasis in original). Thus, an "unintended person [may be] the object of the detention," so long as the detention is "willful" and not merely the consequence of "an unknowing act." A police officer may make a seizure by a show of authority and without the use of physical force, but there is no seizure without actual submission; otherwise, there is at most an attempted seizure, so far as the Fourth Amendment is concerned. See *California v. Hodari D.,* 499 U.S. 621.

When the actions of the police do not show an unambiguous intent to restrain or when an individual's submission to a show of governmental authority takes the form of passive acquiescence, there needs to be some test for telling when a seizure occurs in response to authority, and when it does not. The test was devised by Justice Stewart in *United States v. Mendenhall,* 446 U.S. 544 (1980), who wrote that a seizure occurs if "in view of all of the circumstances surrounding the incident, a reasonable person would have believed that he was not free to leave." Later on, the Court adopted Justice Stewart's touchstone, see, *e.g., Hodari D., supra,* at 627, but added that when a person "has no desire to leave" for reasons unrelated to the police presence, the "coercive effect of the encounter" can be measured better by asking whether "a reasonable person would feel free to decline the officers' requests or otherwise terminate the encounter," *Bostick, supra,* at 435–436.

The law is settled that in Fourth Amendment terms a traffic stop entails a seizure of the driver "even though the purpose of the stop is limited and the resulting detention quite brief." *Delaware v. Prouse,* 440

U.S. 648, 653 (1979). And although we have not, until today, squarely answered the question whether a passenger is also seized, we have said over and over in dicta that during a traffic stop an officer seizes everyone in the vehicle, not just the driver. See, *e.g., Prouse, supra,* at 653. . . .

The State concedes that the police had no adequate justification to pull the car over, but argues that the passenger was not seized and thus cannot claim that the evidence was tainted by an unconstitutional stop. We resolve this question by asking whether a reasonable person in Brendlin's position when the car stopped would have believed himself free to "terminate the encounter" between the police and himself. We think that in these circumstances any reasonable passenger would have understood the police officers to be exercising control to the point that no one in the car was free to depart without police permission.

A traffic stop necessarily curtails the travel a passenger has chosen just as much as it halts the driver, diverting both from the stream of traffic to the side of the road, and the police activity that normally amounts to intrusion on "privacy and personal security" does not normally (and did not here) distinguish between passenger and driver. *United States v. Martinez–Fuerte,* 428 U.S. 543 (1976). An officer who orders one particular car to pull over acts with an implicit claim of right based on fault of some sort, and a sensible person would not expect a police officer to allow people to come and go freely from the physical focal point of an investigation into faulty behavior or wrongdoing. If the likely wrongdoing is not the driving, the passenger will reasonably feel subject to suspicion owing to close association; but even when the wrongdoing is only bad driving, the passenger will expect to be subject to some scrutiny, and his attempt to leave the scene would be so obviously likely to prompt an objection from the officer that no passenger would feel free to leave in the first place.[3]

It is also reasonable for passengers to expect that a police officer at the scene of a crime, arrest, or investigation will not let people move around in ways that could jeopardize his safety. In *Maryland v. Wilson,* 519 U.S. 408 (1997), we held that during a lawful traffic stop an officer may order a passenger out of the car as a precautionary measure, without reasonable suspicion that the passenger poses a safety risk. In fashioning this rule, we invoked our earlier statement that " '[t]he risk of harm to both the police and the occupants is minimized if the officers routinely exercise unquestioned command of the situation.' " *Wilson, supra,* at 414 (quoting *Michigan v. Summers,* 452 U.S. 692 (1981)). What we have said in these opinions probably reflects a societal expectation of " 'unquestioned [police] command' " at odds with any notion that a passenger would feel free to leave, or to terminate the personal encounter any other way, without advance permission. . . .

3. Of course, police may also stop a car solely to investigate a passenger's conduct. Accordingly, a passenger cannot assume, merely from the fact of a traffic stop, that the driver's conduct is the cause of the stop.

The contrary conclusion drawn by the Supreme Court of California, that seizure came only with formal arrest, reflects three premises as to which we respectfully disagree. First, the State Supreme Court reasoned that Brendlin was not seized by the stop because Deputy Sheriff Brokenbrough only intended to investigate Simeroth and did not direct a show of authority toward Brendlin. The court saw Brokenbrough's "flashing lights [as] directed at the driver...." But that view of the facts ignores the objective *Mendenhall* test of what a reasonable passenger would understand. To the extent that there is anything ambiguous in the show of force (was it fairly seen as directed only at the driver or at the car and its occupants?), the test resolves the ambiguity, and here it leads to the intuitive conclusion that all the occupants were subject to like control by the successful display of authority. The State Supreme Court's approach, on the contrary, shifts the issue from the intent of the police as objectively manifested to the motive of the police for taking the intentional action to stop the car, and we have repeatedly rejected attempts to introduce this kind of subjectivity into Fourth Amendment analysis. See, *e.g., Whren,* 517 U.S., at 813.

California defends the State Supreme Court's ruling on this point by citing our cases holding that seizure requires a purposeful, deliberate act of detention.... The intent that counts under the Fourth Amendment is the "intent [that] has been conveyed to the person confronted," and the criterion of willful restriction on freedom of movement is no invitation to look to subjective intent when determining who is seized. Our most recent cases are in accord on this point. In *Lewis,* 523 U.S. 833, we considered whether a seizure occurred when an officer accidentally ran over a passenger who had fallen off a motorcycle during a high-speed chase, and in holding that no seizure took place, we stressed that the officer stopped Lewis's movement by accidentally crashing into him, not "through means intentionally applied." We did not even consider, let alone emphasize, the possibility that the officer had meant to detain the driver only and not the passenger. Nor is *Brower,* 489 U.S. 593, to the contrary, where it was dispositive that "Brower was meant to be stopped by the physical obstacle of the roadblock-and that he was so stopped." California reads this language to suggest that for a specific occupant of the car to be seized he must be the motivating target of an officer's show of authority, as if the thrust of our observation were that Brower, and not someone else, was "meant to be stopped." But our point was not that Brower alone was the target but that officers detained him "through means intentionally applied"; if the car had had another occupant, it would have made sense to hold that he too had been seized when the car collided with the roadblock. [T]he issue is whether a reasonable passenger would have perceived that the show of authority was at least partly directed at him, and that he was thus not free to ignore the police presence and go about his business.

Second, the Supreme Court of California assumed that Brendlin, "as the passenger, had no ability to submit to the deputy's show of authority" because only the driver was in control of the moving vehicle....

Here, Brendlin had no effective way to signal submission while the car was still moving on the roadway, but once it came to a stop he could, and apparently did, submit by staying inside.

Third, the State Supreme Court shied away from the rule we apply today for fear that it "would encompass even those motorists following the vehicle subject to the traffic stop who, by virtue of the original detention, are forced to slow down and perhaps even come to a halt in order to accommodate that vehicle's submission to police authority." But an occupant of a car who knows that he is stuck in traffic because another car has been pulled over (like the motorist who can't even make out why the road is suddenly clogged) would not perceive a show of authority as directed at him or his car. Such incidental restrictions on freedom of movement would not tend to affect an individual's "sense of security and privacy in traveling in an automobile." Nor would the consequential blockage call for a precautionary rule to avoid the kind of "arbitrary and oppressive interference by [law] enforcement officials with the privacy and personal security of individuals" that the Fourth Amendment was intended to limit.

. . . Holding that the passenger in a private car is not (without more) seized in a traffic stop would invite police officers to stop cars with passengers regardless of probable cause or reasonable suspicion of anything illegal. The fact that evidence uncovered as a result of an arbitrary traffic stop would still be admissible against any passengers would be a powerful incentive to run the kind of "roving patrols" that would still violate the driver's Fourth Amendment right. See, *e.g., Almeida–Sanchez v. United States,* 413 U.S. 266 (1973).

Brendlin was seized from the moment Simeroth's car came to a halt on the side of the road, and it was error to deny his suppression motion on the ground that seizure occurred only at the formal arrest. It will be for the state courts to consider in the first instance whether suppression turns on any other issue. The judgment of the Supreme Court of California is vacated, and the case is remanded for further proceedings not inconsistent with this opinion.

It is so ordered.

Problem

One of the issues raised in *Brendlin* is whether "all taxi cab and bus passengers would be 'seized' under the Fourth Amendment if the cab or bus driver is pulled over by the police for running a red light." Suppose that a Greyhound bus is pulled over by a police officer for a safety violation. Have the passengers been seized? Would a reasonable person in the passenger's position feel free to take steps to terminate the encounter? Would you reach the same result if the police pulled over a taxi cab driver for an equipment violation?

On p. 316, at the end of the problems, add the following new problems:

7. *Length of Stop.* Suppose that a police officer validly stops a suspect for a traffic violation. May the police officer extend the stop long enough to run a background check on the suspect (to make sure who she is dealing with) and to check for outstanding warrants? *See People v. Harris*, 228 Ill.2d 222, 319 Ill.Dec. 823, 886 N.E.2d 947 (2008).

8. *More on the Length of Stop.* In the prior problem, after the officer confirms the validity of the suspect's driver's license and the absence of outstanding warrants, the officer is writing a citation when another officer arrives him and informs the first officer that the suspect is believed to be involved in drug activity. The first officer immediately stops writing the ticket, and goes to the suspect's car to question him about illegal drugs. After a very brief conversation, the suspect consents to a search of the vehicle which turned up illegal narcotics and illegal firearms. Under *Royer* and *Muehler*, did the officer act permissibly in prolonging the search to ask about drugs and request consent to search? Does it matter whether you conclude that the officer had a "reasonable suspicion" on which to base the inquiry? *See United States v. Turvin*, 517 F.3d 1097 (9th Cir. 2008); *State v. Louthan*, 275 Neb. 101, 744 N.W.2d 454 (2008).

9. *Scope of Permissible Detention and Questioning.* In *Muehler v. Mena*, 544 U.S. 93 (2005) (previously discussed on p. 133 of the text), the Court upheld the handcuffing and detention of an occupant of a house that police believed to be a gang house. During the search, an officer asked the detainee about her immigration status, and the Court decided that this question did not constitute a separate seizure requiring reasonable suspicion, because "mere police questioning does not constitute a seizure." Instead, the Court emphasized that the duration of the questioning, not the content of the questioning, would be relevant to determine whether the detention was lawful. Does *Muehler* mean that a police officer may lawfully question a stopped motorist about subjects that are unrelated to the purpose of the stop, assuming that such questioning does not prolong the detention? Compare *United States v. Stewart*, 473 F.3d 1265 (10th Cir. 2007) with *United States v. Mendez*, 467 F.3d 1162 (9th Cir. 2006).

On p. 328, before the problems, add the following new case:

LOS ANGELES COUNTY v. RETTELE

127 S.Ct. 1989 (2007).

PER CURIAM.

Deputies of the Los Angeles County Sheriff's Department obtained a valid warrant to search a house, but they were unaware that the suspects being sought had moved out three months earlier. When the deputies searched the house, they found in a bedroom two residents who were of a different race than the suspects. The deputies ordered these innocent residents, who had been sleeping unclothed, out of bed. The deputies required them to stand for a few minutes before allowing them to dress.

The residents brought suit under 42 U.S.C. § 1983, naming the deputies and other parties and accusing them of violating the Fourth

Amendment right to be free from unreasonable searches and seizures. The District Court granted summary judgment to all named defendants. The Court of Appeals for the Ninth Circuit reversed, concluding both that the deputies violated the Fourth Amendment and that they were not entitled to qualified immunity because a reasonable deputy would have stopped the search upon discovering that respondents were of a different race than the suspects and because a reasonable deputy would not have ordered respondents from their bed. We grant the petition for certiorari and reverse the judgment of the Court of Appeals by this summary disposition.

From September to December 2001, Los Angeles County Sheriff's Department Deputy Dennis Watters investigated a fraud and identity-theft crime ring. There were four suspects of the investigation. One had registered a 9–millimeter Glock handgun. The four suspects were known to be African–Americans.

On December 11, Watters obtained a search warrant for two houses in Lancaster, California, where he believed he could find the suspects. The warrant authorized him to search the homes and three of the suspects for documents and computer files. In support of the search warrant an affidavit cited various sources showing the suspects resided at respondents' home. The sources included Department of Motor Vehicles reports, mailing address listings, an outstanding warrant, and an Internet telephone directory. In this Court respondents do not dispute the validity of the warrant or the means by which it was obtained.

What Watters did not know was that one of the houses (the first to be searched) had been sold in September to a Max Rettele. He had purchased the home and moved into it three months earlier with his girlfriend Judy Sadler and Sadler's 17–year-old son Chase Hall. All three, respondents here, are Caucasians.

On the morning of December 19, Watters briefed six other deputies in preparation for the search of the houses. Watters informed them they would be searching for three African–American suspects, one of whom owned a registered handgun. The possibility a suspect would be armed caused the deputies concern for their own safety. Watters had not obtained special permission for a night search, so he could not execute the warrant until 7 a.m. Around 7:15 Watters and six other deputies knocked on the door and announced their presence. Chase Hall answered. The deputies entered the house after ordering Hall to lie face down on the ground.

The deputies' announcement awoke Rettele and Sadler. The deputies entered their bedroom with guns drawn and ordered them to get out of their bed and to show their hands. They protested that they were not wearing clothes. Rettele stood up and attempted to put on a pair of sweatpants, but deputies told him not to move. Sadler also stood up and attempted, without success, to cover herself with a sheet. Rettele and Sadler were held at gunpoint for one to two minutes before Rettele was allowed to retrieve a robe for Sadler. He was then permitted to dress.

Rettele and Sadler left the bedroom within three to four minutes to sit on the couch in the living room.

By that time the deputies realized they had made a mistake. They apologized to Rettele and Sadler, thanked them for not becoming upset, and left within five minutes. They proceeded to the other house the warrant authorized them to search, where they found three suspects. Those suspects were arrested and convicted.

Rettele and Sadler, individually and as guardians ad litem for Hall, filed this § 1983 suit against Los Angeles County, the Los Angeles County Sheriff's Department, Deputy Watters, and other members of the sheriff's department.... The District Court held that the warrant was obtained by proper procedures and the search was reasonable. It concluded in the alternative that any Fourth Amendment rights the deputies violated were not clearly established and that, as a result, the deputies were entitled to qualified immunity.... On appeal respondents did not challenge the validity of the warrant; they did argue that the deputies had conducted the search in an unreasonable manner. A divided panel of the Court of Appeals for the Ninth Circuit reversed in an unpublished opinion.... The Court of Appeals denied rehearing and rehearing en banc.

Because respondents were of a different race than the suspects the deputies were seeking, the Court of Appeals held that "[a]fter taking one look at [respondents], the deputies should have realized that [respondents] were not the subjects of the search warrant and did not pose a threat to the deputies' safety." We need not pause long in rejecting this unsound proposition. When the deputies ordered respondents from their bed, they had no way of knowing whether the African–American suspects were elsewhere in the house. The presence of some Caucasians in the residence did not eliminate the possibility that the suspects lived there as well. [I]t is not uncommon in our society for people of different races to live together. Just as people of different races live and work together, so too might they engage in joint criminal activity. The deputies, who were searching a house where they believed a suspect might be armed, possessed authority to secure the premises before deciding whether to continue with the search.

In *Michigan v. Summers,* 452 U.S. 692 (1981), this Court held that officers executing a search warrant for contraband may "detain the occupants of the premises while a proper search is conducted." In weighing whether the search in *Summers* was reasonable the Court first found that "detention represents only an incremental intrusion on personal liberty when the search of a home has been authorized by a valid warrant." Against that interest, it balanced "preventing flight in the event that incriminating evidence is found"; "minimizing the risk of harm to the officers"; and facilitating "the orderly completion of the search."

In executing a search warrant officers may take reasonable action to secure the premises and to ensure their own safety and the efficacy of the search. The test of reasonableness under the Fourth Amendment is an objective one. Unreasonable actions include the use of excessive force or restraints that cause unnecessary pain or are imposed for a prolonged and unnecessary period of time.

The orders by the police to the occupants, in the context of this lawful search, were permissible, and perhaps necessary, to protect the safety of the deputies. Blankets and bedding can conceal a weapon, and one of the suspects was known to own a firearm, factors which underscore this point. The Constitution does not require an officer to ignore the possibility that an armed suspect may sleep with a weapon within reach. The reports are replete with accounts of suspects sleeping close to weapons. See *United States v. Enslin,* 327 F.3d 788, 791 (C.A.9 2003) ("When [the suspect] put his hands in the air and began to sit up, his movement shifted the covers and the marshals could see a gun in the bed next to him").

The deputies needed a moment to secure the room and ensure that other persons were not close by or did not present a danger. Deputies were not required to turn their backs to allow Rettele and Sadler to retrieve clothing or to cover themselves with the sheets. Rather, "[t]he risk of harm to both the police and the occupants is minimized if the officers routinely exercise unquestioned command of the situation." *Summers,* 452 U.S., at 702–703.

This is not to say, of course, that the deputies were free to force Rettele and Sadler to remain motionless and standing for any longer than necessary. We have recognized that "special circumstances, or possibly a prolonged detention" might render a search unreasonable. There is no accusation that the detention here was prolonged. The deputies left the home less than 15 minutes after arriving. The detention was shorter and less restrictive than the 2- to 3-hour handcuff detention upheld in *Mena.* And there is no allegation that the deputies prevented Sadler and Rettele from dressing longer than necessary to protect their safety. Sadler was unclothed for no more than two minutes, and Rettele for only slightly more time than that. Sadler testified that once the police were satisfied that no immediate threat was presented, "they wanted us to get dressed and they were pressing us really fast to hurry up and get some clothes on."

. . . Officers executing search warrants on occasion enter a house when residents are engaged in private activity; and the resulting frustration, embarrassment, and humiliation may be real, as was true here. When officers execute a valid warrant and act in a reasonable manner to protect themselves from harm, however, the Fourth Amendment is not violated.

As respondents' constitutional rights were not violated, "there is no necessity for further inquiries concerning qualified immunity." The judgment of the Court of Appeals is reversed, and the case is remanded for further proceedings consistent with this opinion.

It is so ordered.

JUSTICE SOUTER would deny the petition for a writ of certiorari.

JUSTICE STEVENS, with whom JUSTICE GINSBURG joins, concurring in the judgment.

[R]egardless of the proper answer to the constitutional question, the defendants were entitled to qualified immunity. I would reverse on that ground and disavow the unwise practice of deciding constitutional questions in advance of the necessity for doing so.... Accordingly, I concur in the Court's judgment.

On p. 328, add new problem ##1 & 2 at the beginning of the problems and renumber the succeeding problems:

1. *The Need to Justify a Protective Sweep.* Suppose that the police go to a suspect's home to arrest him pursuant to a warrant. The warrant was issued because defendant failed to appear in court in response to charges of "disorderly conduct" (he alleged played his stereo too loud late at night). The police are admitted to the house by the suspect's wife, and they call to him from the bottom of the stairs (the suspect is on the second floor of the house) asking him to come downstairs. The suspect does come down, is handcuffed, and is taken away to the kitchen. Before leaving, the police conduct a protective sweep of the upstairs. As you read *Buie*, was the protective sweep permissible? If not, why not? *See State v. McGrane*, 733 N.W.2d 671 (Iowa 2007).

2. *More on the Need to Justify.* As you think about the prior problem, does it matter what crime the defendant is suspected of committing? Suppose that the facts of the case are the same except that the suspect is being arrested on drug charges, and the police have reason to believe that the suspect is dealing drugs out of his house. Does the nature of the charge alter the analysis? *See State v. McGrane*, 733 N.W.2d 671 (Iowa 2007).

On p. 335, following problem #8, add the following new problem:

9. *Driving Slowly.* A police officer on routine patrol observes a driver traveling at 48 mph in a 65 mph zone. Does the officer have reasonable suspicion to stop the car, based on this fact alone? Or must there be additional evidence, such as erratic driving or unusual behavior by the driver to justify a stop? See *State v. Rincon*, 122 Nev. 1170, 147 P.3d 233 (2007).

8. Border Searches

On p. 355, following the problems, add the following new problem:

3. *Computer Searches.* We know that Customs agents have broad authority to conduct searches at international borders. How far does that authority extend? Suppose that defendant is passing through a border checkpoint on the U.S.-Canadian border when a border patrol agent asks him to start his computer. When the agent noticed that there were icons labeled "Kodak Pictures" and "Kodak Memories," he opened and examined them and found child pornography. When he was subsequently convicted of possession of child pornography, defendant claims that the Fourth Amendment prohibited the Customs agent from examining his computer files. Is defendant correct? *See United States v. Arnold*, 523 F.3d 941 (9th Cir. 2008).

4. *Post-Entry Searches.* Internal Revenue Service officials call U.S. Customs agents, and express interest in laptops that will be carried through customs by defendant and a traveling companion both of whom had been working as contractors in Iraq and Kuwait. When defendant arrived in the United States, she was referred to a secondary inspection area where she was searched and released. She proceeded out of the Customs area into the main airport terminal. Subsequently, Customs agents found $10,000 in undeclared cash in the companion's luggage, and the agents became suspicious regarding defendant. The agents located defendant in the terminal, escorted her back to the Customs area, and found (on a subsequent search) that she had committed currency violations as well. Defendant seeks to challenge her subsequent conviction on the basis that Customs officials lacked a warrant and probable cause. Customs officials seek to justify the search as a "border search." Who should prevail and why? *See United States v. McGinnis*, 247 Fed.Appx. 589 (6th Cir. 2007).

9. *Special Needs*

On p. 364, at the end of the problems, add the following new problems:

6. *The Drug Search.* A principal receives a "tip" from a "trustworthy" student stating that another student (Jill) is hiding marijuana in her pants. Jill has a history of non-drug related disciplinary problems. When approached by the principal, Jill acts "suspiciously" in denying the allegations. Based on these facts, does the principal have sufficient grounds to order a strip search of the student, including her underwear? *See Phaneuf v. Fraikin*, 448 F.3d 591 (2d Cir. 2006).

7. *Terrorism and Football.* Florida's Tampa Sports Authority (TSA), concerned about the possibility of terrorists entering Raymond James Stadium, wants to conduct suspicionless pat-down searches of all individuals attending games at the Stadium. You are the attorney for the TSA. What must the TSA show in order to impose the pat-down search requirement? *See Johnston v. Tampa Sports Authority*, 442 F. Supp.2d 1257 (M.D. Fla. 2006).

8. *Terrorism and Subways.* In response to subway attacks in other countries, the New York Police Department (NYPD) would like to implement a program of random, suspicionless, searches of items being carried by, or on, subway passengers. The genesis of the program was the subway bombings in other countries, particularly England. Suppose that you are the legal adviser asked to advise the NYPD? What must the NYPD show in order to create a valid "special needs" program? For example, must it show that it is responding to a particular terrorist threat? Must it show that the program will be effective in deterring potential terrorists? Must the NYPD place warning signs at the entrances to police stations warning potential subway riders that "by choosing to ride on the subway, they agree to consent to random searches of their persons and effects"? Must the program be random? *See MacWade v. Kelly*, 460 F.3d 260 (2d Cir. 2006).

9. *Drug Testing and Librarians.* May a city require drug testing of all applicants for all city jobs? Jane Foeburn is denied a job as a librarian on the basis that she refuses to take a drug test. If hired, Foeburn would have retrieved items from the book drop and returned them to the shelves. In

challenging the denial, Foeburn claims that the city is unable to establish a "special need" for subjecting librarians to drug tests. The city disagrees. Who is correct? *See Lanier v. Woodburn*, 518 F.3d 1147 (9th Cir. 2008). Could a city drug test all welfare recipients as a prerequisite to eligibility? The city's goal is to make sure that the children of needy families are receiving adequate care. *See Marchwinski v. Howard*, 309 F.3d 330 (6th Cir. 2002).

10. *Exigent Circumstances*

On p. 378, at the end of the problems, add the following new problem:

6. *The Abortion Protestors.* Suppose that anti-abortion protestors have trucks with large photos of aborted fetuses. Because of the potentially offensive nature of the material, the protestors cover the photos with tarps when going to and from protest sites. In addition, because of the potential for violence at protest sites, the protestors wear helmets and kevlar vests. A police officer on routine patrol happens to observe the trucks (covered by tarps) being driven by individuals with helmets and kevlar vests. Fearing a terrorist strike, the police decide to stop the trucks and search them. Did the police act properly? *See Center for Bio–Ethical Reform, Inc. v. Springboro*, 477 F.3d 807 (6th Cir. 2007).

Chapter 6

POLICE INTERROGATIONS & CONFESSIONS

C. *MIRANDA'S* APPLICATION

On p. 452, at the end of the problems, add the following new problem:

8. *The Hospital Interrogation.* Jamison, who has suffered a gunshot wound, is taken to the emergency room where he tells a police officer "I've been shot." The officer places bags on Jamison's hands (routine procedure for shooting victims in order to preserve evidence), but does not place Jamison under arrest. In an effort to find out what happened, the officer proceeds to discuss the situation with Jamison who makes incriminating statements. Was Jamison in "custody" so that *Miranda* warnings were required? *See United States v. Jamison*, 509 F.3d 623 (4th Cir. 2007).

On p. 483, at the end of the problems, add the following new problem:

7. *Reinitiation by One of Two Suspects.* Defendant and her boyfriend were subjected to separate custodial interrogations regarding a robbery. Both denied involvement, and then both asserted their *Miranda* right to remain silent. Both were released, but were arrested later that day. On the way to the station, defendant's boyfriend stated that they would speak to the police if they were first allowed to converse with each other. The police agreed. After the two conversed, the police read both defendants their *Miranda* rights again, and honored the boyfriend's request that they be interrogated in the same room. The boyfriend signed a written statement indicating that he was retracting his prior assertion of rights, and was willing to waive his *Miranda* rights. Defendant was not asked to sign a waiver form or even to verbally waive her rights. In the subsequent interrogation, both defendant and her boyfriend made incriminating statements. Did the interrogators act properly under *Miranda*? *See United States v. Lafferty*, 503 F.3d 293 (3d Cir. 2007).

6. *The Uses of Evidence Obtained in Violation of Miranda*

On p. 490, following the note, add the following new note:

2. In *Sanchez-Llamas v. Oregon*, 548 U.S. 331 (2006), the police complied with *Miranda*, but failed to comply with Article 36 of the Vienna

Convention on Consular Relations. Article 36 provides that, when a national of one country is detained by authorities in another, the authorities must notify the consular officers of the detainee's home country if the detainee so requests. Article 36(1)(b) also requires the authorities to notify a detainee of his right to consular assistance. The Court refused to apply the exclusionary rule for non-compliance with Article 36.

Chapter 9

THE EXCLUSIONARY RULE

On p. 616, add the following new note:

In *Sanchez–Llamas v. Oregon*, 548 U.S. 331 (2006), the Court refused to apply the exclusionary rule to a violation of Article 36 of the Vienna Convention on Consular Relations (Vienna Convention or Convention). Article 36 provides that, when a national of one country is detained by authorities in another, the authorities must notify the consular officers of the detainee's home country if the detainee so requests. In addition, the authorities must inform the detainee of his right to request consular assistance. Sanchez–Llamas was detained for shooting a police officer, and given a *Miranda* warning, but not informed of his right to consular assistance. He sought to suppress his statements because of non-compliance with Article 36. Another foreign national raised similar claims as well. After noting that Article 36 does not provide for the remedy of suppression, the Court held that United States law does not require suppression:

> ... Sanchez–Llamas argues only that suppression is required because it is the appropriate remedy for an Article 36 violation under United States law, and urges us to require suppression for Article 36 violations as a matter of our "authority to develop remedies for the enforcement of federal law in state-court criminal proceedings." ...

> To the extent Sanchez–Llamas argues that we should invoke our supervisory authority, the law is clear: "It is beyond dispute that we do not hold a supervisory power over the courts of the several States." *Dickerson v. United States*, 530 U.S. 428 (2000). [O]ur authority to create a judicial remedy applicable in state court must lie, if anywhere, in the treaty itself.... And where a treaty provides for a particular judicial remedy, there is no issue of intruding on the constitutional prerogatives of the States or the other federal branches. Courts must apply the remedy as a requirement of federal law. But where a treaty does not provide a particular remedy, either expressly or implicitly, it is not for the federal courts to impose one on the States through lawmaking of their own.

> Sanchez–Llamas argues that the language of the Convention implicitly requires a judicial remedy because it states that the laws and regulations governing the exercise of Article 36 rights "must enable *full*

effect to be given to the purposes for which the rights ... are intended,'' Art. 36(2), 21 U.S.T., at 101 (emphasis added).... [T]here is little indication that other parties to the Convention have interpreted Article 36 to require a judicial remedy in the context of criminal prosecutions. Nevertheless, even if Sanchez–Llamas is correct that Article 36 implicitly requires a judicial remedy, the Convention equally states that Article 36 rights ''shall be exercised in conformity with the laws and regulations of the receiving State.'' Art. 36(2), 21 U.S.T., at 101. Under our domestic law, the exclusionary rule is not a remedy we apply lightly. ''[O]ur cases have repeatedly emphasized that the rule's 'costly toll' upon truth-seeking and law enforcement objectives presents a high obstacle for those urging application of the rule.'' *Pennsylvania Bd. of Probation and Parole v. Scott,* 524 U.S. 357 (1998). Because the rule's social costs are considerable, suppression is warranted only where the rule's '' 'remedial objectives are thought most efficaciously served.' '' *United States v. Leon,* 468 U.S. 897 (1984) (quoting *United States v. Calandra,* 414 U.S. 338, 348 (1974)).

We have applied the exclusionary rule primarily to deter constitutional violations. In particular, we have ruled that the Constitution requires the exclusion of evidence obtained by certain violations of the Fourth Amendment....

The few cases in which we have suppressed evidence for statutory violations do not help Sanchez–Llamas. In those cases, the excluded evidence arose directly out of statutory violations that implicated important Fourth and Fifth Amendment interests. *McNabb,* for example, involved the suppression of incriminating statements obtained during a prolonged detention of the defendants, in violation of a statute requiring persons arrested without a warrant to be promptly presented to a judicial officer. We noted that the statutory right was intended to ''avoid all the evil implications of secret interrogation of persons accused of crime,'' and later stated that *McNabb* was ''responsive to the same considerations of Fifth Amendment policy that ... face[d] us ... as to the states'' in *Miranda,* 384 U.S., at 463. Similarly, in *Miller,* we required suppression of evidence that was the product of a search incident to an unlawful arrest.

The violation of the right to consular notification, in contrast, is at best remotely connected to the gathering of evidence.... The provision secures only a right of foreign nationals to have their consulate *informed* of their arrest or detention—not to have their consulate intervene, or to have law enforcement authorities cease their investigation pending any such notice or intervention. In most circumstances, there is likely to be little connection between an Article 36 violation and evidence or statements obtained by police.

Moreover, the reasons we often require suppression for Fourth and Fifth Amendment violations are entirely absent from the consular notification context. We require exclusion of coerced confessions both because we disapprove of such coercion and because such confessions tend to be unreliable. *Watkins v. Sowders,* 449 U.S. 341 (1981). We exclude the fruits of unreasonable searches on the theory that without a strong deterrent, the constraints of the Fourth Amendment might be too easily disregarded by law enforcement. *Elkins v. United States,* 364 U.S. 206 (1960). The situation here is quite different. The failure to inform a defendant of his Article 36 rights is unlikely, with any frequency, to produce unreliable confessions. And unlike the search-and-seizure context—where the need to obtain valuable evidence may tempt authorities to transgress Fourth Amendment limitations—police win little, if any, practical advantage from violating Article 36. Suppression would be a vastly disproportionate remedy for an Article 36 violation.

Sanchez–Llamas counters that the failure to inform defendants of their right to consular notification gives them "a misleadingly incomplete picture of [their] legal options," and that suppression will give authorities an incentive to abide by Article 36.

Leaving aside the suggestion that it is the role of police generally to advise defendants of their legal options, we think other constitutional and statutory requirements effectively protect the interests served, in Sanchez–Llamas' view, by Article 36. A foreign national detained on suspicion of crime, like anyone else in our country, enjoys under our system the protections of the Due Process Clause. Among other things, he is entitled to an attorney, and is protected against compelled self-incrimination. Article 36 adds little to these "legal options," and we think it unnecessary to apply the exclusionary rule where other constitutional and statutory protections—many of them already enforced by the exclusionary rule—safeguard the same interests Sanchez–Llamas claims are advanced by Article 36.

Finally, suppression is not the only means of vindicating Vienna Convention rights. A defendant can raise an Article 36 claim as part of a broader challenge to the voluntariness of his statements to police. If he raises an Article 36 violation at trial, a court can make appropriate accommodations to ensure that the defendant secures, to the extent possible, the benefits of consular assistance. Of course, diplomatic avenues—the primary means of enforcing the Convention—also remain open.

In sum, neither the Vienna Convention itself nor our precedents applying the exclusionary rule support suppression of Sanchez–Llamas' statements to police. . . .

Justice Breyer, joined by Justices Stevens and Souter, dissented:

. . . I agree with the majority insofar as it rejects the argument that the Convention creates a *Miranda*-style "automatic exclusionary rule." But I do not agree with the absolute nature of its statement. Rather, *sometimes* suppression could prove the only effective remedy. And, if that is so, then the Convention, which insists upon effective remedies, would require suppression in an appropriate case.

Much depends upon the circumstances. It may be true that in "most circumstances, there is likely to be little connection between an Article 36 violation and evidence or statements obtained by police." *Miranda* surely helps, for it guarantees that police will inform an arrested foreign national of his right to contact a lawyer. But one cannot guarantee in advance that *Miranda* will adequately cure *every* seriously prejudicial failure to inform an arrested person of his right to contact his consular post. One can imagine a case, for example, involving a foreign national who speaks little English, who comes from a country where confessions made to the police cannot be used in court as evidence, who does not understand that a state-provided lawyer can provide him crucial assistance in an interrogation, and whose native community has great fear of police abuse. Indeed, Sanchez–Llamas made allegations similar to these in his case.

While Justice GINSBURG is correct that a defendant who is prejudiced under the Convention may be able to show that his confession is involuntary under *Miranda,* I am not persuaded that this will always be so. A person who fully understands his *Miranda* rights but does not fully understand the implications of these rights for our legal system may or may not be able to show that his confession was involuntary under *Miranda,* but he will certainly have a claim under the Vienna Convention. In such a case suppression of a confession may prove the only effective remedy. I would not rule out the existence of such cases in advance.

Furthermore, the majority is wrong to say that it would "be startling if the Convention were read to require suppression" in such cases because suppression "is an entirely American legal creation." [It] is not "startling" to read the Convention as *sometimes* requiring suppression. That is because those who wrote the Convention were fully aware that the criminal justice systems of different nations differ in important ways. They did not list particular remedies. They used general language. That language requires every member nation to give "full effect" to Article 36(1)'s "purposes." That language leaves it up to each nation to determine how to implement Article 36(1)'s requirements. But as a matter of logic and purpose that language must also insist upon the use of suppression if and when there are circumstances in which suppression provides the only *effective remedy.*

These differences may also help to explain what the majority says is the disturbing circumstance that "nearly all" other signatories to the Convention "refuse to recognize" suppression "as a matter of domestic law," and therefore that "Sanchez–Llamas would [not] be afforded the relief he seeks here in any of the other 169 countries party to the Vienna Convention." In fact, there are several cases from common-law jurisdictions suggesting that suppression is an appropriate remedy for a Convention violation. . . .

Part III

THE ADVERSARY SYSTEM

Chapter 13

PRELIMINARY PROCEEDINGS

A. INITIAL APPEARANCE

On p. 749, insert the following Note, before part B:

Note

In Chapter 3, you learned about the scope of the right to counsel in the criminal justice system. A careful reading of the cases reveals a surprising truth. The Supreme Court has never regarded the initial appearance, when a bail decision is made, as a "critical stage" when a defendant has a right to counsel. As the foregoing materials establish, federal and state rules prescribe notification to the accused about his future right to counsel. However, when most defendants appear in court for the first time, no one is representing them. Thus, when the court typically is making pretrial release decisions, as discussed in Chapter 11, most defendants are representing themselves. Appellate courts constitutionally have confirmed those trial court practices. For example, in *Fenner v. State*, 381 Md. 1, 846 A.2d 1020 (2004), the court held that an indigent defendant's right to counsel does not include representation at the bail-setting proceeding.

Chapter 14

GRAND JURIES

B. THE GRAND JURY AS A SHIELD

1. *Sufficiency of the Evidence*

On page 775, substitute the following corrected citation on lines 3–4:

U.S. Attorneys' Manual § 9–11.231 (Supp. 2006).

Chapter 19

JURY TRIALS

On p. 985, insert the following Note, before part 3:

Note

In the preceding Exercise, item 4(E) discusses voir dire in capital cases. In *Uttecht v. Brown*, 127 S.Ct. 2218 (2007), the Supreme Court recognized the need for a trial judge to balance the prosecution's interest in having jurors who can follow the jury instructions about applying capital punishment without violating the defendant's right to an impartial jury that is not tilted in favor of capital punishment through prosecutorial challenges for cause. The Court believes that a trial judge is in a better position to assess a prospective juror's demeanor, attitude and qualification to sit in the case. A reviewing court should consider the entire voir dire in the defendant's case as well as the questioning of the particular juror. Where "there is lengthy questioning of a prospective juror and trial court has supervised a diligent and thoughtful voir dire, the trial court has broad discretion."

3. *Exercising Peremptory Challenges*

On page 995, insert the following at the end of the first paragraph of Note 3:

Similarly, in *Snyder v. Louisiana*, 128 S.Ct. 1203 (2008), The prosecutor stated that he used a peremptory challenge to remove a black college senior from a capital homicide jury because he would vote to convict on a lesser charge, thereby obviating the need for a capital sentencing proceeding so that he could get back to his studies. The Court found that prosecutor's "explanation given for the strike of [the juror in question] is by itself unconvincing and suffices for the determination that there was *Batson* error." As in *Miller-El*, the Court the prosecutor's failure to strike white jurors who disclosed obligations that conflicted with jury duty and appeared at least as pressing as the black juror.

Chapter 21

SENTENCING

1.   The Problem of Fairness

On p. 1041, insert the following at the beginning of the section:

KENNEDY v. LOUISIANA

128 S.Ct. 2641 (2008).

JUSTICE KENNEDY delivered the opinion of the Court.

The National Government and, beyond it, the separate States are bound by the proscriptive mandates of the Eighth Amendment to the Constitution of the United States, and all persons within those respective jurisdictions may invoke its protection. See Amdts. 8 and 14, § 1; Patrick Kennedy, the petitioner here, seeks to set aside his death sentence under the Eighth Amendment. He was charged by the respondent, the State of Louisiana, with the aggravated rape of his then–8–year-old stepdaughter. After a jury trial petitioner was convicted and sentenced to death under a state statute authorizing capital punishment for the rape of a child under 12 years of age. This case presents the question whether the Constitution bars respondent from imposing the death penalty for the rape of a child where the crime did not result, and was not intended to result, in death of the victim. We hold the Eighth Amendment prohibits the death penalty for this offense. The Louisiana statute is unconstitutional.

I

Petitioner's crime was one that cannot be recounted in these pages in a way sufficient to capture in full the hurt and horror inflicted on his victim or to convey the revulsion society, and the jury that represents it, sought to express by sentencing petitioner to death. At 9:18 a.m. on March 2, 1998, petitioner called 911 to report that his stepdaughter, referred to here as L. H., had been raped. * * *

L.H. was transported to the Children's Hospital. An expert in pediatric forensic medicine testified that L. H.'s injuries were the most

severe he had seen from a sexual assault in his four years of practice.
* * *

The State charged petitioner with aggravated rape of a child under
La. Stat. Ann. § 14:42 and sought the death penalty. * * *

The jury unanimously determined that petitioner should be sentenced to death. The Supreme Court of Louisiana affirmed. The court
rejected petitioner's reliance on *Coker v. Georgia,* 433 U.S. 584 (1977),
noting that, while *Coker* bars the use of the death penalty as punishment
for the rape of an adult woman, it left open the question which, if any,
other nonhomicide crimes can be punished by death consistent with the
Eighth Amendment. Because " 'children are a class that need special
protection,' "the state court reasoned, the rape of a child is unique in
terms of the harm it inflicts upon the victim and our society.

The court acknowledged that petitioner would be the first person
executed for committing child rape since La. Stat. Ann. § 14:42 was
amended in 1995 and that Louisiana is in the minority of jurisdictions
that authorize the death penalty for the crime of child rape. But
following the approach of *Roper v. Simmons,* 543 U.S. 551 (2005), and
Atkins v. Virginia, 536 U.S. 304 (2002), it found significant not the
"numerical counting of which [S]tates ... stand for or against a particular capital prosecution," but "the direction of change." Since 1993, the
court explained, four more States–Oklahoma, South Carolina, Montana,
and Georgia-had capitalized the crime of child rape and at least eight
States had authorized capital punishment for other nonhomicide crimes.
By its count, 14 of the then–38 States permitting capital punishment,
plus the Federal Government, allowed the death penalty for nonhomicide
crimes and 5 allowed the death penalty for the crime of child rape.

The state court next asked whether "child rapists rank among the
worst offenders." It noted the severity of the crime; that the execution of
child rapists would serve the goals of deterrence and retribution; and
that, unlike in *Atkins* and *Roper,* there were no characteristics of
petitioner that tended to mitigate his moral culpability. *Id.,* at 788–789.
It concluded: "[S]hort of first-degree murder, we can think of no other
non-homicide crime more deserving [of capital punishment]." *Id.,* at 789.

On this reasoning the Supreme Court of Louisiana rejected petitioner's argument that the death penalty for the rape of a child under 12
years is disproportionate and upheld the constitutionality of the statute.
Chief Justice Calogero dissented. *Coker, supra,* and *Eberheart v. Georgia,*
433 U.S. 917 (1977), in his view, "set out a bright-line and easily
administered rule" that the Eighth Amendment precludes capital punishment for any offense that does not involve the death of the victim. We
granted certiorari.

II

The Eighth Amendment, applicable to the States through the Fourteenth Amendment, provides that "[e]xcessive bail shall not be required,
nor excessive fines imposed, nor cruel and unusual punishments inflict-

ed." The Amendment proscribes "all excessive punishments, as well as cruel and unusual punishments that may or may not be excessive." *Atkins,* 536 U.S., at 311, n. 7. The Court explained in *Atkins, id.,* at 311, and *Roper, supra,* at 560, that the Eighth Amendment's protection against excessive or cruel and unusual punishments flows from the basic "precept of justice that punishment for [a] crime should be graduated and proportioned to [the] offense." *Weems v. United States,* 217 U.S. 349, 367 (1910). Whether this requirement has been fulfilled is determined not by the standards that prevailed when the Eighth Amendment was adopted in 1791 but by the norms that "currently prevail." *Atkins, supra,* at 311. The Amendment "draw[s] its meaning from the evolving standards of decency that mark the progress of a maturing society." *Trop v. Dulles,* 356 U.S. 86, 101 (1958) (plurality opinion). This is because "[t]he standard of extreme cruelty is not merely descriptive, but necessarily embodies a moral judgment. The standard itself remains the same, but its applicability must change as the basic mores of society change." *Furman v. Georgia,* 408 U.S. 238, 382 (1972) (Burger, C. J., dissenting).

Evolving standards of decency must embrace and express respect for the dignity of the person, and the punishment of criminals must conform to that rule. See *Trop, supra,* at 100 (plurality opinion). As we shall discuss, punishment is justified under one or more of three principal rationales: rehabilitation, deterrence, and retribution. It is the last of these, retribution, that most often can contradict the law's own ends. This is of particular concern when the Court interprets the meaning of the Eighth Amendment in capital cases. When the law punishes by death, it risks its own sudden descent into brutality, transgressing the constitutional commitment to decency and restraint.

For these reasons we have explained that capital punishment must "be limited to those offenders who commit 'a narrow category of the most serious crimes' and whose extreme culpability makes them 'the most deserving of execution.' " *Roper, supra,* at 568. Though the death penalty is not invariably unconstitutional, the Court insists upon confining the instances in which the punishment can be imposed.

Applying this principle, we held in *Roper* and *Atkins* that the execution of juveniles and mentally retarded persons are punishments violative of the Eighth Amendment because the offender had a diminished personal responsibility for the crime. The Court further has held that the death penalty can be disproportionate to the crime itself where the crime did not result, or was not intended to result, in death of the victim. In *Coker,* 433 U.S. 584, for instance, the Court held it would be unconstitutional to execute an offender who had raped an adult woman. And in *Enmund v. Florida,* 458 U.S. 782 (1982), the Court overturned the capital sentence of a defendant who aided and abetted a robbery during which a murder was committed but did not himself kill, attempt to kill, or intend that a killing would take place. On the other hand, in *Tison v. Arizona,* 481 U.S. 137 (1987), the Court allowed the defendants' death sentences to stand where they did not themselves kill the victims but their involvement in the events leading up to the murders was active, recklessly indifferent, and substantial.

In these cases the Court has been guided by "objective indicia of society's standards, as expressed in legislative enactments and state practice with respect to executions." *Roper,* 543 U.S., at 563. The inquiry does not end there, however. Consensus is not dispositive. Whether the death penalty is disproportionate to the crime committed depends as well upon the standards elaborated by controlling precedents and by the Court's own understanding and interpretation of the Eighth Amendment's text, history, meaning, and purpose.

Based both on consensus and our own independent judgment, our holding is that a death sentence for one who raped but did not kill a child, and who did not intend to assist another in killing the child, is unconstitutional under the Eighth and Fourteenth Amendments.

III

A

The existence of objective indicia of consensus against making a crime punishable by death was a relevant concern in *Roper, Atkins, Coker,* and *Enmund,* and we follow the approach of those cases here. The history of the death penalty for the crime of rape is an instructive beginning point.

In 1925, 18 States, the District of Columbia, and the Federal Government had statutes that authorized the death penalty for the rape of a child or an adult. Between 1930 and 1964, 455 people were executed for those crimes. See 5 Historical Statistics of the United States: Earliest Times to the Present, pp. 5–262 to 5–263 (S. Carter et al. eds. 2006) (Table Ec343–357). To our knowledge the last individual executed for the rape of a child was Ronald Wolfe in 1964. See H. Frazier, Death Sentences in Missouri, 1803–2005: A History and Comprehensive Registry of Legal Executions, Pardons, and Commutations 143 (2006).

In 1972, *Furman* invalidated most of the state statutes authorizing the death penalty for the crime of rape; and in *Furman*'s aftermath only six States reenacted their capital rape provisions. Three States—Georgia, North Carolina, and Louisiana—did so with respect to all rape offenses. Three States—Florida, Mississippi, and Tennessee—did so with respect only to child rape. See *Coker, supra,* at 594–595 (plurality opinion). All six statutes were later invalidated under state or federal law.

Louisiana reintroduced the death penalty for rape of a child in 1995. Under the current statute, any anal, vaginal, or oral intercourse with a child under the age of 13 constitutes aggravated rape and is punishable by death. Mistake of age is not a defense, so the statute imposes strict liability in this regard. Five States have since followed Louisiana's lead.

By contrast, 44 States have not made child rape a capital offense. As for federal law, Congress in the Federal Death Penalty Act of 1994 expanded the number of federal crimes for which the death penalty is a permissible sentence, including certain nonhomicide offenses; but it did not do the same for child rape or abuse. See 108 Stat.1972 (codified as amended in scattered sections of 18 U.S.C.). Under 18 U.S.C. § 2245, an offender is death eligible only when the sexual abuse or exploitation results in the victim's death. * * *

Definitive resolution of state-law issues is for the States' own courts, and there may be disagreement over the statistics. It is further true that some States, including States that have addressed the issue in just the last few years, have made child rape a capital offense. The summary recited here, however, does allow us to make certain comparisons with the data cited in the *Atkins, Roper,* and *Enmund* cases.

When *Atkins* was decided in 2002, 30 States, including 12 noncapital jurisdictions, prohibited the death penalty for mentally retarded offenders; 20 permitted it. When *Roper* was decided in 2005, the numbers disclosed a similar division among the States: 30 States prohibited the death penalty for juveniles, 18 of which permitted the death penalty for other offenders; and 20 States authorized it. Both in *Atkins* and in *Roper,* we noted that the practice of executing mentally retarded and juvenile offenders was infrequent. Only five States had executed an offender known to have an IQ below 70 between 1989 and 2002, and only three States had executed a juvenile offender between 1995 and 2005.

The statistics in *Enmund* bear an even greater similarity to the instant case. There eight jurisdictions had authorized imposition of the death penalty solely for participation in a robbery during which an accomplice committed murder, and six defendants between 1954 and 1982 had been sentenced to death for felony murder where the defendant did not personally commit the homicidal assault. These facts, the Court concluded, "weigh[ed] on the side of rejecting capital punishment for the crime."

The evidence of a national consensus with respect to the death penalty for child rapists, as with respect to juveniles, mentally retarded offenders, and vicarious felony murderers, shows divided opinion but, on balance, an opinion against it. Thirty-seven jurisdictions—36 States plus the Federal Government—have the death penalty. As mentioned above, only six of those jurisdictions authorize the death penalty for rape of a child. Though our review of national consensus is not confined to tallying the number of States with applicable death penalty legislation, it is of significance that, in 45 jurisdictions, petitioner could not be executed for child rape of any kind. That number surpasses the 30 States in *Atkins* and *Roper* and the 42 States in *Enmund* that prohibited the death penalty under the circumstances those cases considered.

B

* * * The state courts that have confronted the precise question before us have been uniform in concluding that *Coker* did not address the constitutionality of the death penalty for the crime of child rape. * * *

There is, to be sure, some contrary authority contained in various state-court opinions. But it is either dicta, or from a decision of a state intermediate court that has been superseded by a more specific statement of the law by the State's supreme court. * * *

We conclude on the basis of this review that there is no clear indication that state legislatures have misinterpreted *Coker* to hold that the death penalty for child rape is unconstitutional. The small number of States that have enacted this penalty, then, is relevant to determining whether there is a consensus against capital punishment for this crime.

C

Respondent insists that the six States where child rape is a capital offense, along with the States that have proposed but not yet enacted applicable death penalty legislation, reflect a consistent direction of change in support of the death penalty for child rape. Consistent change might counterbalance an otherwise weak demonstration of consensus. But whatever the significance of consistent change where it is cited to show emerging support for expanding the scope of the death penalty, no showing of consistent change has been made in this case.

Respondent and its *amici* identify five States where, in their view, legislation authorizing capital punishment for child rape is pending. It is not our practice, nor is it sound, to find contemporary norms based upon state legislation that has been proposed but not yet enacted. * * *

Aside from pending legislation, it is true that in the last 13 years there has been change towards making child rape a capital offense. This is evidenced by six new death penalty statutes, three enacted in the last two years. Here, the total number of States to have made child rape a capital offense after *Furman* is six. This is not an indication of a trend or change in direction comparable to the one supported by data in *Roper.* The evidence here bears a closer resemblance to the evidence of state activity in *Enmund,* where we found a national consensus against the death penalty for vicarious felony murder despite eight jurisdictions having authorized the practice.

D

There are measures of consensus other than legislation. Statistics about the number of executions may inform the consideration whether capital punishment for the crime of child rape is regarded as unacceptable in our society. These statistics confirm our determination from our review of state statutes that there is a social consensus against the death penalty for the crime of child rape.

Nine States—Florida, Georgia, Louisiana, Mississippi, Montana, Oklahoma, South Carolina, Tennessee, and Texas—have permitted capital punishment for adult or child rape for some length of time between the Court's 1972 decision in *Furman* and today. Yet no individual has been executed for the rape of an adult or child since 1964, and no execution for any other nonhomicide offense has been conducted since 1963.

After reviewing the authorities informed by contemporary norms, including the history of the death penalty for this and other nonhomicide crimes, current state statutes and new enactments, and the number of executions since 1964, we conclude there is a national consensus against capital punishment for the crime of child rape.

IV

A

As we have said in other Eighth Amendment cases, objective evidence of contemporary values as it relates to punishment for child rape is entitled to great weight, but it does not end our inquiry. "[T]he Constitution contemplates that in the end our own judgment will be brought to bear on the question of the acceptability of the death penalty under the Eighth Amendment." *Coker, supra,* at 597 (plurality opinion). We turn, then, to the resolution of the question before us, which is informed by our precedents and our own understanding of the Constitution and the rights it secures.

It must be acknowledged that there are moral grounds to question a rule barring capital punishment for a crime against an individual that did not result in death. These facts illustrate the point. Here the victim's fright, the sense of betrayal, and the nature of her injuries caused more prolonged physical and mental suffering than, say, a sudden killing by an unseen assassin. The attack was not just on her but on her childhood. For this reason, we should be most reluctant to rely upon the language of the plurality in *Coker,* which posited that, for the victim of rape, "life may not be nearly so happy as it was" but it is not beyond repair. 433 U.S., at 598. Rape has a permanent psychological, emotional, and sometimes physical impact on the child. See C. Bagley & K. King, Child Sexual Abuse: The Search for Healing 2–24, 111–112 (1990); Finkelhor & Browne, Assessing the Long–Term Impact of Child Sexual Abuse: A Review and Conceptualization in Handbook on Sexual Abuse of Children 55–60 (L. Walker ed.1988). We cannot dismiss the years of long anguish that must be endured by the victim of child rape.

It does not follow, though, that capital punishment is a proportionate penalty for the crime. The constitutional prohibition against excessive or cruel and unusual punishments mandates that the State's power to punish "be exercised within the limits of civilized standards." *Trop,* 356 U.S., at 99, 100 (plurality opinion). Evolving standards of decency that mark the progress of a maturing society counsel us to be most hesitant before interpreting the Eighth Amendment to allow the extension of the death penalty, a hesitation that has special force where no life was taken in the commission of the crime. It is an established principle that decency, in its essence, presumes respect for the individual and thus moderation or restraint in the application of capital punishment.

To date the Court has sought to define and implement this principle, for the most part, in cases involving capital murder. One approach has been to insist upon general rules that ensure consistency in determining who receives a death sentence. At the same time the Court has insisted, to ensure restraint and moderation in use of capital punishment, on judging the "character and record of the individual offender and the circumstances of the particular offense as a constitutionally indispensable part of the process of inflicting the penalty of death."

The tension between general rules and case-specific circumstances has produced results not all together satisfactory. This has led some Members of the Court to say we should cease efforts to resolve the tension and simply allow legislatures, prosecutors, courts, and juries greater latitude. For others the failure to limit these same imprecisions by stricter enforcement of narrowing rules has raised doubts concerning the constitutionality of capital punishment itself.

Our response to this case law, which is still in search of a unifying principle, has been to insist upon confining the instances in which capital punishment may be imposed.

Our concern here is limited to crimes against individual persons. We do not address, for example, crimes defining and punishing treason, espionage, terrorism, and drug kingpin activity, which are offenses against the State. As it relates to crimes against individuals, though, the death penalty should not be expanded to instances where the victim's life was not taken.

The same distinction between homicide and other serious violent offenses against the individual informed the Court's analysis in *Enmund,* 458 U.S. 782, where the Court held that the death penalty for the crime of vicarious felony murder is disproportionate to the offense. The Court repeated there the fundamental, moral distinction between a "murderer" and a "robber," noting that while "robbery is a serious crime deserving serious punishment," it is not like death in its "severity and irrevocability." *Id.,* at 797.

Consistent with evolving standards of decency and the teachings of our precedents we conclude that, in determining whether the death penalty is excessive, there is a distinction between intentional first-degree murder on the one hand and nonhomicide crimes against individual persons, even including child rape, on the other. The latter crimes may be devastating in their harm, as here, but "in terms of moral depravity and of the injury to the person and to the public," *Coker,* 433 U.S., at 598, they cannot be compared to murder in their "severity and irrevocability." Ibid.

In reaching our conclusion we find significant the number of executions that would be allowed under respondent's approach. The crime of child rape, considering its reported incidents, occurs more often than first-degree murder. Approximately 5,702 incidents of vaginal, anal, or oral rape of a child under the age of 12 were reported nationwide in 2005; this is almost twice the total incidents of intentional murder for victims of all ages (3,405) reported during the same period. Although we have no reliable statistics on convictions for child rape, we can surmise that, each year, there are hundreds, or more, of these convictions just in jurisdictions that permit capital punishment. As a result of existing rules, only 2.2% of convicted first-degree murderers are sentenced to death. But under respondent's approach, the 36 States that permit the death penalty could sentence to death all persons convicted of raping a child less than 12 years of age. This could not be reconciled with our evolving standards of decency and the necessity to constrain the use of the death penalty.

It might be said that narrowing aggravators could be used in this context, as with murder offenses, to ensure the death penalty's re-strained application. We find it difficult to identify standards that would guide the decisionmaker so the penalty is reserved for the most severe cases of child rape and yet not imposed in an arbitrary way. Even were we to forbid, say, the execution of first-time child rapists, see *supra* at 12, or require as an aggravating factor a finding that the perpetrator's instant rape offense involved multiple victims, the jury still must bal-ance, in its discretion, those aggravating factors against mitigating circumstances. In this context, which involves a crime that in many cases will overwhelm a decent person's judgment, we have no confidence that the imposition of the death penalty would not be so arbitrary as to be "freakis[h]," *Furman,* 408 U.S., at 310 (Stewart, J., concurring). We cannot sanction this result when the harm to the victim, though grave, cannot be quantified in the same way as death of the victim.

As noted above, the resulting imprecision and the tension between evaluating the individual circumstances and consistency of treatment have been tolerated where the victim dies. It should not be introduced into our justice system, though, where death has not occurred.

Our concerns are all the more pronounced where, as here, the death penalty for this crime has been most infrequent. See Part III–D, *supra.* We have developed a foundational jurisprudence in the case of capital murder to guide the States and juries in imposing the death penalty. Starting with *Gregg,* 428 U.S. 153, we have spent more than 32 years articulating limiting factors that channel the jury's discretion to avoid the death penalty's arbitrary imposition in the case of capital murder. Though that practice remains sound, beginning the same process for crimes for which no one has been executed in more than 40 years would require experimentation in an area where a failed experiment would result in the execution of individuals undeserving of the death penalty. Evolving standards of decency are difficult to reconcile with a regime that seeks to expand the death penalty to an area where standards to confine its use are indefinite and obscure.

B

Our decision is consistent with the justifications offered for the death penalty. *Gregg* instructs that capital punishment is excessive when it is grossly out of proportion to the crime or it does not fulfill the two distinct social purposes served by the death penalty: retribution and deterrence of capital crimes.

As in *Coker,* here it cannot be said with any certainty that the death penalty for child rape serves no deterrent or retributive function. * * * This argument does not overcome other objections, however. The incongruity between the crime of child rape and the harshness of the death penalty poses risks of overpunishment and counsels against a constitutional ruling that the death penalty can be expanded to include this offense.

The goal of retribution, which reflects society's and the victim's interests in seeing that the offender is repaid for the hurt he caused. In measuring retribution, as well as other objectives of criminal law, it is appropriate to distinguish between a particularly depraved murder that merits death as a form of retribution and the crime of child rape.

There is an additional reason for our conclusion that imposing the death penalty for child rape would not further retributive purposes. In considering whether retribution is served, among other factors we have looked to whether capital punishment "has the potential . . . to allow the community as a whole, including the surviving family and friends of the victim, to affirm its own judgment that the culpability of the prisoner is so serious that the ultimate penalty must be sought and imposed." *Panetti v. Quarterman,* 551 U.S. ___, ___ (2007). In considering the death penalty for nonhomicide offenses this inquiry necessarily also must include the question whether the death penalty balances the wrong to the victim.

It is not at all evident that the child rape victim's hurt is lessened when the law permits the death of the perpetrator. Capital cases require a long-term commitment by those who testify for the prosecution, especially when guilt and sentencing determinations are in multiple proceedings. In cases like this the key testimony is not just from the family but from the victim herself. During formative years of her adolescence, made all the more daunting for having to come to terms with the brutality of her experience, L.H. was required to discuss the case at length with law enforcement personnel. In a public trial she was required to recount once more all the details of the crime to a jury as the State pursued the death of her stepfather. Cf. G. Goodman et al., Testifying in Criminal Court: Emotional Effects on Child Sexual Assault Victims 50, 62, 72 (1992); Brief for National Association of Social Workers et al. as *Amici Curiae* 17–21. And in the end the State made L.H. a central figure in its decision to seek the death penalty, telling the jury in closing statements: "[L. H.] is asking you, asking you to set up a time and place when he dies."

Society's desire to inflict the death penalty for child rape by enlisting the child victim to assist it over the course of years in asking for capital punishment forces a moral choice on the child, who is not of mature age to make that choice. The way the death penalty here involves the child victim in its enforcement can compromise a decent legal system; and this is but a subset of fundamental difficulties capital punishment can cause in the administration and enforcement of laws proscribing child rape.

There are, moreover, serious systemic concerns in prosecuting the crime of child rape that are relevant to the constitutionality of making it a capital offense. The problem of unreliable, induced, and even imagined child testimony means there is a "special risk of wrongful execution" in some child rape cases. *Atkins, supra,* at 321. This undermines, at least to some degree, the meaningful contribution of the death penalty to legitimate goals of punishment.

Similar criticisms pertain to other cases involving child witnesses; but child rape cases present heightened concerns because the central narrative and account of the crime often comes from the child herself. She and the accused are, in most instances, the only ones present when the crime was committed. * * * Although capital punishment does bring retribution, and the legislature here has chosen to use it for this end, its judgment must be weighed, in deciding the constitutional question, against the special risks of unreliable testimony with respect to this crime.

With respect to deterrence, if the death penalty adds to the risk of non-reporting, that, too, diminishes the penalty's objectives. Underreporting is a common problem with respect to child sexual abuse. See Hanson, Resnick, Saunders, Kilpatrick, & Best, Factors Related to the Reporting of Childhood Rape, 23 Child Abuse & Neglect 559, 564 (1999) (finding that about 88% of female rape victims under the age of 18 did not disclose their abuse to authorities); Smith et al., Delay in Disclosure of Childhood Rape: Results From A National Survey, 24 Child Abuse & Neglect 273, 278–279 (2000) (finding that 72% of women raped as children disclosed their abuse to someone, but that only 12% of the victims reported the rape to authorities). Although we know little about what differentiates those who report from those who do not report, see Hanson, *supra,* at 561, one of the most commonly cited reasons for nondisclosure is fear of negative consequences for the perpetrator, a concern that has special force where the abuser is a family member. The experience of the *amici* who work with child victims indicates that, when the punishment is death, both the victim and the victim's family members may be more likely to shield the perpetrator from discovery, thus increasing underreporting. As a result, punishment by death may not result in more deterrence or more effective enforcement.

In addition, by in effect making the punishment for child rape and murder equivalent, a State that punishes child rape by death may remove a strong incentive for the rapist not to kill the victim. Assuming the offender behaves in a rational way, as one must to justify the penalty on grounds of deterrence, the penalty in some respects gives less protection, not more, to the victim, who is often the sole witness to the crime. It might be argued that, even if the death penalty results in a marginal increase in the incentive to kill, this is counterbalanced by a marginally increased deterrent to commit the crime at all. Whatever balance the legislature strikes, however, uncertainty on the point makes the argument for the penalty less compelling than for homicide crimes.

Each of these propositions, standing alone, might not establish the unconstitutionality of the death penalty for the crime of child rape. Taken in sum, however, they demonstrate the serious negative consequences of making child rape a capital offense. These considerations lead us to conclude, in our independent judgment, that the death penalty is not a proportional punishment for the rape of a child.

V

Our determination that there is a consensus against the death penalty for child rape raises the question whether the Court's own institutional position and its holding will have the effect of blocking further or later consensus in favor of the penalty from developing. The Court, it will be argued, by the act of addressing the constitutionality of the death penalty, intrudes upon the consensus-making process. By imposing a negative restraint, the argument runs, the Court makes it more difficult for consensus to change or emerge. The Court, according to the criticism, itself becomes enmeshed in the process, part judge and part the maker of that which it judges.

These concerns overlook the meaning and full substance of the established proposition that the Eighth Amendment is defined by "the evolving standards of decency that mark the progress of a maturing society." *Trop,* 356 U.S., at 101. Confirmed by repeated, consistent rulings of this Court, this principle requires that use of the death penalty be restrained. The rule of evolving standards of decency with specific marks on the way to full progress and mature judgment means that resort to the penalty must be reserved for the worst of crimes and limited in its instances of application. In most cases justice is not better served by terminating the life of the perpetrator rather than confining him and preserving the possibility that he and the system will find ways to allow him to understand the enormity of his offense. Difficulties in administering the penalty to ensure against its arbitrary and capricious application require adherence to a rule reserving its use, at this stage of evolving standards and in cases of crimes against individuals, for crimes that take the life of the victim.

The judgment of the Supreme Court of Louisiana upholding the capital sentence is reversed. This case is remanded for further proceedings not inconsistent with this opinion. It is so ordered.

JUSTICE ALITO, with whom THE CHIEF JUSTICE, JUSTICE SCALIA, and JUSTICE THOMAS join, dissenting.

The Court today holds that the Eighth Amendment categorically prohibits the imposition of the death penalty for the crime of raping a child. This is so, according to the Court, no matter how young the child, no matter how many times the child is raped, no matter how many children the perpetrator rapes, no matter how sadistic the crime, no matter how much physical or psychological trauma is inflicted, and no matter how heinous the perpetrator's prior criminal record may be. The Court provides two reasons for this sweeping conclusion: First, the Court claims to have identified "a national consensus" that the death penalty is never acceptable for the rape of a child; second, the Court concludes, based on its "independent judgment," that imposing the death penalty for child rape is inconsistent with " 'the evolving standards of decency that mark the progress of a maturing society.' " Because neither of these justifications is sound, I respectfully dissent.

I

A

I turn first to the Court's claim that there is "a national consensus" that it is never acceptable to impose the death penalty for the rape of a child. The Eighth Amendment's requirements, the Court writes, are "determined not by the standards that prevailed" when the Amendment was adopted but "by the norms that 'currently prevail.' " In assessing current norms, the Court relies primarily on the fact that only 6 of the 50 States now have statutes that permit the death penalty for this offense. But this statistic is a highly unreliable indicator of the views of state lawmakers and their constituents. As I will explain, dicta in this Court's decision in *Coker v. Georgia,* 433 U.S. 584 (1977), has stunted legislative consideration of the question whether the death penalty for the targeted offense of raping a young child is consistent with prevailing standards of decency. The *Coker* dicta gave state legislators and others good reason to fear that any law permitting the imposition of the death penalty for this crime would meet precisely the fate that has now befallen the Louisiana statute that is currently before us, and this threat strongly discouraged state legislators-regardless of their own values and those of their constituents-from supporting the enactment of such legislation. * * *

For the past three decades, these interpretations have posed a very high hurdle for state legislatures considering the passage of new laws permitting the death penalty for the rape of a child. The enactment and implementation of any new state death penalty statute—and particularly a new type of statute such as one that specifically targets the rape of young children—imposes many costs. There is the burden of drafting an innovative law that must take into account this Court's exceedingly complex Eighth Amendment jurisprudence. Securing passage of controversial legislation may interfere in a variety of ways with the enactment of other bills on the legislative agenda. Once the statute is enacted, there is the burden of training and coordinating the efforts of those who must implement the new law. Capital prosecutions are qualitatively more difficult than noncapital prosecutions and impose special emotional burdens on all involved. When a capital sentence is imposed under the new law, there is the burden of keeping the prisoner on death row and the lengthy and costly project of defending the constitutionality of the statute on appeal and in collateral proceedings. And if the law is eventually overturned, there is the burden of new proceedings on remand. Moreover, conscientious state lawmakers, whatever their personal views about the morality of imposing the death penalty for child rape, may defer to this Court's dicta, either because they respect our authority and expertise in interpreting the Constitution or merely because they do not relish the prospect of being held to have violated the Constitution and contravened prevailing "standards of decency." Accordingly, the *Coker* dicta gave state legislators a strong incentive not to push for the enactment of new capital child-rape laws even though these legislators and their constituents may have believed that the laws would be appropriate and desirable.

B

The Court expresses doubt that the *Coker* dicta had this effect, but the skepticism is unwarranted. It would be quite remarkable if state legislators were not influenced by the considerations noted above. And although state legislatures typically do not create legislative materials like those produced by Congress, there is evidence that proposals to permit the imposition of the death penalty for child rape were opposed on the ground that enactment would be futile and costly. * * *

C

Because of the effect of the *Coker* dicta, the Court is plainly wrong in comparing the situation here to that in *Atkins* or *Roper v. Simmons,* 543 U.S. 551 (2005). Thirteen years earlier, in *Penry v. Lynaugh,* 492 U.S. 302 (1989), the Court had held that this was permitted by the Eighth Amendment, and therefore, during the time between *Penry* and *Atkins,* state legislators had reason to believe that this Court would follow its prior precedent and uphold statutes allowing such punishment.

The situation in *Roper* was similar. *Roper* concerned a challenge to the constitutionality of imposing the death penalty on a defendant who had not reached the age of 18 at the time of the crime. Sixteen years earlier in *Stanford v. Kentucky,* 492 U.S. 361(1989), the Court had rejected a similar challenge, and therefore state lawmakers had cause to believe that laws allowing such punishment would be sustained.

When state lawmakers believe that their decision will prevail on the question whether to permit the death penalty for a particular crime or class of offender, the legislators' resolution of the issue can be interpreted as an expression of their own judgment, informed by whatever weight they attach to the values of their constituents. But when state legislators think that the enactment of a new death penalty law is likely to be futile, inaction cannot reasonably be interpreted as an expression of their understanding of prevailing societal values. In that atmosphere, legislative inaction is more likely to evidence acquiescence.

D

If anything can be inferred from state legislative developments, the message is very different from the one that the Court perceives. In just the past few years, despite the shadow cast by the *Coker* dicta, five States have enacted targeted capital child-rape laws. If, as the Court seems to think, our society is "[e]volving" toward ever higher "standards of decency," these enactments might represent the beginning of a new evolutionary line.

Such a development would not be out of step with changes in our society's thinking since *Coker* was decided. During that time, reported instances of child abuse have increased dramatically; and there are many indications of growing alarm about the sexual abuse of children. In 1994, Congress enacted the Jacob Wetterling Crimes Against Children and Sexually Violent Offender Registration Program, 42 U.S.C. § 14071 (2000 ed. and Supp. V), which requires States receiving certain federal funds to establish registration systems for convicted sex offenders and to notify the public about persons convicted of the sexual abuse of minors. All 50 States have now enacted such statutes. In addition, at least 21 States and the District of Columbia now have statutes permitting the involuntary commitment of sexual predators, and at least 12 States have enacted residency restrictions for sex offenders. * * *

E

Aside from its misleading tally of current state laws, the Court points to two additional "objective indicia" of a "national consensus," but these arguments are patent makeweights. The Court notes that Congress has not enacted a law permitting the death penalty for the rape of a child, but due to the territorial limits of the relevant federal statutes, very few rape cases, not to mention child-rape cases, are prosecuted in federal court. Congress' failure to enact a death penalty statute for this tiny set of cases is hardly evidence of Congress' assessment of our society's values.

Finally, the Court argues that statistics about the number of executions in rape cases support its perception of a "national consensus," but here too the statistics do not support the Court's position. The Court notes that the last execution for the rape of a child occurred in 1964, but the Court fails to mention that litigation regarding the constitutionality of the death penalty brought executions to a halt across the board in the late 1960's. In 1965 and 1966, there were a total of eight executions for all offenses, and from 1968 until 1977, the year when *Coker* was decided, there were no executions for any crimes. The Court also fails to mention that in Louisiana, since the state law was amended in 1995 to make child rape a capital offense, prosecutors have asked juries to return death verdicts in four cases. This 50% record is hardly evidence that juries share the Court's view that the death penalty for the rape of a young child is unacceptable under even the most aggravated circumstances.

F

In light of the points discussed above, I believe that the "objective indicia" of our society's "evolving standards of decency" can be fairly summarized as follows. Neither Congress nor juries have done anything that can plausibly be interpreted as evidencing the "national consensus" that the Court perceives. State legislatures, for more than 30 years, have operated under the ominous shadow of the *Coker* dicta and thus have not been free to express their own understanding of our society's standards of decency. And in the months following our grant of certiorari in this case, state legislatures have had an additional reason to pause. Yet despite the inhibiting legal atmosphere that has prevailed since 1977, six States have recently enacted new, targeted child-rape laws.

I do not suggest that six new state laws necessarily establish a "national consensus" or even that they are sure evidence of an ineluctable trend. In terms of the Court's metaphor of moral evolution, these enactments might have turned out to be an evolutionary dead end. But they might also have been the beginning of a strong new evolutionary line. We will never know, because the Court today snuffs out the line in its incipient stage.

II

B

That sweeping holding is also not justified by the Court's concerns about the reliability of the testimony of child victims. First, the Eighth Amendment provides a poor vehicle for addressing problems regarding the admissibility or reliability of evidence, and problems presented by the testimony of child victims are not unique to capital cases. Second, concerns about the reliability of the testimony of child witnesses are not present in every child-rape case. In the case before us, for example, there was undisputed medical evidence that the victim was brutally raped, as well as strong independent evidence that petitioner was the perpetrator. Third, if the Court's evidentiary concerns have Eighth Amendment relevance, they could be addressed by allowing the death penalty in only those child-rape cases in which the independent evidence is sufficient to prove all the elements needed for conviction and imposition of a death sentence. There is precedent for requiring special corroboration in certain criminal cases. For example, some jurisdictions do not allow a conviction based on the uncorroborated testimony of an accomplice. A State wishing to permit the death penalty in child-rape cases could impose an analogous corroboration requirement.

C

After all the arguments noted above are put aside, what is left? What remaining grounds does the Court provide to justify its independent judgment that the death penalty for child rape is categorically unacceptable? I see two.

1

The first is the proposition that we should be "most hesitant before interpreting the Eighth Amendment to allow the *extension* of the death penalty." But holding that the Eighth Amendment does not categorically prohibit the death penalty for the rape of a young child would not "extend" or "expand" the death penalty. Laws enacted by the state legislatures are presumptively constitutional. Consequently, upholding the constitutionality of such a law would not "extend" or "expand" the death penalty; rather, it would confirm the status of presumptive constitutionality that such laws have enjoyed up to this point. And in any event, this Court has previously made it clear that "[t]he Eighth Amendment is not a ratchet, whereby a temporary consensus on leniency for a particular crime fixes a permanent constitutional maximum, disabling States from giving effect to altered beliefs and responding to changed social conditions." *Harmelin v. Michigan,* 501 U.S. 957, 990 (1991).

2

The Court's final-and, it appears, principal-justification for its holding is that murder, the only crime for which defendants have been executed since this Court's 1976 death penalty decisions, is unique in its moral depravity and in the severity of the injury that it inflicts on the victim and the public. But the Court makes little attempt to defend these conclusions.

With respect to the question of moral depravity, is it really true that every person who is convicted of capital murder and sentenced to death is more morally depraved than every child rapist? Consider the following two cases. In the first, a defendant robs a convenience store and watches as his accomplice shoots the store owner. The defendant acts recklessly, but was not the triggerman and did not intend the killing. See, *e.g., Tison v. Arizona,* 481 U.S. 137 (1987). In the second case, a previously convicted child rapist kidnaps, repeatedly rapes, and tortures multiple child victims. Is it clear that the first defendant is more morally depraved than the second?

The Court's decision here stands in stark contrast to *Atkins* and *Roper,* in which the Court concluded that characteristics of the affected defendants-mental retardation in *Atkins* and youth in *Roper*-diminished their culpability. Nor is this case comparable to *Enmund v. Florida,* 458 U.S. 782 (1982), in which the Court held that the Eighth Amendment prohibits the death penalty where the defendant participated in a robbery during which a murder was committed but did not personally intend for lethal force to be used. I have no doubt that, under the prevailing standards of our society, robbery, the crime that the petitioner in *Enmund* intended to commit, does not evidence the same degree of moral depravity as the brutal rape of a young child. Indeed, I have little doubt that, in the eyes of ordinary Americans, the very worst child rapists-predators who seek out and inflict serious physical and emotional injury on defenseless young children-are the epitome of moral depravity.

With respect to the question of the harm caused by the rape of child in relation to the harm caused by murder, it is certainly true that the loss of human life represents a unique harm, but that does not explain why other grievous harms are insufficient to permit a death sentence. And the Court does not take the position that no harm other than the loss of life is sufficient. The Court takes pains to limit its holding to "crimes against individual persons" and to exclude "offenses against the State," a category that the Court stretches-without explanation-to include "drug kingpin activity." But the Court makes no effort to explain why the harm caused by such crimes is necessarily greater than the harm caused by the rape of young children. This is puzzling in light of the Court's acknowledgment that "[r]ape has a permanent psychological, emotional, and sometimes physical impact on the child." As the Court aptly recognizes, "[w]e cannot dismiss the years of long anguish that must be endured by the victim of child rape." *Ibid.*

The rape of any victim inflicts great injury, and "[s]ome victims are so grievously injured physically or psychologically that life *is* beyond repair." *Coker,* 433 U.S., at 603 (opinion of Powell, J.). * * * Long-term studies show that sexual abuse is "grossly intrusive in the lives of children and is harmful to their normal psychological, emotional and sexual development in ways which no just or humane society can tolerate." C. Bagley & K. King, Child Sexual Abuse: The Search for Healing 2 (1990).

It has been estimated that as many as 40% of 7– to 13–year-old sexual assault victims are considered "seriously disturbed." A. Lurigio, M. Jones, & B. Smith, Child Sexual Abuse: Its Causes, Consequences, and Implications for Probation Practice, 59 Sep Fed. Probation 69, 70 (1995). Psychological problems include sudden school failure, unprovoked crying, dissociation, depression, insomnia, sleep disturbances, nightmares, feelings of guilt and inferiority, and self-destructive behavior, including an increased incidence of suicide. Meister, *supra,* at 209; Broughton, *supra,* at 38; Glazer, Child Rapists Beware! The Death Penalty and Louisiana's Amended Aggravated Rape Statute, 25 Am. J.Crim. L. 79, 88 (1997).

The deep problems that afflict child-rape victims often become society's problems as well. Commentators have noted correlations between childhood sexual abuse and later problems such as substance abuse, dangerous sexual behaviors or dysfunction, inability to relate to others on an interpersonal level, and psychiatric illness. Broughton, *supra,* at 38; Glazer, *supra,* at 89; Handbook on Sexual Abuse of Children 7 (L. Walker ed.1988). Victims of child rape are nearly 5 times more likely than nonvictims to be arrested for sex crimes and nearly 30 times more likely to be arrested for prostitution. *Ibid.*

The harm that is caused to the victims and to society at large by the worst child rapists is grave. It is the judgment of the Louisiana lawmakers and those in an increasing number of other States that these harms justify the death penalty. The Court provides no cogent explanation why this legislative judgment should be overridden. Conclusory references to "decency," "moderation," "restraint," "full progress," and "moral judgment" are not enough.

III

* * * The party attacking the constitutionality of a state statute bears the "heavy burden" of establishing that the law is unconstitution-

al. That burden has not been discharged here, and I would therefore affirm the decision of the Louisiana Supreme Court.

D.   SENTENCING PROCEDURES

On p. 1075, insert the following to replace the last sentence of the second paragraph of Note 1:

No appellate court has held that *Booker* is retroactive, thereby relieving the potential for added litigation in the federal courts. See, e.g., *Padilla v. United States*, 416 F.3d 424, 427 (5th Cir. 2005); *Humphress v. United States*, 398 F.3d 855, 860 (6th Cir. 2005); *Wilson v. United States*, 414 F.3d 829, 831–32 (7th Cir. 2005); *Never Misses a Shot v. United States*, 413 F.3d 781, 783–84 (8th Cir. 2005).

On p. 1076, insert the following to replace Note 4:

4. *What is a "reasonable" sentence?* Justice Breyer's opinion held that the remedy for the constitutional violation was to make the Guidelines advisory and to replace *de novo* appellate review of sentences with a reasonableness standard of review. Appellate courts may apply a presumption of reasonableness to within-guidelines sentences. *Rita v. United States*, 127 S.Ct. 2456 (2007). However, that an appellate court may adopt a presumption of reasonableness does not mean that courts may adopt a presumption of unreasonableness' for nonguidelines sentences. Judges may impose a nonguidelines sentence on the basis of policy disagreements with the guidelines. *Kimbrough v. United States*, 128 S.Ct. 558 (2007).

In *Gall v. United States*, 128 S.Ct. 586 (2007), the Court held that "while the extent of the difference between a particular sentence and the recommended Guidelines range is surely relevant, courts of appeals must review all sentences—whether inside, just outside, or significantly outside the Guidelines range—under a deferential abuse of discretion standard."

The Court "reject[ed] . . . an appellate rule that requires 'extraordinary' circumstances to justify a sentence outside the Guidelines range." The *Gall* Court explained the duties of the sentencing and appellate courts.

> [A] a district court should begin all sentencing proceedings by correctly calculating the applicable Guidelines range. * * * Accordingly, after giving both parties an opportunity to argue for whatever sentence they deem appropriate, the district judge should then consider all of the [Guideline] factors to determine whether they support the sentence requested by a party. In so doing, he may not presume that the Guidelines range is reasonable. He must make an individualized assessment based on the facts presented. If he decides that an outside-Guidelines sentence is warranted, he must consider the extent of the deviation and ensure that the justification is sufficiently compelling to support the degree of the variance. * * * [A] major departure should be supported by a more significant justification than a minor one. After settling on the appropriate sentence, he must adequately explain the chosen sentence to allow for meaningful appellate review and to promote the perception of fair sentencing.

Regardless of whether the sentence imposed is inside or outside the Guidelines range, the appellate court must review the sentence under an abuse-of-discretion standard. It must first ensure that the district court committed no significant procedural error, such as failing to calculate (or improperly calculating) the Guidelines range, treating the Guidelines as mandatory, failing to consider the [statutory] factors, selecting a sentence based on clearly erroneous facts, or failing to adequately explain the chosen sentence-including an explanation for any deviation from the Guidelines range. Assuming that the district court's sentencing decision is procedurally sound, the appellate court should then consider the substantive reasonableness of the sentence imposed under an abuse-of-discretion standard. When conducting this review, the court will, of course, take into account the totality of the circumstances, including the extent of any variance from the Guidelines range. If the sentence is within the Guidelines range, the appellate court may, but is not required to, apply a presumption of reasonableness. But if the sentence is outside the Guidelines range, the court may not apply a presumption of unreasonableness. It may consider the extent of the deviation, but must give due deference to the district court's decision that the [statutory] factors, on a whole, justify the extent of the variance. The fact that the appellate court might reasonably have concluded that a different sentence was appropriate is insufficient to justify reversal of the district court.

See *United States v. Cutler*, 520 F.3d 136 (2d Cir. 2008), for application of the *Gall* standard to a below-the-Guidelines sentence. The court carefully examined both the trial court's sentencing procedure as well as the factual underpinnings and reasonableness of the ultimate sentences.

On p. 1076, insert the following at the end of Note 3:

After *Booker*, several circuits reviewing federal sentences presumed that a sentence imposed within the Sentencing Guidelines range was reasonable. *Rita v. United States*, 127 S.Ct. 2456 (2007) held that the use of that presumption by the appellate courts is proper.

Chapter 23

APPEALS

On p. 1111, insert in Part B, after the second paragraph, the following:

A party cannot file an appeal in federal court outside the time period prescribed by a federal statute or a rule of appellate procedure, even if the filing extension relies on a trial court's erroneous calculation of the filing deadline. *Bowles v. Russell*, 127 S.Ct. 2360 (2007). The 5–4 decision found that, because statutory time limits for filing appeals are jurisdictional, an appellate court has no authority to decide appeals that fail to satisfy a timeliness requirement.

On p. 1119, insert the following Note immediately after the Chapman opinion:

Note

Regardless of whether a state court recognized a trial error under *Brecht* or applied the more deferential "harmless beyond a reasonable doubt" standard from *Chapman*, a federal habeas court applies the *Brecht* standard when reviewing a constitutional error in a state conviction. *Fry v. Pliler*, 127 S.Ct. 2321 (2007).

Chapter 24

COLLATERAL REMEDIES

A. INTRODUCTION

On page 1138, insert the following as Note 2 and designate the existing Note as Note 1:

2. The writ of habeas corpus may be suspended under the circumstances described in Art. I, § 2, cl. 2 of the Constitution: "The Privilege of the Writ of Habeas Corpus shall not be suspended, unless when in Cases of Rebellion or Invasion the public Safety may require it." *Boumediene v. Bush*, 128 S.Ct. 2229 (2008) held that, in the case of enemy combatants held at Guantanamo Bay, Cuba, Congress had violated the Suspension Clause by improperly denying access to habeas corpus relief.

> Where a person is detained by executive order, rather than, say, after being tried and convicted in a court, the need for collateral review is most pressing. A criminal conviction in the usual course occurs after a judicial hearing before a tribunal disinterested in the outcome and committed to procedures designed to ensure its own independence. These dynamics are not inherent in executive detention orders or executive review procedures. In this context the need for habeas corpus is more urgent. The intended duration of the detention and the reasons for it bear upon the precise scope of the inquiry. Habeas corpus proceedings need not resemble a criminal trial, even when the detention is by executive order. But the writ must be effective. The habeas court must have sufficient authority to conduct a meaningful review of both the cause for detention and the Executive's power to detain.

On p. 1139, insert the following sentence on the next to last line of the page, after the citation:

The tolling provision of § 2244(d)(2) also applies when there is a final state judgment, but a petition for certiorari has been filed with the Supreme Court. *Lawrence v. Florida*, 127 S.Ct. 1079 (2007).

On p. 1157, insert the following, before part D:

CAREY v. MUSLADIN

549 U.S. 70 (2006).

JUSTICE THOMAS delivered the opinion of the Court.

This Court has recognized that certain courtroom practices are so inherently prejudicial that they deprive the defendant of a fair trial. *Estelle v. Williams*, 425 U.S. 501 (1976); *Holbrook v. Flynn*, 475 U.S. 560 (1986). In this case, a state court held that buttons displaying the victim's image worn by the victim's family during respondent's trial did not deny respondent his right to a fair trial. We must decide whether that holding was contrary to or an unreasonable application of clearly established federal law, as determined by this Court. 28 U.S.C. § 2254(d)(1). We hold that it was not.

On May 13, 1994, respondent Mathew Musladin shot and killed Tom Studer outside the home of Musladin's estranged wife, Pamela. At trial, Musladin admitted that he killed Studer but argued that he did so in self-defense. A California jury rejected Musladin's self-defense argument and convicted him of first-degree murder and three related offenses.

During Musladin's trial, several members of Studer's family sat in the front row of the spectators' gallery. On at least some of the trial's 14 days, some members of Studer's family wore buttons with a photo of Studer on them. Prior to opening statements, Musladin's counsel moved the court to order the Studer family not to wear the buttons during the trial. The court denied the motion, stating that it saw "no possible prejudice to the defendant."

Musladin appealed his conviction to the California Court of Appeal in 1997. He argued that the buttons deprived him of his Fourteenth Amendment and Sixth Amendment rights. At the outset of its analysis, the Court of Appeal stated that Musladin had to show actual or inherent prejudice to succeed on his claim and cited *Flynn*, as providing the test for inherent prejudice. The Court of Appeal, quoting part of *Flynn*'s test, made clear that it "consider[ed] the wearing of photographs of victims in a courtroom to be an 'impermissible factor coming into play,' the practice of which should be discouraged." (quoting *Flynn*). Nevertheless, the court concluded, again quoting *Flynn*, that the buttons had not "branded defendant 'with an unmistakable mark of guilt' in the eyes of the jurors" because "[t]he simple photograph of Tom Studer was unlikely to have been taken as a sign of anything other than the normal grief occasioned by the loss of [a] family member."

At the conclusion of the state appellate process, Musladin filed an application for writ of habeas corpus in federal district court pursuant to § 2254. In his application, Musladin argued that the buttons were inherently prejudicial and that the California Court of Appeal erred by holding that the Studers' wearing of the buttons did not deprive him of a fair trial. The District Court denied habeas relief but granted a certificate of appealability on the buttons issue.

The Court of Appeals for the Ninth Circuit reversed and remanded for issuance of the writ, finding that under § 2254 the state court's decision "was contrary to, or involved an unreasonable application of, clearly established Federal law, as determined by the Supreme Court of the United States." § 2254(d)(1). According to the Court of Appeals, this Court's decisions in *Williams* and *Flynn* clearly established a rule of federal law applicable to Musladin's case. Specifically, the Court of Appeals cited its own precedent in support of its conclusion that *Williams* and *Flynn* clearly established the test for inherent prejudice applicable to spectators' courtroom conduct. The Court of Appeals held that the state court's application of a test for inherent prejudice that differed from the one stated in *Williams* and *Flynn* "was contrary to clearly established federal law and constituted an unreasonable application of that law." . . . We granted certiorari, and now vacate.

[In] *Williams v. Taylor*, we explained that "clearly established Federal law" in § 2254(d)(1) "refers to the holdings, as opposed to the dicta, of this Court's decisions as of the time of the relevant state-court decision." Therefore, federal habeas relief may be granted here if the California Court of Appeal's decision was contrary to or involved an unreasonable application of this Court's applicable holdings.

In *Estelle v. Williams* and *Flynn*, this Court addressed the effect of courtroom practices on defendants' fair-trial rights. In *Williams*, the Court considered "whether an accused who is compelled to wear identifiable prison clothing at his trial by a jury is denied due process or equal protection of the laws." The Court stated that "the State cannot, consistently with the Fourteenth Amendment, compel an accused to stand trial before a jury while dressed in identifiable prison clothes," but held that the defendant in that case had waived any objection to being tried in prison clothes by failing to object at trial.

In *Flynn*, the Court addressed whether seating "four uniformed state troopers" in the row of spectators' seats immediately behind the defendant at trial denied the defendant his right to a fair trial. The Court held that the presence of the troopers was not so inherently prejudicial that it denied the defendant a fair trial. In reaching that holding, the Court stated that "the question must be ... whether 'an unacceptable risk is presented of impermissible factors coming into play.'"

Both *Williams* and *Flynn* dealt with government-sponsored practices: In *Williams*, the State compelled the defendant to stand trial in prison clothes, and in *Flynn*, the State seated the troopers immediately behind the defendant. Moreover, in both cases, this Court noted that some practices are so inherently prejudicial that they must be justified by an "essential state" policy or interest. . . .

In contrast to state-sponsored courtroom practices, the effect on a defendant's fair-trial rights of the spectator conduct to which Musladin objects is an open question in our jurisprudence. This Court has never addressed a claim that such private-actor courtroom conduct was so inherently prejudicial that it deprived a defendant of a fair trial. And although the Court articulated the test for inherent prejudice that applies to state conduct in *Williams* and *Flynn*, we have never applied that test to spectators' conduct. Indeed, part of the legal test of *Williams* and *Flynn*—asking whether the practices furthered an essential state interest—suggests that those cases apply only to state-sponsored practices.

Reflecting the lack of guidance from this Court, lower courts have diverged widely in their treatment of defendants' spectator-conduct claims. . . .

Given the lack of holdings from this Court regarding the potentially prejudicial effect of spectators' courtroom conduct of the kind involved here, it cannot be said that the state court "unreasonabl[y] appli[ed] clearly established Federal law." § 2254(d)(1). No holding of this Court required the California Court of Appeal to apply the test of *Williams* and *Flynn* to the spectators' conduct here. Therefore, the state court's decision was not contrary to or an unreasonable application of clearly established federal law.

The Court of Appeals improperly concluded that the California Court of Appeal's decision was contrary to or an unreasonable application of clearly established federal law as determined by this Court. For these reasons, the judgment of the Court of Appeals is vacated, and the case is remanded for further proceedings consistent with this opinion.

It is so ordered.

Notes

1. Justice Kennedy was the only Justice in the majority of the 2007 habeas corpus cases decided by a vote of 5–4 under the AEDPA. For example, in *Schriro v. Landrigan*, 127 S.Ct. 1933 (2007) (previously discussed on p. 19 of this supplement), the Court upheld the denial of an evidentiary hearing in a case where the defendant refused to permit his counsel to present mitigating evidence on the penalty phase of a capital case. Under § 2254's deferential standards, the federal district court did not abuse its discretion in denying the petition for habeas relief; regardless of what information defense counsel might have produced, because the defendant would not have permitted him to present it.

2. In *Uttecht v. Brown*, 127 S.Ct. 2218 (2007), the Supreme Court reminded us again of the AEDPA's "independent, high standard" before a habeas corpus writ can issue to set aside a state court ruling. At trial, defense counsel did not object to the removal of a juror whose voir dire responses raised a question about his ability to consider the death penalty. The Court held that a reviewing court should consider the entire voir dire in the defendant's case as well as the questioning of the particular juror. Where "there is lengthy questioning of a prospective juror and trial court has supervised a diligent and thoughtful voir dire, the trial court has broad discretion." Here, the trial court's decision "was not contrary to, or an

unreasonable application of, clearly established federal law" under 28 U.S.C. § 2254(d).

3.   On the other hand, the Court at times has found that a decision denying habeas relief violated 28 U.S.C. § 2254(d) because it was "contrary to" and "involved an unreasonable application of, clearly established Federal law, as determined by the Supreme Court of the United States." In *Abdul-Kabir v. Quarterman*, 127 S.Ct. 1654 (2007) and *Brewer v. Quarterman*, 127 S.Ct. 1706 (2007) held that a trial court's jury instructions prevented the jury from giving meaningful consideration and effect to relevant mitigating evidence during the capital trial's penalty phase, in the same manner as had occurred in *Penry v. Lynaugh*, 492 U.S. 302(1989).

On page 1163, insert the following Note 3, before Part 2:

3.   If a prisoner wants to file a "second or successive" application for habeas corpus in federal district court, the AEDPA requires him first to seek and obtain permission from the "appropriate court of appeals for an order authorizing the district court to consider the application." 28 U.S.C. § 2244(b)(3)(A). The Court of Appeals' three-judge panel may authorize that application only if the claim raised satisfies one of two statutory grounds in § 2244(b).

Burton's 1998 application for habeas corpus challenged the constitutionality of his convictions without raising any sentencing issues. While the Ninth Circuit found that he had a "legitimate excuse for failing to raise" the constitutionality of his sentencing until his 2002 petition. the Court held that the 2002 application was a "second or subsequent" application: at the time of the 2002 application, he was still being held pursuant to the same judgment as when he had filed the 1998 application. Given its status as a "second or subsequent" application, the district court lacked jurisdiction to consider the later application because Burton never sought or obtained statutory authority from the Court of Appeals to file the 2002 application. *Burton v. Stewart*, 549 U.S. 147 (2007).

Appendix A

SELECTED PROVISIONS OF THE UNITED STATES CONSTITUTION

ARTICLE I

Section 9. * * *

[2] The privilege of the Writ of Habeas Corpus shall not be suspended, unless when in Cases of Rebellion or Invasion the public Safety may require it.

[3] No Bill of Attainder or ex post facto Law shall be passed.

ARTICLE III

Section 1. The judicial Power of the United States, shall be vested in one supreme Court, and in such inferior Courts as the Congress may from time to time ordain and establish. The Judges, both of the supreme and inferior Courts, shall hold their Offices during good Behaviour, and shall, at stated Times, receive for their Services a Compensation, which shall not be diminished during their Continuance in Office.

Section 2. [1] The judicial Power shall extend to all Cases, in Law and Equity, arising under this Constitution, the Laws of the United States, and Treaties made, or which shall be made, under their Authority;—to all Cases affecting Ambassadors, other public Ministers and Consuls;—to all Cases of admiralty and maritime Jurisdiction;—to Controversies to which the United States shall be a Party;—to Controversies between two or more States;—between a State and Citizens of another State;—between Citizens of different States;—between Citizens of the same State claiming Lands under the Grants of different States, and between a State, or the Citizens thereof, and foreign States, Citizens or Subjects.

[3] The trial of all Crimes, except in Cases of Impeachment, shall be by Jury; and such Trial shall be held in the State where the said Crimes shall have been committed; but when not committed within any State, the Trial shall be at such Place or Places as the Congress may by Law have directed.

Section 3. [1] Treason against the United States, shall consist only in levying War against them, or, in adhering to their Enemies, giving them Aid and Comfort. No Person shall be convicted of Treason unless on the Testimony of two Witnesses to the same overt Act, or on Confession in open Court.

89

[2] The Congress shall have Power to declare the Punishment of Treason, but no Attainder of Treason shall work Corruption of Blood, or Forfeiture except during the Life of the Person attainted.

ARTICLE IV

Section 2.   [1] The Citizens of each State shall be entitled to all Privileges and Immunities of Citizens in the several States.

[2] A Person charged in any State with Treason, Felony, or other Crime, who shall flee from Justice, and be found in another State, shall on demand of the executive Authority of the State from which he fled, be delivered up, to be removed to the State having Jurisdiction of the Crime.

ARTICLE VI

[2] This Constitution, and the Laws of the United States which shall be made in Pursuance thereof; and all Treaties made, or which shall be made, under the Authority of the United States, shall be the supreme Law.

AMENDMENT I [1791]

Congress shall make no law respecting an establishment of religion, or prohibiting the free exercise thereof; or abridging the freedom of speech, or of the press; or the right of the people peaceably to assemble, and to petition the Government for a redress of grievances.

AMENDMENT II [1791]

A well regulated Militia, being necessary to the security of a free State, the right of the people to keep and bear Arms, shall not be infringed.

AMENDMENT III [1791]

No Soldier shall, in time of peace be quartered in any house, without the consent of the Owner, nor in time of war, but in a manner to be prescribed by law.

AMENDMENT IV [1791]

The right of the people to be secure in their persons, houses, papers, and effects, against unreasonable searches and seizures, shall not be violated, and no Warrants shall issue, but upon probable cause, supported by Oath or affirmation, and particularly describing the place to be searched, and the persons or things to be seized.

AMENDMENT V [1791]

No person shall be held to answer for a capital, or otherwise infamous crime, unless on a presentment or indictment of a Grand Jury, except in cases arising in the land or naval forces, or in the Militia, when in actual service in time of War or public danger; nor shall any person be subject for the same offence to be twice put in jeopardy of life or limb; nor shall be compelled in any criminal case to be a witness against himself, nor be deprived of life, liberty, or property, without due process of law; nor shall private property be taken for public use, without just compensation.

AMENDMENT VI [1791]

In all criminal prosecutions, the accused shall enjoy the right to a speedy and public trial, by an impartial jury of the State and district wherein the crime shall have been committed, which district shall have been previously ascertained by law, and to be informed of the nature and cause of the accusation; to be confronted with the witnesses against him; to have compulsory process for obtaining witnesses in his favor, and to have the Assistance of Counsel for his defence.

AMENDMENT VII [1791]

In Suits at common law, where the value in controversy shall exceed twenty dollars, the right of trial by jury shall be preserved, and no fact tried by jury, shall be otherwise re-examined in any Court of the United States, than according to the rules of the common law.

AMENDMENT VIII [1791]

Excessive bail shall not be required, nor excessive fines imposed, nor cruel and unusual punishments inflicted.

AMENDMENT IX [1791]

The enumeration in the Constitution, of certain rights, shall not be construed to deny or disparage others retained by the people.

AMENDMENT X [1791]

The powers not delegated to the United States by the Constitution, nor prohibited by it to the States, are reserved to the States respectively, or to the people.

AMENDMENT XIII [1865]

Section 1.   Neither slavery nor involuntary servitude, except as a punishment for crime whereof the party shall have been duly convicted, shall exist within the United States, or any place subject to their jurisdiction.

Section 2.   Congress shall have power to enforce this article by appropriate legislation.

AMENDMENT XIV [1868]

Section 1.   All persons born or naturalized in the United States, and subject to the jurisdiction thereof, are citizens of the United States and of the State wherein they reside.   No State shall make or enforce any law which shall abridge the privileges or immunities of citizens of the United States; nor shall any State deprive any person of life, liberty, or property, without due process of law; nor deny to any person within its jurisdiction the equal protection of the laws.

Section 5.   The Congress shall have power to enforce, by appropriate legislation, the provisions of the article.

AMENDMENT XV [1870]

Section 1.   The right of citizens of the United States to vote shall not be denied or abridged by the United States or by any State on account of race, color, or previous condition of servitude.

Section 2.   The Congress shall have power to enforce this article by appropriate legislation.

Appendix B

SELECTED FEDERAL STATUTORY PROVISIONS

Analysis

Wire and Electronic Communications Interception and Interception of Oral Communications (18 U.S.C. §§ 2510–2511, 2515–2518, 2520–2521)

Searches and Seizures (18 U.S.C.A. §§ 3103a, 3105, 3109)

Bail Reform Act of 1984 (18 U.S.C. §§ 3141–3150)

Speedy Trial Act of 1974 (As Amended) (18 U.S.C. §§ 3161–3162, 3164)

Jencks Act (18 U.S.C. § 3500)

Litigation Concerning Sources of Evidence (18 U.S.C. § 3504)

Criminal Appeals Act of 1970 (As Amended) (18 U.S.C. § 3731)

Crime Victims' Rights (18 U.S.C. § 3771)

Jury Selection and Service Act of 1968 (As Amended) (28 U.S.C. §§ 1861–1863, 1865–1867)

Habeas Corpus (28 U.S.C. §§ 2241–2244, 2253–2255, 2261–2266)

Privacy Protection Act of 1980 (42 U.S.C. §§ 2000aa—2000aa–12); Guidelines (28 C.F.R. § 59.4)

Foreign Intelligence Surveillance Act (50 U.S.C.A. § 1861)

WIRE AND ELECTRONIC COMMUNICATIONS INTERCEPTION AND INTERCEPTION OF ORAL COMMUNICATIONS

(18 U.S.C. §§ 2510–2511, 2515–2518, 2520–2521).

§ 2510. Definitions

As used in this chapter

(1) "wire communication means any aural transfer made in whole or in part through the use of facilities for the transmission of communications by the aid of wire, cable, or other like connection between the point of origin and the point of reception (including the use of such connection in a switching station) furnished or operated by any person engaged in providing or operating such facilities for the transmission of interstate or foreign communications or communications affecting interstate or foreign commerce;

93

(2) "oral communication" means any oral communication uttered by a person exhibiting an expectation that such communication is not subject to interception under circumstances justifying such expectation, but such term does not include any electronic communication;

(3) "State" means any State of the United States, the District of Columbia, the Commonwealth of Puerto Rico, and any territory or possession of the United States;

(4) "intercept" means the aural or other acquisition of the contents of any wire, electronic, or oral communication through the use of any electronic, mechanical, or other device.

(5) "electronic, mechanical, or other device" means any device or apparatus which can be used to intercept a wire, oral, or electronic communication other than—

    (a) any telephone or telegraph instrument, equipment or facility, or any component thereof, (i) furnished to the subscriber or user by a provider of wire or electronic communication service in the ordinary course of its business and being used by the subscriber or user in the ordinary course of its business or furnished by such subscriber or user for connection to the facilities of such service and used in the ordinary course of its business; or (ii) being used by a provider of wire or electronic communication service in the ordinary course of its business, or by an investigative or law enforcement officer in the ordinary course of his duties;

    (b) a hearing aid or similar device being used to correct subnormal hearing to not better than normal;

(6) "person" means any employee, or agent of the United States or any State or political subdivision thereof, and any individual, partnership, association, joint stock company, trust, or corporation;

(7) "Investigative or law enforcement officer" means any officer of the United States or of a State or political subdivision thereof, who is empowered by law to conduct investigations of or to make arrests for offenses enumerated in this chapter, and any attorney authorized by law to prosecute or participate in the prosecution of such offenses;

(8) "contents", when used with respect to any wire, oral, or electronic communication, includes any information concerning the substance, purport, or meaning of that communication;

(9) "Judge of competent jurisdiction" means—

    (a) a judge of a United States district court or a United States court of appeals; and

    (b) a judge of any court of general criminal jurisdiction of a State who is authorized by a statute of that State to enter orders authorizing interceptions of wire, oral, or electronic communications;

(10) "communication common carrier" has the meaning given that term in section 3 of the Communications Act of 1934;

(11) "aggrieved person" means a person who was a party to any intercepted wire, oral, or electronic communication or a person against whom the interception was directed;

(12) "electronic communication" means any transfer of signs, signals, writing, images, sounds, data, or intelligence of any nature transmitted in whole or in part by a wire, radio, electromagnetic, photoelectronic or photooptical system that affects interstate or foreign commerce, but does not include—

(A) any wire or oral communication;

(B) any communication made through a tone-only paging device;

(C) any communication from a tracking device (as defined in section 3117 of this title); or

(D) electronic funds transfer information stored by a financial institution in a communications system used for the electronic storage and transfer of funds;

(13) "user" means any person or entity who—

(A) uses an electronic communication service; and

(B) is duly authorized by the provider of such service to engage in such use;

(14) "electronic communications system" means any wire, radio, electromagnetic, photooptical or photoelectronic facilities for the transmission of wire or electronic communications, and any computer facilities or related electronic equipment for the electronic storage of such communications;

(15) "electronic communication service" means any service which provides to users thereof the ability to send or receive wire or electronic communications;

(16) "readily accessible to the general public" means, with respect to a radio communication, that such communication is not—

(A) scrambled or encrypted;

(B) transmitted using modulation techniques whose essential parameters have been withheld from the public with the intention of preserving the privacy of such communication;

(C) carried on a subcarrier or other signal subsidiary to a radio transmission;

(D) transmitted over a communication system provided by a common carrier, unless the communication is a tone only paging system communication; or

(E) transmitted on frequencies allocated under part 25, subpart D, E, or F of part 74, or part 94 of the Rules of the Federal Communications Commission, unless, in the case of a communication transmitted on a frequency allocated under part 74 that is not exclusively allocated to broadcast auxiliary services, the communication is a two-way voice communication by radio;

(17) "electronic storage" means—

(A) any temporary, intermediate storage of a wire or electronic communication incidental to the electronic transmission thereof; and

(B) any storage of such communication by an electronic communication service for purposes of backup protection of such communication;

(18) "aural transfer" means a transfer containing the human voice at any point between and including the point of origin and the point of reception;

(19) "foreign intelligence information", for purposes of section 2517(6) of this title, means—

(A) information, whether or not concerning a United States person, that relates to the ability of the United States to protect against—

(i) actual or potential attack or other grave hostile acts of a foreign power or an agent of a foreign power;

(ii) sabotage or international terrorism by a foreign power or an agent of a foreign power; or

(iii) clandestine intelligence activities by an intelligence service or network of a foreign power or by an agent of a foreign power; or

(B) information, whether or not concerning a United States person, with respect to a foreign power or foreign territory that relates to—

(i) the national defense or the security of the United States; or

(ii) the conduct of the foreign affairs of the United States;

(20) "protected computer" has the meaning set forth in section 1030; and

(21) "computer trespasser"—

(A) means a person who accesses a protected computer without authorization and thus has no reasonable expectation of privacy in any communication transmitted to, through, or from the protected computer; and

(B) does not include a person known by the owner or operator of the protected computer to have an existing contractual relationship with the owner or operator of the protected computer for access to all or part of the protected computer.

§ 2511. Interception and disclosure of wire, oral, or electronic communications prohibited

(1) Except as otherwise specifically provided in this chapter any person who—

(a) intentionally intercepts, endeavors to intercept, or procures any other person to intercept or endeavor to intercept, any wire, oral, or electronic communication;

(b) intentionally uses, endeavors to use, or procures any other person to use or endeavor to use any electronic, mechanical, or other device to intercept any oral communication when—

(i) such device is affixed to, or otherwise transmits a signal through, a wire, cable, or other like connection used in wire communication; or

(ii) such device transmits communications by radio, or interferes with the transmission of such communication; or

(iii) such person knows, or has reason to know, that such device or any component thereof has been sent through the mail or transported in interstate or foreign commerce; or

(iv) such use or endeavor to use (A) takes place on the premises of any business or other commercial establishment the operations of which affect interstate or foreign commerce; or (B) obtains or is for the purpose of obtaining information relating to the operations of any business or other commercial establishment the operations of which affect interstate or foreign commerce; or

(v) such person acts in the District of Columbia, the Commonwealth of Puerto Rico, or any territory or possession of the United States;

(c) intentionally discloses, or endeavors to disclose, to any other person the contents of any wire, oral, or electronic communication, knowing or having reason to know that the information was obtained through the interception of a wire, oral, or electronic communication in violation of this subsection;

(d) intentionally uses, or endeavors to use, the contents of any wire, oral, or electronic communication, knowing or having reason to know that the information was obtained through the interception of a wire, oral, or electronic communication in violation of this subsection; or

(e)(i) intentionally discloses, or endeavors to disclose, to any other person the contents of any wire, oral, or electronic communication, intercepted by means authorized by sections 2511(2)(a)(ii), 2511(2)(b)–(c), 2511(2)(e), 2516, and 2518 of this chapter, (ii) knowing or having reason to know that the information was obtained through the interception of such a communication in connection with a criminal investigation, (iii) having obtained or received the information in connection with a criminal investigation, and (iv) with intent to improperly obstruct, impede, or interfere with a duly authorized criminal investigation, shall be punished as provided in subsection (4) or shall be subject to suit as provided in subsection (5).

(2)(a)(i) It shall not be unlawful under this chapter for an operator of a switchboard, or an officer, employee, or agent of a provider of wire or electronic communication service, whose facilities are used in the transmission of a wire or electronic communication, to intercept, disclose, or use that communication in the normal course of his employment while engaged in any activity which is a necessary incident to the rendition of his service or to the protection of the rights or property of the provider of that service, except that a provider of wire communication service to the public shall not utilize service observing or random monitoring except for mechanical or service quality control checks.

(ii) Notwithstanding any other law, providers of wire or electronic communication service, their officers, employees, and agents, landlords, custodians, or other persons, are authorized to provide information, facilities, or technical assistance to persons authorized by law to intercept wire, oral, or electronic communications or to conduct electronic surveillance, as defined in section 101 of the Foreign Intelligence Surveillance Act of 1978, if such provider, its officers, employees, or agents, landlord, custodian, or other specified person, has been provided with—

(A) a court order directing such assistance signed by the authorizing judge, or

(B) a certification in writing by a person specified in section 2518(7) of this title or the Attorney General of the United States that no warrant or court order is required by law, that all statutory requirements have been met, and that the specified assistance is required,

setting forth the period of time during which the provision of the information, facilities, or technical assistance is authorized and specifying the information, facilities, or technical assistance required. No provider of wire or electronic communication service, officer, employee, or agent thereof, or landlord, custodian, or other specified person shall disclose the existence of any interception or surveillance or the device used to accomplish the interception or surveillance with respect to which the person has been furnished a court order or certification under this chapter, except as may otherwise be required by legal process and then only after prior notification to the Attorney General or to the principal prosecuting attorney of a State or any political subdivision of a State, as may be appropriate. Any such disclosure, shall render such person liable for the civil damages provided for in section 2520. No cause of action shall lie in any court against any provider of wire or electronic communication service, its officers, employees, or agents, landlord, custodian, or other specified person for providing information, facilities, or assistance in accordance with the terms of a court order, statutory authorization, or certification under this chapter.

(b) It shall not be unlawful under this chapter for an officer, employee, or agent of the Federal Communications Commission, in the normal course of his employment and in discharge of the monitoring responsibilities exercised by the Commission in the enforcement of chapter 5 of title 47 of the United States Code, to intercept a wire or electronic communication, or oral communication transmitted by radio, or to disclose or use the information thereby obtained.

(c) It shall not be unlawful under this chapter for a person acting under color of law to intercept a wire, oral, or electronic communication, where such person is a party to the communication or one of the parties to the communication has given prior consent to such interception.

(d) It shall not be unlawful under this chapter for a person not acting under color of law to intercept a wire, oral, or electronic communication where such person is a party to the communication or where one of the parties to the communication has given prior consent to such interception unless such communication is intercepted for the purpose of committing any criminal or tortious act in violation of the Constitution or laws of the United States or of any State.

(e) Notwithstanding any other provision of this title or section 705 or 706 of the Communications Act of 1934, it shall not be unlawful for an officer, employee, or agent of the United States in the normal course of his official duty to conduct electronic surveillance, as defined in section 101 of the Foreign Intelligence Surveillance Act of 1978, as authorized by that Act.

(f) Nothing contained in this chapter or chapter 121 or 206 of this title, or section 705 of the Communications Act of 1934, shall be deemed to affect the acquisition by the United States Government of foreign intelligence information from international or foreign communications, or foreign intelligence activities conducted in accordance with otherwise applicable Federal law involving a foreign electronic communications system, utilizing a means other than electronic surveillance as defined in section 101 of the Foreign Intelligence Surveillance Act of 1978, and procedures in this chapter or chapter 121 and the Foreign Intelligence Surveillance Act of 1978 shall be the exclusive means by which electronic surveillance, as defined in section 101 of such Act, and the interception of domestic wire, oral, and electronic communications may be conducted.

(g) It shall not be unlawful under this chapter or chapter 121 of this title for any person—

(i) to intercept or access an electronic communication made through an electronic communication system that is configured so that such electronic communication is readily accessible to the general public;

(ii) to intercept any radio communication which is transmitted—

(I) by any station for the use of the general public, or that relates to ships, aircraft, vehicles, or persons in distress;

(II) by any governmental, law enforcement, civil defense, private land mobile, or public safety communications system, including police and fire, readily accessible to the general public;

(III) by a station operating on an authorized frequency within the bands allocated to the amateur, citizens band, or general mobile radio services; or

(IV) by any marine or aeronautical communications system;

(iii) to engage in any conduct which—

(I) is prohibited by section 633 of the Communications Act of 1934; or

(II) is excepted from the application of section 705(a) of the Communications Act of 1934 by section 705(b) of that Act;

(iv) to intercept any wire or electronic communication the transmission of which is causing harmful interference to any lawfully operating station or consumer electronic equipment, to the extent necessary to identify the source of such interference; or

(v) for other users of the same frequency to intercept any radio communication made through a system that utilizes frequencies monitored by individuals engaged in the provision or the use of such system, if such communication is not scrambled or encrypted.

(h) It shall not be unlawful under this chapter—

(i) to use a pen register or a trap and trace device (as those terms are defined for the purposes of chapter 206 (relating to pen registers and trap and trace devices) of this title); or

(ii) for a provider of electronic communication service to record the fact that a wire or electronic communication was initiated or completed in order to protect such provider, another provider furnishing service toward the completion of the wire or electronic communication, or a user of that service, from fraudulent, unlawful or abusive use of such service.

(i) It shall not be unlawful under this chapter for a person acting under color of law to intercept the wire or electronic communications of a computer trespasser transmitted to, through, or from the protected computer, if—

(I) the owner or operator of the protected computer authorizes the interception of the computer trespasser's communications on the protected computer;

(II) the person acting under color of law is lawfully engaged in an investigation;

(III) the person acting under color of law has reasonable grounds to believe that the contents of the computer trespasser's communications will be relevant to the investigation; and

(IV) such interception does not acquire communications other than those transmitted to or from the computer trespasser.

(3)(a) Except as provided in paragraph (b) of this subsection, a person or entity providing an electronic communication service to the public shall not intentionally divulge the contents of any communication (other than one to such person or entity, or an agent thereof) while in transmission on that service to any person or entity other than an addressee or intended recipient of such communication or an agent of such addressee or intended recipient.

(b) A person or entity providing electronic communication service to the public may divulge the contents of any such communication—

(i) as otherwise authorized in section 2511(2)(a) or 2517 of this title;

(ii) with the lawful consent of the originator or any addressee or intended recipient of such communication;

(iii) to a person employed or authorized, or whose facilities are used, to forward such communication to its destination; or

(iv) which were inadvertently obtained by the service provider and which appear to pertain to the commission of a crime, if such divulgence is made to a law enforcement agency.

(4)(a) Except as provided in paragraph (b) of this subsection or in subsection (5), whoever violates subsection (1) of this section shall be fined under this title or imprisoned not more than five years, or both.

(b) Conduct otherwise an offense under this subsection that consists of or relates to the interception of a satellite transmission that is not encrypted or scrambled and that is transmitted—

(i) to a broadcasting station for purposes of retransmission to the general public; or

(ii) as an audio subcarrier intended for redistribution to facilities open to the public, but not including data transmissions or telephone calls,

is not an offense under this subsection unless the conduct is for the purposes of direct or indirect commercial advantage or private financial gain.

[(c) Redesignated (b)]

(5)(a)(i) If the communication is—

(A) a private satellite video communication that is not scrambled or encrypted and the conduct in violation of this chapter is the private viewing of that communication and is not for a tortious or illegal purpose or for purposes of direct or indirect commercial advantage or private commercial gain; or

(B) a radio communication that is transmitted on frequencies allocated under subpart D of part 74 of the rules of the Federal Communications Commission that is not scrambled or encrypted and the conduct in violation of this chapter is not for a tortious or illegal purpose or for purposes of direct or indirect commercial advantage or private commercial gain,

then the person who engages in such conduct shall be subject to suit by the Federal Government in a court of competent jurisdiction.

(ii) In an action under this subsection—

(A) if the violation of this chapter is a first offense for the person under paragraph (a) of subsection (4) and such person has not been found liable in a civil action under section 2520 of this title, the Federal Government shall be entitled to appropriate injunctive relief; and

(B) if the violation of this chapter is a second or subsequent offense under paragraph (a) of subsection (4) or such person has been found liable in any prior civil action under section 2520, the person shall be subject to a mandatory $500 civil fine.

(b) The court may use any means within its authority to enforce an injunction issued under paragraph (ii)(A), and shall impose a civil fine of not less than $500 for each violation of such an injunction.

§ 2515. Prohibition of use as evidence of intercepted wire or oral communications

Whenever any wire or oral communication has been intercepted, no part of the contents of such communication and no evidence derived therefrom may be received in evidence in any trial, hearing, or other proceeding in or before any court, grand jury, department, officer, agency, regulatory body, legislative committee, or other authority of the United States, a State, or a political subdivision thereof if the disclosure of that information would be in violation of this chapter.

§ 2516. Authorization for interception of wire, oral, or electronic communications

(1) The Attorney General, Deputy Attorney General, Associate Attorney General, or any Assistant Attorney General, any acting Assistant Attorney General, or any Deputy Assistant Attorney General or acting Deputy Assistant Attorney General in the Criminal Division specially designated by the Attorney General, may authorize an application to a Federal judge of competent jurisdiction for, and such judge may grant in conformity with section 2518 of this chapter an order authorizing or approving the interception of wire or oral communications by the Federal Bureau of Investigation, or a Federal agency having responsibility for the investigation of the offense as to which the application is made, when such interception may provide or has provided evidence of—

(a) any offense punishable by death or by imprisonment for more than one year under sections 2122 and 2274 through 2277 of title 42 of the United States Code (relating to the enforcement of the Atomic Energy Act of 1954), section 2284 of title 42 of the United States Code (relating to sabotage of nuclear facilities or fuel), or under the following chapters of this title: chapter 37 (relating to espionage), chapter 55 (relating to kidnapping), chapter 90 (relating to protection of trade secrets), chapter 105 (relating to sabotage), chapter 115 (relating to treason), chapter 102 (relating to riots), chapter 65 (relating to malicious mischief), chapter 111 (relating to destruction of vessels), or chapter 81 (relating to piracy);

(b) a violation of section 186 or section 501(c) of title 29, United States Code (dealing with restrictions on payments and loans to labor organizations), or any offense which involves murder, kidnapping, robbery, or extortion, and which is punishable under this title;

(c) any offense which is punishable under the following sections of this title: section 201 (bribery of public officials and witnesses), section 215 (relating to bribery of bank officials), section 224 (bribery in sporting contests), subsection (d), (e), (f), (g), (h), or (i) of section 844 (unlawful use of explosives), section 1032 (relating to concealment of assets), section 1084 (transmission of wagering information), section 751 (relating to escape), section 1014 (relating to loans and credit applications generally; renewals and discounts), sections 1503, 1512, and 1513 (influencing or injuring an officer, juror, or witness generally), section 1510 (obstruction of criminal investigations), section 1511 (obstruction of State or local law enforcement), section 1591 (sex trafficking of children by force, fraud, or coercion), section 1751 (Presidential and Presidential staff assassination, kidnapping, and assault), section 1951 (interference with commerce by threats or violence), section 1952 (interstate and foreign travel or transportation in aid of racketeering enterprises), section 1958 (relating to use of interstate commerce facilities in the commission of murder for hire), section 1959 (relating to violent crimes in aid of racketeering activity), section 1954 (offer, acceptance, or solicitation to influence operations of employee benefit plan), section 1955 (prohibition of business enterprises of gambling), section 1956 (laundering of monetary instruments), section 1957 (relating to engaging in monetary transactions in property derived from specified unlawful activity), section 659 (theft from interstate shipment), section 664 (embezzlement from pension and welfare funds), section 1343 (fraud by wire, radio, or television), section 1344 (relating to bank fraud), sections 2251 and 2252 (sexual exploitation of children), section 2251A (selling or buying of children), section 2252A (relating to material constituting or containing child pornography), section 1466A (relating to child obscenity), section 2260 (production of sexually explicit depictions of a minor for importation into the United States), sections 2421, 2422, 2423, and 2425 (relating to transportation for illegal sexual activity and related crimes), sections 2312, 2313, 2314, and 2315 (interstate transportation of stolen property), section 2321 (relating to trafficking in certain motor vehicles or motor vehicle parts), section 1203 (relating to hostage taking), section 1029 (relating to fraud and related activity in connection with access devices), section 3146 (relating to penalty for failure to appear), section 3521(b)(3) (relating to witness relocation and assistance), section 32 (relating to destruction of aircraft or aircraft facilities), section 38 (relating to aircraft parts fraud), section 1963 (violations with respect to racketeer influenced and corrupt organizations), section 115 (relating to threatening or retaliating against a Federal official), section 1341 (relating to mail fraud), a felony violation of section 1030 (relating to computer fraud and abuse), section 351 (violations with respect to congressional, Cabinet, or Supreme Court assassinations, kidnapping, and assault), section 831 (relating to prohibited transactions involving nuclear materials), section 33 (relating to destruction of motor vehicles or motor vehicle facilities), section 175 (relating to biological weapons), section 175c (relating to variola virus), section 1992 (relating to wrecking trains), a felony violation of section 1028 (relating to production of false identification documentation), section 1425 (relating to the procurement of citizenship or nationalization unlawfully), section 1426 (relating to the reproduction of naturalization or citizenship papers), section 1427 (relating to the sale of naturalization or citizenship papers), section 1541 (relating to passport issuance without authority), section 1542 (relating to false statements in passport applications), section 1543 (relating to forgery or false use of passports), section 1544 (relating to misuse of passports), or section 1546 (relating to fraud and misuse of visas, permits, and other documents);

(d) any offense involving counterfeiting punishable under section 471, 472, or 473 of this title;

(e) any offense involving fraud connected with a case under title 11 or the manufacture, importation, receiving, concealment, buying, selling, or otherwise dealing in narcotic drugs, marihuana, or other dangerous drugs, punishable under any law of the United States;

(f) any offense including extortionate credit transactions under sections 892, 893, or 894 of this title;

(g) a violation of section 5322 of title 31, United States Code (dealing with the reporting of currency transactions);

(h) any felony violation of sections 2511 and 2512 (relating to interception and disclosure of certain communications and to certain intercepting devices) of this title;

(i) any felony violation of chapter 71 (relating to obscenity) of this title;

(j) any violation of section 60123(b) (relating to destruction of a natural gas pipeline) or section 46502 (relating to aircraft piracy) of title 49;

(k) any criminal violation of section 2778 of title 22 (relating to the Arms Export Control Act);

(*l*) the location of any fugitive from justice from an offense described in this section;

(m) a violation of section 274, 277, or 278 of the Immigration and Nationality Act (8 U.S.C. 1324, 1327, or 1328) (relating to the smuggling of aliens);

(n) any felony violation of sections 922 and 924 of title 18, United States Code (relating to firearms);

(*o*) any violation of section 5861 of the Internal Revenue Code of 1986 (relating to firearms);

(p) a felony violation of section 1028 (relating to production of false identification documents), section 1542 (relating to false statements in passport applications), section 1546 (relating to fraud and misuse of visas, permits, and other documents) of this title or a violation of section 274, 277, or 278 of the Immigration and Nationality Act (relating to the smuggling of aliens);

(q) any criminal violation of section 229 (relating to chemical weapons); or sections 2332, 2332a, 2332b, 2332d, 2332f, 2332g, 2332h, 2339A, 2339B, or 2339C of this title (relating to terrorism); or

(r) any conspiracy to commit any offense described in any subparagraph of this paragraph.

(2) The principal prosecuting attorney of any State, or the principal prosecuting attorney of any political subdivision thereof, if such attorney is authorized by a statute of that State to make application to a State court judge of competent jurisdiction for an order authorizing or approving the interception of wire, oral, or electronic communications, may apply to such judge for, and such judge may grant in conformity with section 2518 of this chapter and with the applicable State statute an order authorizing, or approving the interception of wire, oral, or electronic communications by investigative or law enforcement officers having responsibility for the investigation of the offense as to which the application is made, when such interception may provide or has provided evidence of the commission of the offense of murder, kidnapping, gambling, robbery, bribery, extortion, or dealing in narcotic drugs, marihuana or other dangerous drugs, or other crime dangerous to life, limb, or property, and punishable by imprisonment for more than one year, designated in any applicable State statute authoriz-

ing such interception, or any conspiracy to commit any of the foregoing offenses.

(3) Any attorney for the Government (as such term is defined for the purposes of the Federal Rules of Criminal Procedure) may authorize an application to a Federal judge of competent jurisdiction for, and such judge may grant, in conformity with section 2518 of this title, an order authorizing or approving the interception of electronic communications by an investigative or law enforcement officer having responsibility for the investigation of the offense as to which the application is made, when such interception may provide or has provided evidence of any Federal felony.

§ 2517.   Authorization for disclosure and use of intercepted wire, oral, or electronic communications

(1) Any investigative or law enforcement officer who, by any means authorized by this chapter, has obtained knowledge of the contents of any wire, oral, or electronic communication, or evidence derived therefrom, may disclose such contents to another investigative or law enforcement officer to the extent that such disclosure is appropriate to the proper performance of the official duties of the officer making or receiving the disclosure.

(2) Any investigative or law enforcement officer who, by any means authorized by this chapter, has obtained knowledge of the contents of any wire, oral, or electronic communication or evidence derived therefrom may use such contents to the extent such use is appropriate to the proper performance of his official duties.

(3) Any person who has received, by any means authorized by this chapter, any information concerning a wire, oral, or electronic communication, or evidence derived therefrom intercepted in accordance with the provisions of this chapter may disclose the contents of that communication or such derivative evidence while giving testimony under oath or affirmation in any proceeding held under the authority of the United States or of any State or political subdivision thereof.

(4) No otherwise privileged wire, oral, or electronic communication intercepted in accordance with, or in violation of, the provisions of this chapter shall lose its privileged character.

(5) When an investigative or law enforcement officer, while engaged in intercepting wire, oral, or electronic communications in the manner authorized herein, intercepts wire, oral, or electronic communications relating to offenses other than those specified in the order of authorization or approval, the contents thereof, and evidence derived therefrom, may be disclosed or used as provided in subsections (1) and (2) of this section. Such contents and any evidence derived therefrom may be used under subsection (3) of this section when authorized or approved by a judge of competent jurisdiction where such judge finds on subsequent application that the contents were otherwise intercepted in accordance with the provisions of this chapter. Such application shall be made as soon as practicable.

(6) Any investigative or law enforcement officer, or attorney for the Government, who by any means authorized by this chapter, has obtained knowledge of the contents of any wire, oral, or electronic communication, or

evidence derived therefrom, may disclose such contents to any other Federal law enforcement, intelligence, protective, immigration, national defense, or national security official to the extent that such contents include foreign intelligence or counterintelligence (as defined in section 3 of the National Security Act of 1947 (50 U.S.C. 401a)), or foreign intelligence information (as defined in subsection (19) of section 2510 of this title), to assist the official who is to receive that information in the performance of his official duties. Any Federal official who receives information pursuant to this provision may use that information only as necessary in the conduct of that person's official duties subject to any limitations on the unauthorized disclosure of such information.

(7) Any investigative or law enforcement officer, or other Federal official in carrying out official duties as such Federal official, who by any means authorized by this chapter, has obtained knowledge of the contents of any wire, oral, or electronic communication, or evidence derived therefrom, may disclose such contents or derivative evidence to a foreign investigative or law enforcement officer to the extent that such disclosure is appropriate to the proper performance of the official duties of the officer making or receiving the disclosure, and foreign investigative or law enforcement officers may use or disclose such contents or derivative evidence to the extent such use or disclosure is appropriate to the proper performance of their official duties.

(8) Any investigative or law enforcement officer, or other Federal official in carrying out official duties as such Federal official, who by any means authorized by this chapter, has obtained knowledge of the contents of any wire, oral, or electronic communication, or evidence derived therefrom, may disclose such contents or derivative evidence to any appropriate Federal, State, local, or foreign government official to the extent that such contents or derivative evidence reveals a threat of actual or potential attack or other grave hostile acts of a foreign power or an agent of a foreign power, domestic or international sabotage, domestic or international terrorism, or clandestine intelligence gathering activities by an intelligence service or network of a foreign power or by an agent of a foreign power, within the United States or elsewhere, for the purpose of preventing or responding to such a threat. Any official who receives information pursuant to this provision may use that information only as necessary in the conduct of that person's official duties subject to any limitations on the unauthorized disclosure of such information, and any State, local, or foreign official who receives information pursuant to this provision may use that information only consistent with such guidelines as the Attorney General and Director of Central Intelligence shall jointly issue.

§ 2518. Procedure for interception of wire, oral, or electronic communications

(1) Each application for an order authorizing or approving the interception of a wire, oral, or electronic communication under this chapter shall be made in writing upon oath or affirmation to a judge of competent jurisdiction and shall state the applicant's authority to make such application. Each application shall include the following information:

(a) the identity of the investigative or law enforcement officer making the application, and the officer authorizing the application;

(b) a full and complete statement of the facts and circumstances relied upon by the applicant, to justify his belief that an order should be issued, including (i) details as to the particular offense that has been, is being, or is about to be committed, (ii) except as provided in subsection (11), a particular description of the nature and location of the facilities from which or the place where the communication is to be intercepted, (iii) a particular description of the type of communications sought to be intercepted, (iv) the identity of the person, if known, committing the offense and whose communications are to be intercepted;

(c) a full and complete statement as to whether or not other investigative procedures have been tried and failed or why they reasonably appear to be unlikely to succeed if tried or to be too dangerous;

(d) a statement of the period of time for which the interception is required to be maintained. If the nature of the investigation is such that the authorization for interception should not automatically terminate when the described type of communication has been first obtained, a particular description of facts establishing probable cause to believe that additional communications of the same type will occur thereafter;

(e) a full and complete statement of the facts concerning all previous applications known to the individual authorizing and making the application, made to any judge for authorization to intercept, or for approval of interceptions of, wire, oral, or electronic communications involving any of the same persons, facilities or places specified in the application, and the action taken by the judge on each such application; and

(f) where the application is for the extension of an order, a statement setting forth the results thus far obtained from the interception, or a reasonable explanation of the failure to obtain such results.

(2) The judge may require the applicant to furnish additional testimony or documentary evidence in support of the application.

(3) Upon such application the judge may enter an ex parte order, as requested or as modified, authorizing or approving interception of wire, oral, or electronic communications within the territorial jurisdiction of the court in which the judge is sitting (and outside that jurisdiction but within the United States in the case of a mobile interception device authorized by a Federal court within such jurisdiction), if the judge determines on the basis of the facts submitted by the applicant that—

(a) there is probable cause for belief that an individual is committing, has committed, or is about to commit a particular offense enumerated in section 2516 of this chapter;

(b) there is probable cause for belief that particular communications concerning that offense will be obtained through such interception;

(c) normal investigative procedures have been tried and have failed or reasonably appear to be unlikely to succeed if tried or to be too dangerous;

(d) except as provided in subsection (11), there is probable cause for belief that the facilities from which, or the place where, the wire, oral, or electronic communications are to be intercepted are being used, or are about to be used, in connection with the commission of such offense, or are leased to, listed in the name of, or commonly used by such person.

(4) Each order authorizing or approving the interception of any wire, oral, or electronic communication under this chapter shall specify—

(a) the identity of the person, if known, whose communications are to be intercepted;

(b) the nature and location of the communications facilities as to which, or the place where, authority to intercept is granted;

(c) a particular description of the type of communication sought to be intercepted, and a statement of the particular offense to which it relates;

(d) the identity of the agency authorized to intercept the communications, and of the person authorizing the application; and

(e) the period of time during which such interception is authorized, including a statement as to whether or not the interception shall automatically terminate when the described communication has been first obtained.

An order authorizing the interception of a wire, oral, or electronic communication under this chapter shall, upon request of the applicant, direct that a provider of wire or electronic communication service, landlord, custodian or other person shall furnish the applicant forthwith all information, facilities, and technical assistance necessary to accomplish the interception unobtrusively and with a minimum of interference with the services that such service provider, landlord, custodian, or person is according the person whose communications are to be intercepted. Any provider of wire or electronic communication service, landlord, custodian or other person furnishing such facilities or technical assistance shall be compensated therefor by the applicant for reasonable expenses incurred in providing such facilities or assistance. Pursuant to section 2522 of this chapter, an order may also be issued to enforce the assistance capability and capacity requirements under the Communications Assistance for Law Enforcement Act.

(5) No order entered under this section may authorize or approve the interception of any wire, oral, or electronic communication for any period longer than is necessary to achieve the objective of the authorization, nor in any event longer than thirty days. Such thirty-day period begins on the earlier of the day on which the investigative or law enforcement officer first begins to conduct an interception under the order or ten days after the order is entered. Extensions of an order may be granted, but only upon application for an extension made in accordance with subsection (1) of this section and the court making the findings required by subsection (3) of this section. The period of extension shall be no longer than the authorizing judge deems necessary to achieve the purposes for which it was granted and in no event for longer than thirty days. Every order and extension thereof shall contain a provision that the authorization to intercept shall be executed as soon as practicable, shall be conducted in such a way as to minimize the interception

of communications not otherwise subject to interception under this chapter, and must terminate upon attainment of the authorized objective, or in any event in thirty days. In the event the intercepted communication is in a code or foreign language, and an expert in that foreign language or code is not reasonably available during the interception period, minimization may be accomplished as soon as practicable after such interception. An interception under this chapter may be conducted in whole or in part by Government personnel, or by an individual operating under a contract with the Government, acting under the supervision of an investigative or law enforcement officer authorized to conduct the interception.

(6) Whenever an order authorizing interception is entered pursuant to this chapter, the order may require reports to be made to the judge who issued the order showing what progress has been made toward achievement of the authorized objective and the need for continued interception. Such reports shall be made at such intervals as the judge may require.

(7) Notwithstanding any other provision of this chapter, any investigative or law enforcement officer, specially designated by the Attorney General, the Deputy Attorney General, the Associate Attorney General, or by the principal prosecuting attorney of any State or subdivision thereof acting pursuant to a statute of that State, who reasonably determines that—

(a) an emergency situation exists that involves—

(i) immediate danger of death or serious physical injury to any person,

(ii) conspiratorial activities threatening the national security interest, or

(iii) conspiratorial activities characteristic of organized crime,

that requires a wire, oral, or electronic communication to be intercepted before an order authorizing such interception can, with due diligence, be obtained, and

(b) there are grounds upon which an order could be entered under this chapter to authorize such interception,

may intercept such wire, oral, or electronic communication if an application for an order approving the interception is made in accordance with this section within forty-eight hours after the interception has occurred, or begins to occur. In the absence of an order, such interception shall immediately terminate when the communication sought is obtained or when the application for the order is denied, whichever is earlier. In the event such application for approval is denied, or in any other case where the interception is terminated without an order having been issued, the contents of any wire, oral, or electronic communication intercepted shall be treated as having been obtained in violation of this chapter, and an inventory shall be served as provided for in subsection (d) of this section on the person named in the application.

(8) (a) The contents of any wire, oral, or electronic communication intercepted by any means authorized by this chapter shall, if possible, be recorded on tape or wire or other comparable device. The recording of the contents of any wire, oral, or electronic communication under this subsection

shall be done in such a way as will protect the recording from editing or other alterations. Immediately upon the expiration of the period of the order, or extensions thereof, such recordings shall be made available to the judge issuing such order and sealed under his directions. Custody of the recordings shall be wherever the judge orders. They shall not be destroyed except upon an order of the issuing or denying judge and in any event shall be kept for ten years. Duplicate recordings may be made for use or disclosure pursuant to the provisions of subsections (1) and (2) of section 2517 of this chapter for investigations. The presence of the seal provided for by this subsection, or a satisfactory explanation for the absence thereof, shall be a prerequisite for the use or disclosure of the contents of any wire, oral, or electronic communication or evidence derived therefrom under subsection (3) of section 2517.

(b) Applications made and orders granted under this chapter shall be sealed by the judge. Custody of the applications and orders shall be wherever the judge directs. Such applications and orders shall be disclosed only upon a showing of good cause before a judge of competent jurisdiction and shall not be destroyed except on order of the issuing or denying judge, and in any event shall be kept for ten years.

(c) Any violation of the provisions of this subsection may be punished as contempt of the issuing or denying judge.

(d) Within a reasonable time but not later than ninety days after the filing of an application for an order of approval under section 2518(7)(b) which is denied or the termination of the period of an order or extensions thereof, the issuing or denying judge shall cause to be served, on the persons named in the order or the application, and such other parties to intercepted communications as the judge may determine in his discretion that is in the interest of justice, an inventory which shall include notice of—

(1) the fact of the entry of the order or the application;

(2) the date of the entry and the period of authorized, approved or disapproved interception, or the denial of the application; and

(3) the fact that during the period wire, oral, or electronic communications were or were not intercepted.

The judge, upon the filing of a motion, may in his discretion make available to such person or his counsel for inspection such portions of the intercepted communications, applications and orders as the judge determines to be in the interest of justice. On an ex parte showing of good cause to a judge of competent jurisdiction the serving of the inventory required by this subsection may be postponed.

(9) The contents of any wire, oral, or electronic communication intercepted pursuant to this chapter or evidence derived therefrom shall not be received in evidence or otherwise disclosed in any trial, hearing, or other proceeding in a Federal or State court unless each party, not less than ten days before the trial, hearing, or proceeding, has been furnished with a copy of the court order, and accompanying application, under which the interception was authorized or approved. This ten-day period may be waived by the judge if he finds that it was not possible to furnish the party with the above

information ten days before the trial, hearing, or proceeding and that the party will not be prejudiced by the delay in receiving such information.

(10)(a) Any aggrieved person in any trial, hearing, or proceeding in or before any court, department, officer, agency, regulatory body, or other authority of the United States, a State, or a political subdivision thereof, may move to suppress the contents of any wire or oral communication intercepted pursuant to this chapter, or evidence derived therefrom, on the grounds that—

(i) the communication was unlawfully intercepted;

(ii) the order of authorization or approval under which it was intercepted is insufficient on its face; or

(iii) the interception was not made in conformity with the order of authorization or approval.

Such motion shall be made before the trial, hearing, or proceeding unless there was no opportunity to make such motion or the person was not aware of the grounds of the motion. If the motion is granted, the contents of the intercepted wire or oral communication, or evidence derived therefrom, shall be treated as having been obtained in violation of this chapter. The judge, upon the filing of such motion by the aggrieved person, may in his discretion make available to the aggrieved person or his counsel for inspection such portions of the intercepted communication or evidence derived therefrom as the judge determines to be in the interests of justice.

(b) In addition to any other right to appeal, the United States shall have the right to appeal from an order granting a motion to suppress made under paragraph (a) of this subsection, or the denial of an application for an order of approval, if the United States attorney shall certify to the judge or other official granting such motion or denying such application that the appeal is not taken for purposes of delay. Such appeal shall be taken within thirty days after the date the order was entered and shall be diligently prosecuted.

(c) The remedies and sanctions described in this chapter with respect to the interception of electronic communications are the only judicial remedies and sanctions for nonconstitutional violations of this chapter involving such communications.

(11) The requirements of subsections (1)(b)(ii) and (3)(d) of this section relating to the specification of the facilities from which, or the place where, the communication is to be intercepted do not apply if—

(a) in the case of an application with respect to the interception of an oral communication—

(i) the application is by a Federal investigative or law enforcement officer and is approved by the Attorney General, the Deputy Attorney General, the Associate Attorney General, an Assistant Attorney General, or an acting Assistant Attorney General;

(ii) the application contains a full and complete statement as to why such specification is not practical and identifies the person committing the offense and whose communications are to be intercepted; and

(iii) the judge finds that such specification is not practical; and

(b) in the case of an application with respect to a wire or electronic communication—

(i) the application is by a Federal investigative or law enforcement officer and is approved by the Attorney General, the Deputy Attorney General, the Associate Attorney General, an Assistant Attorney General, or an acting Assistant Attorney General;

(ii) the application identifies the person believed to be committing the offense and whose communications are to be intercepted and the applicant makes a showing that there is probable cause to believe that the person's actions could have the effect of thwarting interception from a specified facility;

(iii) the judge finds that such showing has been adequately made; and

(iv) the order authorizing or approving the interception is limited to interception only for such time as it is reasonable to presume that the person identified in the application is or was reasonably proximate to the instrument through which such communication will be or was transmitted.

(12) An interception of a communication under an order with respect to which the requirements of subsections (1)(b)(ii) and (3)(d) of this section do not apply by reason of subsection (11)(a) shall not begin until the place where the communication is to be intercepted is ascertained by the person implementing the interception order. A provider of wire or electronic communications service that has received an order as provided for in subsection (11)(b) may move the court to modify or quash the order on the ground that its assistance with respect to the interception cannot be performed in a timely or reasonable fashion. The court, upon notice to the government, shall decide such a motion expeditiously.

§ 2520. Recovery of civil damages authorized

(a) In general.—Except as provided in section 2511(2)(a)(ii), any person whose wire, oral, or electronic communication is intercepted, disclosed, or intentionally used in violation of this chapter may in a civil action recover from the person or entity, other than the United States, which engaged in that violation such relief as may be appropriate.

(b) Relief.—In an action under this section, appropriate relief includes—

(1) such preliminary and other equitable or declaratory relief as may be appropriate;

(2) damages under subsection (c) and punitive damages in appropriate cases; and

(3) a reasonable attorney's fee and other litigation costs reasonably incurred.

(c) Computation of damages.—(1) In an action under this section, if the conduct in violation of this chapter is the private viewing of a private satellite video communication that is not scrambled or encrypted or if the communication is a radio communication that is transmitted on frequencies allocated under subpart D of part 74 of the rules of the Federal Communications Commission that is not scrambled or encrypted and the conduct is not for a tortious or illegal purpose or for purposes of direct or indirect commercial advantage or private commercial gain, then the court shall assess damages as follows:

(A) If the person who engaged in that conduct has not previously been enjoined under section 2511(5) and has not been found liable in a prior civil action under this section, the court shall assess the greater of the sum of actual damages suffered by the plaintiff, or statutory damages of not less than $50 and not more than $500.

(B) If, on one prior occasion, the person who engaged in that conduct has been enjoined under section 2511(5) or has been found liable in a civil action under this section, the court shall assess the greater of the sum of actual damages suffered by the plaintiff, or statutory damages of not less than $100 and not more than $1000.

(2) In any other action under this section, the court may assess as damages whichever is the greater of—

(A) the sum of the actual damages suffered by the plaintiff and any profits made by the violator as a result of the violation; or

(B) statutory damages of whichever is the greater of $100 a day for each day of violation or $10,000.

(d) Defense.—A good faith reliance on—

(1) a court warrant or order, a grand jury subpoena, a legislative authorization, or a statutory authorization;

(2) a request of an investigative or law enforcement officer under section 2518(7) of this title; or

(3) a good faith determination that section 2511(3) or 2511(2)(i) of this title permitted the conduct complained of;

is a complete defense against any civil or criminal action brought under this chapter or any other law.

(e) Limitation.—A civil action under this section may not be commenced later than two years after the date upon which the claimant first has a reasonable opportunity to discover the violation.

(f) Administrative discipline.—If a court or appropriate department or agency determines that the United States or any of its departments or agencies has violated any provision of this chapter, and the court or appropriate department or agency finds that the circumstances surrounding the violation raise serious questions about whether or not an officer or employee of the United States acted willfully or intentionally with respect to the violation, the department or agency shall, upon receipt of a true and correct copy of the decision and findings of the court or appropriate department or agency promptly initiate a proceeding to determine whether disciplinary action against the officer or employee is warranted. If the head of the department or agency involved determines that disciplinary action is not warranted, he or she shall notify the Inspector General with jurisdiction over the department or agency concerned and shall provide the Inspector General with the reasons for such determination.

(g) Improper disclosure is violation.—Any willful disclosure or use by an investigative or law enforcement officer or governmental entity of information beyond the extent permitted by section 2517 is a violation of this chapter for purposes of section 2520(a).

§ 2521. Injunction against illegal interception

Whenever it shall appear that any person is engaged or is about to engage in any act which constitutes or will constitute a felony violation of this chapter, the Attorney General may initiate a civil action in a district court of the United States to enjoin such violation. The court shall proceed as soon as practicable to the hearing and determination of such an action, and may, at any time before final determination, enter such a restraining order or prohibition, or take such other action, as is warranted to prevent a continuing and substantial injury to the United States or to any person or class of persons for whose protection the action is brought. A proceeding under this section is governed by the Federal Rules of Civil Procedure, except that, if an indictment has been returned against the respondent, discovery is governed by the Federal Rules of Criminal Procedure.

SEARCHES AND SEIZURES

(18 U.S.C.A. §§ 3103a, 3105, 3109).

§ 3103a. Additional grounds for issuing warrant

(a) In general.—In addition to the grounds for issuing a warrant in section 3103 of this title, a warrant may be issued to search for and seize any property that constitutes evidence of a criminal offense in violation of the laws of the United States.

(b) Delay.—With respect to the issuance of any warrant or court order under this section, or any other rule of law, to search for and seize any property or material that constitutes evidence of a criminal offense in violation of the laws of the United States, any notice required, or that may be required, to be given may be delayed if—

(1) the court finds reasonable cause to believe that providing immediate notification of the execution of the warrant may have an adverse result (as defined in section 2705);

(2) the warrant prohibits the seizure of any tangible property, any wire or electronic communication (as defined in section 2510), or, except as expressly provided in chapter 121, any stored wire or electronic information, except where the court finds reasonable necessity for the seizure; and

(3) the warrant provides for the giving of such notice within a reasonable period of its execution, which period may thereafter be extended by the court for good cause shown.

§ 3105. Persons authorized to serve search warrant

A search warrant may in all cases be served by any of the officers mentioned in its direction or by an officer authorized by law to serve such warrant, but by no other person, except in aid of the officer on his requiring it, he being present and acting in its execution.

§ 3109. Breaking doors or windows for entry or exit

The officer may break open any outer or inner door or window of a house, or any part of a house, or anything therein, to execute a search warrant, if, after notice of his authority and purpose, he is refused admittance or when necessary to liberate himself or a person aiding him in the execution of the warrant.

BAIL REFORM ACT OF 1984

(18 U.S.C. §§ 3141–3150).

§ 3141. Release and detention authority generally

(a) Pending trial.—A judicial officer authorized to order the arrest of a person under section 3041 of this title before whom an arrested person is brought shall order that such person be released or detained, pending judicial proceedings, under this chapter.

(b) Pending sentence or appeal.—A judicial officer of a court of original jurisdiction over an offense, or a judicial officer of a Federal appellate court, shall order that, pending imposition or execution of sentence, or pending appeal of conviction or sentence, a person be released or detained under this chapter.

§ 3142. Release or detention of a defendant pending trial

(a) In general.—Upon the appearance before a judicial officer of a person charged with an offense, the judicial officer shall issue an order that, pending trial, the person be—

(1) released on personal recognizance or upon execution of an unsecured appearance bond, under subsection (b) of this section;

(2) released on a condition or combination of conditions under subsection (c) of this section;

(3) temporarily detained to permit revocation of conditional release, deportation, or exclusion under subsection (d) of this section; or

(4) detained under subsection (e) of this section.

(b) Release on personal recognizance or unsecured appearance bond.— The judicial officer shall order the pretrial release of the person on personal recognizance, or upon execution of an unsecured appearance bond in an amount specified by the court, subject to the condition that the person not commit a Federal, State, or local crime during the period of release, unless the judicial officer determines that such release will not reasonably assure the appearance of the person as required or will endanger the safety of any other person or the community.

(c) Release on conditions.—(1) If the judicial officer determines that the release described in subsection (b) of this section will not reasonably assure the appearance of the person as required or will endanger the safety of any other person or the community, such judicial officer shall order the pretrial release of the person—

(A) subject to the condition that the person not commit a Federal, State, or local crime during the period of release; and

(B) subject to the least restrictive further condition, or combination of conditions, that such judicial officer determines will reasonably assure the appearance of the person as required and the safety of any other person and the community, which may include the condition that the person—

(i) remain in the custody of a designated person, who agrees to assume supervision and to report any violation of a release condition to the court, if the designated person is able reasonably to assure the judicial officer that the person will appear as required and will not pose a danger to the safety of any other person or the community;

(ii) maintain employment, or, if unemployed, actively seek employment;

(iii) maintain or commence an educational program;

(iv) abide by specified restrictions on personal associations, place of abode, or travel;

(v) avoid all contact with an alleged victim of the crime and with a potential witness who may testify concerning the offense;

(vi) report on a regular basis to a designated law enforcement agency, pretrial services agency, or other agency;

(vii) comply with a specified curfew;

(viii) refrain from possessing a firearm, destructive device, or other dangerous weapon;

(ix) refrain from excessive use of alcohol, or any use of a narcotic drug or other controlled substance, as defined in section 102 of the Controlled Substances Act (21 U.S.C. 802), without a prescription by a licensed medical practitioner;

(x) undergo available medical, psychological, or psychiatric treatment, including treatment for drug or alcohol dependency, and remain in a specified institution if required for that purpose;

(xi) execute an agreement to forfeit upon failing to appear as required, property of a sufficient unencumbered value, including money, as is reasonably necessary to assure the appearance of the person as required, and shall provide the court with proof of ownership and the value of the property along with information regarding existing encumbrances as the judicial office may require;

(xii) execute a bail bond with solvent sureties; who will execute an agreement to forfeit in such amount as is reasonably necessary to assure appearance of the person as required and shall provide the court with information regarding the value of the assets and liabilities of the surety if other than an approved surety and the nature and extent of encumbrances against the surety's property; such surety shall have a net worth which shall have sufficient unencumbered value to pay the amount of the bail bond;

(xiii) return to custody for specified hours following release for employment, schooling, or other limited purposes; and

(xiv) satisfy any other condition that is reasonably necessary to assure the appearance of the person as required and to assure the safety of any other person and the community.

(2) The judicial officer may not impose a financial condition that results in the pretrial detention of the person.

(3) The judicial officer may at any time amend the order to impose additional or different conditions of release.

(d) Temporary detention to permit revocation of conditional release, deportation, or exclusion.—If the judicial officer determines that—

(1) such person—

(A) is, and was at the time the offense was committed, on—

(i) release pending trial for a felony under Federal, State, or local law;

(ii) release pending imposition or execution of sentence, appeal of sentence or conviction, or completion of sentence, for any offense under Federal, State, or local law; or

(iii) probation or parole for any offense under Federal, State, or local law; or

(B) is not a citizen of the United States or lawfully admitted for permanent residence, as defined in section 101(a)(20) of the Immigration and Nationality Act (8 U.S.C. 1101(a)(20)); and

(2) such person may flee or pose a danger to any other person or the community;

such judicial officer shall order the detention of such person, for a period of not more than ten days, excluding Saturdays, Sundays, and holidays, and direct the attorney for the Government to notify the appropriate court, probation or parole official, or State or local law enforcement official, or the appropriate official of the Immigration and Naturalization Service. If the official fails or declines to take such person into custody during that period, such person shall be treated in accordance with the other provisions of this section, notwithstanding the applicability of other provisions of law governing release pending trial or deportation or exclusion proceedings. If temporary detention is sought under paragraph (1)(B) of this subsection, such person has the burden of proving to the court such person's United States citizenship or lawful admission for permanent residence.

(e) Detention.—If, after a hearing pursuant to the provisions of subsection (f) of this section, the judicial officer finds that no condition or combination of conditions will reasonably assure the appearance of the person as required and the safety of any other person and the community, such judicial officer shall order the detention of the person before trial. In a case described in subsection (f)(1) of this section, a rebuttable presumption arises that no condition or combination of conditions will reasonably assure the safety of any other person and the community if such judicial officer finds that—

(1) the person has been convicted of a Federal offense that is described in subsection (f)(1) of this section, or of a State or local offense that would have been an offense described in subsection (f)(1) of this section if a circumstance giving rise to Federal jurisdiction had existed;

(2) the offense described in paragraph (1) of this subsection was committed while the person was on release pending trial for a Federal, State, or local offense; and

(3) a period of not more than five years has elapsed since the date of conviction, or the release of the person from imprisonment, for the offense described in paragraph (1) of this subsection, whichever is later.

Subject to rebuttal by the person, it shall be presumed that no condition or combination of conditions will reasonably assure the appearance of the person as required and the safety of the community if the judicial officer finds that there is probable cause to believe that the person committed an offense for which a maximum term of imprisonment of ten years or more is prescribed in the Controlled Substances Act (21 U.S.C. 801 et seq.), the Controlled Substances Import and Export Act (21 U.S.C. 951 et seq.), or the Maritime Drug Law Enforcement Act (46 U.S.C. App. 1901 et seq.), an offense under section 924(c), 956(a), or 2332b of this title, or an offense listed in section 2332b(g)(5)(B) of title 18, United States Code, for which a maximum term of imprisonment of 10 years or more is prescribed or an offense involving a minor victim under section 1201, 1591, 2241, 2242, 2244(a)(1), 2245, 2251, 2251A, 2252(a)(1), 2252(a)(2), 2252(a)(3), 2252A(a)(1), 2252A(a)(2), 2252A(a)(3), 2252A(a)(4), 2260, 2421, 2422, 2423, or 2425 of this title.

(f) Detention hearing.—The judicial officer shall hold a hearing to determine whether any condition or combination of conditions set forth in subsection (c) of this section will reasonably assure the appearance of such person as required and the safety of any other person and the community—

(1) upon motion of the attorney for the Government, in a case that involves—

(A) a crime of violence, or an offense listed in section 2332b(g)(5)(B) for which a maximum term of imprisonment of 10 years or more is prescribed;

(B) an offense for which the maximum sentence is life imprisonment or death;

(C) an offense for which a maximum term of imprisonment of ten years or more is prescribed in the Controlled Substances Act (21 U.S.C. 801 et seq.), the Controlled Substances Import and Export Act (21 U.S.C. 951 et seq.), or the Maritime Drug Law Enforcement Act (46 U.S.C. App. 1901 et seq.); or

(D) any felony if such person has been convicted of two or more offenses described in subparagraphs (A) through (C) of this paragraph, or two or more State or local offenses that would have been offenses described in subparagraphs (A) through (C) of this paragraph if a circumstance giving rise to Federal jurisdiction had existed, or a combination of such offenses; or

(2) Upon motion of the attorney for the Government or upon the judicial officer's own motion, in a case that involves—

(A) a serious risk that such person will flee; or

(B) a serious risk that such person will obstruct or attempt to obstruct justice, or threaten, injure, or intimidate, or attempt to threaten, injure, or intimidate, a prospective witness or juror.

The hearing shall be held immediately upon the person's first appearance before the judicial officer unless that person, or the attorney for the Government, seeks a continuance. Except for good cause, a continuance on motion of such person may not exceed five days (not including any intermediate Saturday, Sunday, or legal holiday), and a continuance on motion of the attorney for the Government may not exceed three days (not including any intermediate Saturday, Sunday, or legal holiday). During a continuance, such person shall be detained, and the judicial officer, on motion of the attorney for the Government or sua sponte, may order that, while in custody, a person who appears to be a narcotics addict receive a medical examination to determine whether such person is an addict. At the hearing, such person has the right to be represented by counsel, and, if financially unable to obtain adequate representation, to have counsel appointed. The person shall be afforded an opportunity to testify, to present witnesses, to cross-examine witnesses who appear at the hearing, and to present information by proffer or otherwise. The rules concerning admissibility of evidence in criminal trials do not apply to the presentation and consideration of information at the hearing. The facts the judicial officer uses to support a finding pursuant to subsection (e) that no condition or combination of conditions will reasonably assure the safety of any other person and the community shall be supported by clear and convincing evidence. The person may be detained pending completion of the hearing. The hearing may be reopened, before or after a determination by the judicial officer, at any time before trial if the judicial officer finds that information exists that was not known to the movant at the time of the hearing and that has a material bearing on the issue whether there are conditions of release that will reasonably assure the appearance of such person as required and the safety of any other person and the community.

(g) Factors to be considered.—The judicial officer shall, in determining whether there are conditions of release that will reasonably assure the appearance of the person as required and the safety of any other person and the community, take into account the available information concerning—

(1) The nature and circumstances of the offense charged, including whether the offense is a crime of violence, or an offense listed in section 2332b(g)(5)(B) for which a maximum term of imprisonment of 10 years or more is prescribed or involves a narcotic drug;

(2) the weight of the evidence against the person;

(3) the history and characteristics of the person, including—

(A) the person's character, physical and mental condition, family ties, employment, financial resources, length of residence in the community, community ties, past conduct, history relating to drug or alcohol abuse, criminal history, and record concerning appearance at court proceedings; and

(B) whether, at the time of the current offense or arrest, the person was on probation, on parole, or on other release pending trial, sentencing, appeal, or completion of sentence for an offense under Federal, State, or local law; and

(4) the nature and seriousness of the danger to any person or the community that would be posed by the person's release. In considering the conditions of release described in subsection (c)(1)(B)(xi) or (c)(1)(B)(xii) of this section, the judicial officer may upon his own motion, or shall upon the motion of the Government, conduct an inquiry into the source of the property to be designated for potential forfeiture or offered as collateral to secure a bond, and shall decline to accept the designation, or the use as collateral, of property that, because of its source, will not reasonably assure the appearance of the person as required.

(h) Contents of release order.—In a release order issued under subsection (b) or (c) of this section, the judicial officer shall—

(1) include a written statement that sets forth all the conditions to which the release is subject, in a manner sufficiently clear and specific to serve as a guide for the person's conduct; and

(2) advise the person of—

(A) the penalties for violating a condition of release, including the penalties for committing an offense while on pretrial release;

(B) the consequences of violating a condition of release, including the immediate issuance of a warrant for the person's arrest; and

(C) sections 1503 of this title (relating to intimidation of witnesses, jurors, and officers of the court), 1510 (relating to obstruction of criminal investigations), 1512 (tampering with a witness, victim, or an informant), and 1513 (retaliating against a witness, victim, or an informant).

(i) Contents of detention order.—In a detention order issued under subsection (e) of this section, the judicial officer shall—

(1) include written findings of fact and a written statement of the reasons for the detention;

(2) direct that the person be committed to the custody of the Attorney General for confinement in a corrections facility separate, to the extent practicable, from persons awaiting or serving sentences or being held in custody pending appeal;

(3) direct that the person be afforded reasonable opportunity for private consultation with counsel; and

(4) direct that, on order of a court of the United States or on request of an attorney for the Government, the person in charge of the corrections facility in which the person is confined deliver the person to

a United States marshal for the purpose of an appearance in connection with a court proceeding.

The judicial officer may, by subsequent order, permit the temporary release of the person, in the custody of a United States marshal or another appropriate person, to the extent that the judicial officer determines such release to be necessary for preparation of the person's defense or for another compelling reason.

(j) Presumption of innocence.—Nothing in this section shall be construed as modifying or limiting the presumption of innocence.

§ 3143. Release or detention of a defendant pending sentence or appeal

(a) Release or detention pending sentence.—(1) Except as provided in paragraph (2), the judicial officer shall order that a person who has been found guilty of an offense and who is awaiting imposition or execution of sentence, other than a person for whom the applicable guideline promulgated pursuant to 28 U.S.C. 994 does not recommend a term of imprisonment, be detained, unless the judicial officer finds by clear and convincing evidence that the person is not likely to flee or pose a danger to the safety of any other person or the community if released under section 3142(b) or (c). If the judicial officer makes such a finding, such judicial officer shall order the release of the person in accordance with section 3142(b) or (c).

(2) The judicial officer shall order that a person who has been found guilty of an offense in a case described in subparagraph (A), (B), or (C) of subsection (f)(1) of section 3142 and is awaiting imposition or execution of sentence be detained unless—

(A)(i) the judicial officer finds there is a substantial likelihood that a motion for acquittal or new trial will be granted; or

(ii) an attorney for the Government has recommended that no sentence of imprisonment be imposed on the person; and

(B) the judicial officer finds by clear and convincing evidence that the person is not likely to flee or pose a danger to any other person or the community.

(b) Release or detention pending appeal by the defendant.—(1) Except as provided in paragraph (2), the judicial officer shall order that a person who has been found guilty of an offense and sentenced to a term of imprisonment, and who has filed an appeal or a petition for a writ of certiorari, be detained, unless the judicial officer finds—

(A) by clear and convincing evidence that the person is not likely to flee or pose a danger to the safety of any other person or the community if released under section 3142(b) or (c) of this title; and

(B) that the appeal is not for the purpose of delay and raises a substantial question of law or fact likely to result in—

(i) reversal,

(ii) an order for a new trial,

(iii) a sentence that does not include a term of imprisonment, or

(iv) a reduced sentence to a term of imprisonment less than the total of the time already served plus the expected duration of the appeal process.

If the judicial officer makes such findings, such judicial officer shall order the release of the person in accordance with section 3142(b) or (c) of this title, except that in the circumstance described in subparagraph (B)(iv) of this paragraph, the judicial officer shall order the detention terminated at the expiration of the likely reduced sentence.

(2) The judicial officer shall order that a person who has been found guilty of an offense in a case described in subparagraph (A), (B), or (C) of subsection (f)(1) of section 3142 and sentenced to a term of imprisonment, and who has filed an appeal or a petition for a writ of certiorari, be detained.

(c) Release or detention pending appeal by the government.—The judicial officer shall treat a defendant in a case in which an appeal has been taken by the United States under section 3731 of this title, in accordance with section 3142 of this title, unless the defendant is otherwise subject to a release or detention order.

Except as provided in subsection (b) of this section, the judicial officer, in a case in which an appeal has been taken by the United States under section 3742, shall—

(1) if the person has been sentenced to a term of imprisonment, order that person detained; and

(2) in any other circumstance, release or detain the person under section 3142.

§ 3144.   Release or detention of a material witness

If it appears from an affidavit filed by a party that the testimony of a person is material in a criminal proceeding, and if it is shown that it may become impracticable to secure the presence of the person by subpoena, a judicial officer may order the arrest of the person and treat the person in accordance with the provisions of section 3142 of this title. No material witness may be detained because of inability to comply with any condition of release if the testimony of such witness can adequately be secured by deposition, and if further detention is not necessary to prevent a failure of justice. Release of a material witness may be delayed for a reasonable period of time until the deposition of the witness can be taken pursuant to the Federal Rules of Criminal Procedure.

§ 3145.   Review and appeal of a release or detention order

(a) Review of a release order.—If a person is ordered released by a magistrate judge, or by a person other than a judge of a court having original jurisdiction over the offense and other than a Federal appellate court—

(1) the attorney for the Government may file, with the court having original jurisdiction over the offense, a motion for revocation of the order or amendment of the conditions of release; and

(2) the person may file, with the court having original jurisdiction over the offense, a motion for amendment of the conditions of release.

The motion shall be determined promptly.

(b) Review of a detention order.—If a person is ordered detained by a magistrate judge, or by a person other than a judge of a court having original jurisdiction over the offense and other than a Federal appellate court, the person may file, with the court having original jurisdiction over the offense, a motion for revocation or amendment of the order. The motion shall be determined promptly.

(c) Appeal from a release or detention order.—An appeal from a release or detention order, or from a decision denying revocation or amendment of such an order, is governed by the provisions of section 1291 of title 28 and section 3731 of this title. The appeal shall be determined promptly. A person subject to detention pursuant to section 3143(a)(2) or (b)(2), and who meets the conditions of release set forth in section 3143(a)(1) or (b)(1), may be ordered released, under appropriate conditions, by the judicial officer, if it is clearly shown that there are exceptional reasons why such person's detention would not be appropriate.

§ 3146. Penalty for failure to appear

(a) Offense.—Whoever, having been released under this chapter knowingly—

(1) fails to appear before a court as required by the conditions of release; or

(2) fails to surrender for service of sentence pursuant to a court order;

shall be punished as provided in subsection (b) of this section.

(b) Punishment.—(1) The punishment for an offense under this section is—

(A) if the person was released in connection with a charge of, or while awaiting sentence, surrender for service of sentence, or appeal or certiorari after conviction for—

(i) an offense punishable by death, life imprisonment, or imprisonment for a term of 15 years or more, a fine under this title or imprisonment for not more than ten years, or both;

(ii) an offense punishable by imprisonment for a term of five years or more, a fine under this title or imprisonment for not more than five years, or both;

(iii) any other felony, a fine under this title or imprisonment for not more than two years, or both; or

(iv) a misdemeanor, a fine under this title or imprisonment for not more than one year, or both; and

(B) if the person was released for appearance as a material witness, a fine under this chapter or imprisonment for not more than one year, or both.

(2) A term of imprisonment imposed under this section shall be consecutive to the sentence of imprisonment for any other offense.

(c) Affirmative defense.—It is an affirmative defense to a prosecution under this section that uncontrollable circumstances prevented the person from appearing or surrendering, and that the person did not contribute to the creation of such circumstances in reckless disregard of the requirement to appear or surrender, and that the person appeared or surrendered as soon as such circumstances ceased to exist.

(d) Declaration of forfeiture.—If a person fails to appear before a court as required, and the person executed an appearance bond pursuant to section 3142(b) of this title or is subject to the release condition set forth in clause (xi) or (xii) of section 3142(c)(1)(B) of this title, the judicial officer may, regardless of whether the person has been charged with an offense under this section, declare any property designated pursuant to that section to be forfeited to the United States.

§ 3147.   Penalty for an offense committed while on release

A person convicted of an offense committed while released under this chapter shall be sentenced, in addition to the sentence prescribed for the offense to—

> (1) a term of imprisonment of not more than ten years if the offense is a felony; or

> (2) a term of imprisonment of not more than one year if the offense is a misdemeanor.

A term of imprisonment imposed under this section shall be consecutive to any other sentence of imprisonment.

§ 3148.   Sanctions for violation of a release condition

(a) Available sanctions.—A person who has been released under section 3142 of this title, and who has violated a condition of his release, is subject to a revocation of release, an order of detention, and a prosecution for contempt of court.

(b) Revocation of release.—The attorney for the Government may initiate a proceeding for revocation of an order of release by filing a motion with the district court. A judicial officer may issue a warrant for the arrest of a person charged with violating a condition of release, and the person shall be brought before a judicial officer in the district in which such person's arrest was ordered for a proceeding in accordance with this section. To the extent practicable, a person charged with violating the condition of release that such person not commit a Federal, State, or local crime during the period of release, shall be brought before the judicial officer who ordered the release and whose order is alleged to have been violated. The judicial officer shall enter an order of revocation and detention if, after a hearing, the judicial officer—

> (1) finds that there is—

>> (A) probable cause to believe that the person has committed a Federal, State, or local crime while on release; or

(B) clear and convincing evidence that the person has violated any other condition of release; and

(2) finds that—

(A) based on the factors set forth in section 3142(g) of this title, there is no condition or combination of conditions of release that will assure that the person will not flee or pose a danger to the safety of any other person or the community; or

(B) the person is unlikely to abide by any condition or combination of conditions of release.

If there is probable cause to believe that, while on release, the person committed a Federal, State, or local felony, a rebuttable presumption arises that no condition or combination of conditions will assure that the person will not pose a danger to the safety of any other person or the community. If the judicial officer finds that there are conditions of release that will assure that the person will not flee or pose a danger to the safety of any other person or the community, and that the person will abide by such conditions, the judicial officer shall treat the person in accordance with the provisions of section 3142 of this title and may amend the conditions of release accordingly.

(c) Prosecution for contempt.—The judicial officer may commence a prosecution for contempt, under section 401 of this title, if the person has violated a condition of release.

§ 3149. Surrender of an offender by a surety

A person charged with an offense, who is released upon the execution of an appearance bond with a surety, may be arrested by the surety, and if so arrested, shall be delivered promptly to a United States marshal and brought before a judicial officer. The judicial officer shall determine in accordance with the provisions of section 3148(b) whether to revoke the release of the person, and may absolve the surety of responsibility to pay all or part of the bond in accordance with the provisions of Rule 46 of the Federal Rules of Criminal Procedure. The person so committed shall be held in official detention until released pursuant to this chapter or another provision of law.

§ 3150. Applicability to a case removed from a State court

The provisions of this chapter apply to a criminal case removed to a Federal court from a State court.

SPEEDY TRIAL ACT OF 1974 (AS AMENDED)

(18 U.S.C. §§ 3161–3162, 3164).

§ 3161. Time limits and exclusions

(a) In any case involving a defendant charged with an offense, the appropriate judicial officer, at the earliest practicable time, shall, after consultation with the counsel for the defendant and the attorney for the Government, set the case for trial on a day certain, or list it for trial on a weekly or other short-term trial calendar at a place within the judicial district, so as to assure a speedy trial.

(b) Any information or indictment charging an individual with the commission of an offense shall be filed within thirty days from the date on which such individual was arrested or served with a summons in connection with such charges. If an individual has been charged with a felony in a district in which no grand jury has been in session during such thirty-day period, the period of time for filing of the indictment shall be extended an additional thirty days.

(c)(1) In any case in which a plea of not guilty is entered, the trial of a defendant charged in an information or indictment with the commission of an offense shall commence within seventy days from the filing date (and making public) of the information or indictment, or from the date the defendant has appeared before a judicial officer of the court in which such charge is pending, whichever date last occurs. If a defendant consents in writing to be tried before a magistrate judge on a complaint, the trial shall commence within seventy days from the date of such consent.

(2) Unless the defendant consents in writing to the contrary, the trial shall not commence less than thirty days from the date on which the defendant first appears through counsel or expressly waives counsel and elects to proceed pro se.

(d)(1) If any indictment or information is dismissed upon motion of the defendant, or any charge contained in a complaint filed against an individual is dismissed or otherwise dropped, and thereafter a complaint is filed against such defendant or individual charging him with the same offense or an offense based on the same conduct or arising from the same criminal episode, or an information or indictment is filed charging such defendant with the same offense or an offense based on the same conduct or arising from the same criminal episode, the provisions of subsections (b) and (c) of this section shall be applicable with respect to such subsequent complaint, indictment, or information, as the case may be.

(2) If the defendant is to be tried upon an indictment or information dismissed by a trial court and reinstated following an appeal, the trial shall commence within seventy days from the date the action occasioning the trial becomes final, except that the court retrying the case may extend the period for trial not to exceed one hundred and eighty days from the date the action occasioning the trial becomes final if the unavailability of witnesses or other factors resulting from the passage of time shall make trial within seventy days impractical. The periods of delay enumerated in section 3161(h) are excluded in computing the time limitations specified in this section. The sanctions of section 3162 apply to this subsection.

(e) If the defendant is to be tried again following a declaration by the trial judge of a mistrial or following an order of such judge for a new trial, the trial shall commence within seventy days from the date the action occasioning the retrial becomes final. If the defendant is to be tried again following an appeal or a collateral attack, the trial shall commence within seventy days from the date the action occasioning the retrial becomes final, except that the court retrying the case may extend the period for retrial not to exceed one hundred and eighty days from the date the action occasioning the retrial becomes final if unavailability of witnesses or other factors resulting from passage of time shall make trial within seventy days impractical. The periods of delay enumerated in section 3161(h) are excluded in computing the time limitations specified in this section. The sanctions of section 3162 apply to this subsection.

(f) Notwithstanding the provisions of subsection (b) of this section, for the first twelve-calendar-month period following the effective date of this section as set forth in section 3163(a) of this chapter the time limit imposed with respect to the period between arrest and indictment by subsection (b) of this section shall be sixty days, for the second such twelve-month period such time limit shall be forty-five days and for the third such period such time limit shall be thirty-five days.

(g) Notwithstanding the provisions of subsection (c) of this section, for the first twelve-calendar-month period following the effective date of this section as set forth in section 3163(b) of this chapter, the time limit with respect to the period between arraignment and trial imposed by subsection (c) of this section shall be one hundred and eighty days, for the second such twelve-month period such time limit shall be one hundred and twenty days, and for the third such period such time limit with respect to the period between arraignment and trial shall be eighty days.

(h) The following periods of delay shall be excluded in computing the time within which an information or an indictment must be filed, or in computing the time within which the trial of any such offense must commence:

(1) Any period of delay resulting from other proceedings concerning the defendant, including but not limited to—

(A) delay resulting from any proceeding, including any examinations, to determine the mental competency or physical capacity of the defendant;

(B) delay resulting from any proceeding, including any examination of the defendant, pursuant to section 2902 of title 28, United States Code;

(C) delay resulting from deferral of prosecution pursuant to section 2902 of title 28, United States Code;

(D) delay resulting from trial with respect to other charges against the defendant;

(E) delay resulting from any interlocutory appeal;

(F) delay resulting from any pretrial motion, from the filing of the motion through the conclusion of the hearing on, or other prompt disposition of, such motion;

(G) delay resulting from any proceeding relating to the transfer of a case or the removal of any defendant from another district under the Federal Rules of Criminal Procedure;

(H) delay resulting from transportation of any defendant from another district, or to and from places of examination or hospitalization, except that any time consumed in excess of ten days from the date an order of removal or an order directing such transportation, and the defendant's arrival at the destination shall be presumed to be unreasonable;

(I) delay resulting from consideration by the court of a proposed plea agreement to be entered into by the defendant and the attorney for the Government; and

(J) delay reasonably attributable to any period, not to exceed thirty days, during which any proceeding concerning the defendant is actually under advisement by the court.

(2) Any period of delay during which prosecution is deferred by the attorney for the Government pursuant to written agreement with the defendant, with the approval of the court, for the purpose of allowing the defendant to demonstrate his good conduct.

(3)(A) Any period of delay resulting from the absence or unavailability of the defendant or an essential witness.

(B) For purposes of subparagraph (A) of this paragraph, a defendant or an essential witness shall be considered absent when his whereabouts are unknown and, in addition, he is attempting to avoid apprehension or prosecution or his whereabouts cannot be determined by due diligence. For purposes of such subparagraph, a defendant or an essential witness shall be considered unavailable whenever his whereabouts are known but his presence for trial cannot be obtained by due diligence or he resists appearing at or being returned for trial.

(4) Any period of delay resulting from the fact that the defendant is mentally incompetent or physically unable to stand trial.

(5) Any period of delay resulting from the treatment of the defendant pursuant to section 2902 of title 28, United States Code.

(6) If the information or indictment is dismissed upon motion of the attorney for the Government and thereafter a charge is filed against the defendant for the same offense, or any offense required to be joined with that offense, any period of delay from the date the charge was dismissed to the date the time limitation would commence to run as to the subsequent charge had there been no previous charge.

(7) A reasonable period of delay when the defendant is joined for trial with a codefendant as to whom the time for trial has not run and no motion for severance has been granted.

(8)(A) Any period of delay resulting from a continuance granted by any judge on his own motion or at the request of the defendant or his counsel or at the request of the attorney for the Government, if the judge granted such continuance on the basis of his findings that the ends of justice served by taking such action outweigh the best interest of the public and the defendant in a speedy trial. No such period of delay resulting from a continuance granted by the court in accordance with this paragraph shall be excludable under this subsection unless the court sets forth, in the record of the case, either orally or in writing, its reasons for finding that the ends of justice served by the granting of such continuance outweigh the best interests of the public and the defendant in a speedy trial.

(B) The factors, among others, which a judge shall consider in determining whether to grant a continuance under subparagraph (A) of this paragraph in any case are as follows:

(i) Whether the failure to grant such a continuance in the proceeding would be likely to make a continuation of such proceeding impossible, or result in a miscarriage of justice.

(ii) Whether the case is so unusual or so complex, due to the number of defendants, the nature of the prosecution, or the existence of novel questions of fact or law, that it is unreasonable to expect adequate preparation for pretrial proceedings or for the trial itself within the time limits established by this section.

(iii) Whether, in a case in which arrest precedes indictment, delay in the filing of the indictment is caused because the arrest occurs at a time such that it is unreasonable to expect return and filing of the indictment within the period specified in section 3161(b), or because the facts upon which the grand jury must base its determination are unusual or complex.

(iv) Whether the failure to grant such a continuance in a case which, taken as a whole, is not so unusual or so complex as to fall within clause (ii), would deny the defendant reasonable time to obtain counsel, would unreasonably deny the defendant or the Government continuity of counsel, or would deny counsel for the defendant or the attorney for the Government the reasonable time necessary for effective preparation, taking into account the exercise of due diligence.

(C) No continuance under subparagraph (A) of this paragraph shall be granted because of general congestion of the court's calendar, or lack of diligent preparation or failure to obtain available witnesses on the part of the attorney for the Government.

(9) Any period of delay, not to exceed one year, ordered by a district court upon an application of a party and a finding by a preponderance of the evidence that an official request, as defined in section 3292 of this title, has been made for evidence of any such offense and that it reasonably appears, or reasonably appeared at the time the request was made, that such evidence is, or was, in such foreign country.

(i) If trial did not commence within the time limitation specified in section 3161 because the defendant had entered a plea of guilty or nolo contendere subsequently withdrawn to any or all charges in an indictment or information, the defendant shall be deemed indicted with respect to all charges therein contained within the meaning of section 3161, on the day the order permitting withdrawal of the plea becomes final.

(j)(1) If the attorney for the Government knows that a person charged with an offense is serving a term of imprisonment in any penal institution, he shall promptly—

(A) undertake to obtain the presence of the prisoner for trial; or

(B) cause a detainer to be filed with the person having custody of the prisoner and request him to so advise the prisoner and to advise the prisoner of his right to demand trial.

(2) If the person having custody of such prisoner receives a detainer, he shall promptly advise the prisoner of the charge and of the prisoner's right to demand trial. If at any time thereafter the prisoner informs the person having custody that he does demand trial, such person shall cause notice to that effect to be sent promptly to the attorney for the Government who caused the detainer to be filed.

(3) Upon receipt of such notice, the attorney for the Government shall promptly seek to obtain the presence of the prisoner for trial.

(4) When the person having custody of the prisoner receives from the attorney for the Government a properly supported request for temporary custody of such prisoner for trial, the prisoner shall be made available to that attorney for the Government (subject, in cases of interjurisdictional transfer, to any right of the prisoner to contest the legality of his delivery).

(k)(1) If the defendant is absent (as defined by subsection (h)(3)) on the day set for trial, and the defendant's subsequent appearance before the court on a bench warrant or other process or surrender to the court occurs more than 21 days after the day set for trial, the defendant shall be deemed to have first appeared before a judicial officer of the court in which the information or indictment is pending within the meaning of subsection (c) on the date of the defendant's subsequent appearance before the court.

(2) If the defendant is absent (as defined by subsection (h)(3)) on the day set for trial, and the defendant's subsequent appearance before the court on a bench warrant or other process or surrender to the court occurs not more than 21 days after the day set for trial, the time limit required by subsection (c), as extended by subsection (h), shall be further extended by 21 days.

§ 3162. Sanctions

(a)(1) If, in the case of any individual against whom a complaint is filed charging such individual with an offense, no indictment or information is filed within the time limit required by section 3161(b) as extended by section 3161(h) of this chapter, such charge against that individual contained in such complaint shall be dismissed or otherwise dropped. In determining whether to dismiss the case with or without prejudice, the court shall consider, among others, each of the following factors: the seriousness of the offense; the facts and circumstances of the case which led to the dismissal; and the impact of a reprosecution on the administration of this chapter and on the administration of justice.

(2) If a defendant is not brought to trial within the time limit required by section 3161(c) as extended by section 3161(h), the information or indictment shall be dismissed on motion of the defendant. The defendant shall have the burden of proof of supporting such motion but the Government shall have the burden of going forward with the evidence in connection with any exclusion of time under subparagraph 3161(h) (3). In determining whether to dismiss the case with or without prejudice, the court shall

consider, among others, each of the following factors: the seriousness of the offense; the facts and circumstances of the case which led to the dismissal; and the impact of a reprosecution on the administration of this chapter and on the administration of justice. Failure of the defendant to move for dismissal prior to trial or entry of a plea of guilty or nolo contendere shall constitute a waiver of the right to dismissal under this section.

(b) In any case in which counsel for the defendant or the attorney for the Government (1) knowingly allows the case to be set for trial without disclosing the fact that a necessary witness would be unavailable for trial; (2) files a motion solely for the purpose of delay which he knows is totally frivolous and without merit; (3) makes a statement for the purpose of obtaining a continuance which he knows to be false and which is material to the granting of a continuance; or (4) otherwise willfully fails to proceed to trial without justification consistent with section 3161 of this chapter, the court may punish any such counsel or attorney, as follows:

(A) in the case of an appointed defense counsel, by reducing the amount of compensation that otherwise would have been paid to such counsel pursuant to section 3006A of this title in an amount not to exceed 25 per centum thereof;

(B) in the case of a counsel retained in connection with the defense of a defendant, by imposing on such counsel a fine of not to exceed 25 per centum of the compensation to which he is entitled in connection with his defense of such defendant;

(C) by imposing on any attorney for the Government a fine of not to exceed $250;

(D) by denying any such counsel or attorney for the Government the right to practice before the court considering such case for a period of not to exceed ninety days; or

(E) by filing a report with an appropriate disciplinary committee.

The authority to punish provided for by this subsection shall be in addition to any other authority or power available to such court.

(c) The court shall follow procedures established in the Federal Rules of Criminal Procedure in punishing any counsel or attorney for the Government pursuant to this section.

§ 3164. Persons detained or designated as being of high risk

(a) The trial or other disposition of cases involving—

(1) a detained person who is being held in detention solely because he is awaiting trial, and

(2) a released person who is awaiting trial and has been designated by the attorney for the Government as being of high risk,

shall be accorded priority.

(b) The trial of any person described in subsection (a) (1) or (a) (2) of this section shall commence not later than ninety days following the beginning of such continuous detention or designation of high risk by the attorney for the Government. The periods of delay enumerated in section 3161(h) are excluded in computing the time limitation specified in this section.

(c) Failure to commence trial of a detainee as specified in subsection (b), through no fault of the accused or his counsel, or failure to commence trial of a designated releasee as specified in subsection (b), through no fault of the attorney for the Government, shall result in the automatic review by the court of the conditions of release. No detainee, as defined in subsection (a), shall be held in custody pending trial after the expiration of such ninety-day period required for the commencement of his trial. A designated releasee, as defined in subsection (a), who is found by the court to have intentionally delayed the trial of his case shall be subject to an order of the court modifying his nonfinancial conditions of release under this title to insure that he shall appear at trial as required.

JENCKS' ACT

(18 U.S.C. § 3500).

§ 3500. Demands for production of statements and reports of witnesses

(a) In any criminal prosecution brought by the United States, no statement or report in the possession of the United States which was made by a Government witness or prospective Government witness (other than the defendant) shall be the subject of subpena, discovery, or inspection until said witness has testified on direct examination in the trial of the case.

(b) After a witness called by the United States has testified on direct examination, the court shall, on motion of the defendant, order the United States to produce any statement (as hereinafter defined) of the witness in the possession of the United States which relates to the subject matter as to which the witness has testified. If the entire contents of any such statement relate to the subject matter of the testimony of the witness, the court shall order it to be delivered directly to the defendant for his examination and use.

(c) If the United States claims that any statement ordered to be produced under this section contains matter which does not relate to the subject matter of the testimony of the witness, the court shall order the United States to deliver such statement for the inspection of the court in camera. Upon such delivery the court shall excise the portions of such statement which do not relate to the subject matter of the testimony of the witness. With such material excised, the court shall then direct delivery of such statement to the defendant for his use. If, pursuant to such procedure, any portion of such statement is withheld from the defendant and the defendant objects to such withholding, and the trial is continued to an adjudication of the guilt of the defendant, the entire text of such statement shall be preserved by the United States and, in the event the defendant appeals, shall be made available to the appellate court for the purpose of determining the correctness of the ruling of the trial judge. Whenever any statement is delivered to a defendant pursuant to this section, the court in its discretion, upon application of said defendant, may recess proceedings in the trial for such time as it may determine to be reasonably required for the examination of such statement by said defendant and his preparation for its use in the trial.

(d) If the United States elects not to comply with an order of the court under subsection (b) or (c) hereof to deliver to the defendant any such statement, or such portion thereof as the court may direct, the court shall strike from the record the testimony of the witness, and the trial shall proceed unless the court in its discretion shall determine that the interests of justice require that a mistrial be declared.

(e) The term "statement", as used in subsections (b), (c), and (d) of this section in relation to any witness called by the United States, means—

(1) a written statement made by said witness and signed or otherwise adopted or approved by him;

(2) a stenographic, mechanical, electrical, or other recording, or a transcription thereof, which is a substantially verbatim recital of an oral statement made by said witness and recorded contemporaneously with the making of such oral statement; or

(3) a statement, however taken or recorded, or a transcription thereof, if any, made by said witness to a grand jury.

LITIGATION CONCERNING SOURCES OF EVIDENCE

(18 U.S.C. § 3504).

§ 3504. Litigation concerning sources of evidence

(a) In any trial, hearing, or other proceeding in or before any court, grand jury, department, officer, agency, regulatory body, or other authority of the United States—

(1) upon a claim by a party aggrieved that evidence is inadmissible because it is the primary product of an unlawful act or because it was obtained by the exploitation of an unlawful act, the opponent of the claim shall affirm or deny the occurrence of the alleged unlawful act;

(2) disclosure of information for a determination if evidence is inadmissible because it is the primary product of an unlawful act occurring prior to June 19, 1968, or because it was obtained by the exploitation of an unlawful act occurring prior to June 19, 1968, shall not be required unless such information may be relevant to a pending claim of such inadmissibility; and

(3) no claim shall be considered that evidence of an event is inadmissible on the ground that such evidence was obtained by the exploitation of an unlawful act occurring prior to June 19, 1968, if such event occurred more than five years after such allegedly unlawful act.

(b) As used in this section "unlawful act" means any act the use of any electronic, mechanical, or other device (as defined in section 2510(5) of this title) in violation of the Constitution or laws of the United States or any regulation or standard promulgated pursuant thereto.

CRIMINAL APPEALS ACT OF 1970 (AS AMENDED)

(18 U.S.C. § 3731).

§ 3731. Appeal by United States

In a criminal case an appeal by the United States shall lie to a court of appeals from a decision, judgment, or order of a district court dismissing an indictment or information or granting a new trial after verdict or judgment, as to any one or more counts, or any part thereof, except that no appeal shall lie where the double jeopardy clause of the United States Constitution prohibits further prosecution.

An appeal by the United States shall lie to a court of appeals from a decision or order of a district court suppressing or excluding evidence or requiring the return of seized property in a criminal proceeding, not made after the defendant has been put in jeopardy and before the verdict or finding on an indictment or information, if the United States attorney certifies to the district court that the appeal is not taken for purpose of delay and that the evidence is a substantial proof of a fact material in the proceeding.

An appeal by the United States shall lie to a court of appeals from a decision or order, entered by a district court of the United States, granting the release of a person charged with or convicted of an offense, or denying a motion for revocation of, or modification of the conditions of, a decision or order granting release.

The appeal in all such cases shall be taken within thirty days after the decision, judgment or order has been rendered and shall be diligently prosecuted.

The provisions of this section shall be liberally construed to effectuate its purposes.

CRIME VICTIMS' RIGHTS

(18 U.S.C. § 3771).

§ 3771. Crime victims' rights

(a) Rights of crime victims.—A crime victim has the following rights:

(1) The right to be reasonably protected from the accused.

(2) The right to reasonable, accurate, and timely notice of any public court proceeding, or any parole proceeding, involving the crime or of any release or escape of the accused.

(3) The right not to be excluded from any such public court proceeding, unless the court, after receiving clear and convincing evidence, determines that testimony by the victim would be materially altered if the victim heard other testimony at that proceeding.

(4) The right to be reasonably heard at any public proceeding in the district court involving release, plea, sentencing, or any parole proceeding.

(5) The reasonable right to confer with the attorney for the Government in the case.

(6) The right to full and timely restitution as provided in law.

(7) The right to proceedings free from unreasonable delay.

(8) The right to be treated with fairness and with respect for the victim's dignity and privacy.

(b) Rights afforded.—In any court proceeding involving an offense against a crime victim, the court shall ensure that the crime victim is afforded the rights described in subsection (a). Before making a determination described in subsection (a)(3), the court shall make every effort to permit the fullest attendance possible by the victim and shall consider reasonable alternatives to the exclusion of the victim from the criminal proceeding. The reasons for any decision denying relief under this chapter shall be clearly stated on the record.

(c) Best efforts to accord rights.—

(1) Government.—Officers and employees of the Department of Justice and other departments and agencies of the United States engaged in the detection, investigation, or prosecution of crime shall make their best efforts to see that crime victims are notified of, and accorded, the rights described in subsection (a).

(2) Advice of attorney.—The prosecutor shall advise the crime victim that the crime victim can seek the advice of an attorney with respect to the rights described in subsection (a).

(3) Notice.—Notice of release otherwise required pursuant to this chapter shall not be given if such notice may endanger the safety of any person.

(d) Enforcement and limitations.—

(1) Rights.—The crime victim or the crime victim's lawful representative, and the attorney for the Government may assert the rights described in subsection (a). A person accused of the crime may not obtain any form of relief under this chapter.

(2) Multiple crime victims.—In a case where the court finds that the number of crime victims makes it impracticable to accord all of the crime victims the rights described in subsection (a), the court shall fashion a reasonable procedure to give effect to this chapter that does not unduly complicate or prolong the proceedings.

(3) Motion for relief and writ of mandamus.—The rights described in subsection (a) shall be asserted in the district court in which a defendant is being prosecuted for the crime or, if no prosecution is underway, in the district court in the district in which the crime occurred. The district court shall take up and decide any motion asserting a victim's right forthwith. If the district court denies the relief sought, the movant may petition the court of appeals for a writ of mandamus. The court of appeals may issue the writ on the order of a single judge pursuant to circuit rule or the Federal Rules of Appellate Procedure. The court of appeals shall take up and decide such application forthwith within 72 hours after the petition has been filed. In no

event shall proceedings be stayed or subject to a continuance of more than five days for purposes of enforcing this chapter. If the court of appeals denies the relief sought, the reasons for the denial shall be clearly stated on the record in a written opinion.

(4) Error.—In any appeal in a criminal case, the Government may assert as error the district court's denial of any crime victim's right in the proceeding to which the appeal relates.

(5) Limitation on relief.—In no case shall a failure to afford a right under this chapter provide grounds for a new trial. A victim may make a motion to re-open a plea or sentence only if—

(A) the victim has asserted the right to be heard before or during the proceeding at issue and such right was denied;

(B) the victim petitions the court of appeals for a writ of mandamus within 10 days; and

(C) in the case of a plea, the accused has not pled to the highest offense charged.

This paragraph does not affect the victim's right to restitution as provided in title 18, United States Code.

(6) No cause of action.—Nothing in this chapter shall be construed to authorize a cause of action for damages or to create, to enlarge, or to imply any duty or obligation to any victim or other person for the breach of which the United States or any of its officers or employees could be held liable in damages. Nothing in this chapter shall be construed to impair the prosecutorial discretion of the Attorney General or any officer under his direction.

(e) Definitions.—For the purposes of this chapter, the term "crime victim" means a person directly and proximately harmed as a result of the commission of a Federal offense or an offense in the District of Columbia. In the case of a crime victim who is under 18 years of age, incompetent, incapacitated, or deceased, the legal guardians of the crime victim or the representatives of the crime victim's estate, family members, or any other persons appointed as suitable by the court, may assume the crime victim's rights under this chapter, but in no event shall the defendant be named as such guardian or representative.

(f) Procedures to promote compliance.—

(1) Regulations.—Not later than 1 year after the date of enactment of this chapter, the Attorney General of the United States shall promulgate regulations to enforce the rights of crime victims and to ensure compliance by responsible officials with the obligations described in law respecting crime victims.

(2) Contents.—The regulations promulgated under paragraph (1) shall—

(A) designate an administrative authority within the Department of Justice to receive and investigate complaints relating to the provision or violation of the rights of a crime victim;

(B) require a course of training for employees and offices of the Department of Justice that fail to comply with provisions of Federal law pertaining to the treatment of crime victims, and otherwise assist such employees and offices in responding more effectively to the needs of crime victims;

(C) contain disciplinary sanctions, including suspension or termination from employment, for employees of the Department of Justice who willfully or wantonly fail to comply with provisions of Federal law pertaining to the treatment of crime victims; and

(D) provide that the Attorney General, or the designee of the Attorney General, shall be the final arbiter of the complaint, and that there shall be no judicial review of the final decision of the Attorney General by a complainant.

JURY SELECTION AND SERVICE ACT OF 1968 (AS AMENDED)

(28 U.S.C. §§ 1861–1863, 1865–1867).

§ 1861. Declaration of policy

It is the policy of the United States that all litigants in Federal courts entitled to trial by jury shall have the right to grand and petit juries selected at random from a fair cross section of the community in the district or division wherein the court convenes. It is further the policy of the United States that all citizens shall have the opportunity to be considered for service on grand and petit juries in the district courts of the United States, and shall have an obligation to serve as jurors when summoned for that purpose.

§ 1862. Discrimination prohibited

No citizen shall be excluded from service as a grand or petit juror in the district courts of the United States or in the Court of International Trade on account of race, color, religion, sex, national origin, or economic status.

§ 1863. Plan for random jury selection

(a) Each United States district court shall devise and place into operation a written plan for random selection of grand and petit jurors that shall be designed to achieve the objectives of sections 1861 and 1862 of this title, and that shall otherwise comply with the provisions of this title. The plan shall be placed into operation after approval by a reviewing panel consisting of the members of the judicial council of the circuit and either the chief judge of the district whose plan is being reviewed or such other active district judge of that district as the chief judge of the district may designate. The panel shall examine the plan to ascertain that it complies with the provisions of this title. If the reviewing panel finds that the plan does not comply, the panel shall state the particulars in which the plan fails to comply and direct the district court to present within a reasonable time an alternative plan remedying the defect or defects. Separate plans may be adopted for each division or combination of divisions within a judicial district. The district court may modify a plan at any time and it shall modify the plan when so directed by the reviewing panel. The district court shall promptly notify the panel, the Administrative Office of the United States Courts, and the Attorney General of the United States, of the initial adoption and future modifications of the plan by filing copies therewith. Modifications of the plan made at the instance of the district court shall become effective after approval by the panel. Each district court shall submit a report on the jury selection process within its jurisdiction to the Administrative Office of the United States Courts in such form and at such times as the Judicial Conference of the United States may specify. The Judicial Conference of the United States may, from time to time, adopt rules and regulations governing the provisions and the operation of the plans formulated under this title.

(b) Among other things, such plan shall—

(1) either establish a jury commission, or authorize the clerk of the court, to manage the jury selection process. If the plan establishes a jury commission, the district court shall appoint one citizen to serve with the clerk of the court as the jury commission: *Provided, however*, That the plan for the District of Columbia may establish a jury commission consisting of three citizens. The citizen jury commissioner shall not belong to the same political party as the clerk serving with him. The clerk or the jury commission, as the case may be, shall act under the supervision and control of the chief judge of the district court or such other judge of the district court as the plan may provide. Each jury commissioner shall, during his tenure in office, reside in the judicial district or division for which he is appointed. Each citizen jury commissioner shall receive compensation to be fixed by the district court plan at a rate not to exceed $50 per day for each day necessarily employed in the performance of his duties, plus reimbursement for travel, subsistence, and other necessary expenses incurred by him in the performance of such duties. The Judicial Conference of the United States may establish standards for allowance of travel, subsistence, and other necessary expenses incurred by jury commissioners.

(2) specify whether the names of prospective jurors shall be selected from the voter registration lists or the lists of actual voters of the political subdivisions within the district or division. The plan shall prescribe some other source or sources of names in addition to voter lists where necessary to foster the policy and protect the rights secured by sections 1861 and 1862 of this title. The plan for the District of Columbia may require the names of prospective jurors to be selected from the city directory rather than from voter lists. The plans for the districts of Puerto Rico and the Canal Zone may prescribe some other source or sources of names of prospective jurors in lieu of voter lists, the use of which shall be consistent with the policies declared and rights secured by sections 1861 and 1862 of this title. The plan for the district of Massachusetts may require the names of prospective jurors to be selected from the resident list provided for in chapter 234A, Massachusetts General Laws, or comparable authority, rather than from voter lists.

(3) specify detailed procedures to be followed by the jury commission or clerk in selecting names from the sources specified in paragraph

(2) of this subsection. These procedures shall be designed to ensure the random selection of a fair cross section of the persons residing in the community in the district or division wherein the court convenes. They shall ensure that names of persons residing in each of the counties, parishes, or similar political subdivisions within the judicial district or division are placed in a master jury wheel; and shall ensure that each county, parish, or similar political subdivision within the district or division is substantially proportionally represented in the master jury wheel for that judicial district, division, or combination of divisions. For the purposes of determining proportional representation in the master jury wheel, either the number of actual voters at the last general election in each county, parish, or similar political subdivision, or the number of registered voters if registration of voters is uniformly required throughout the district or division, may be used.

(4) provide for a master jury wheel (or a device similar in purpose and function) into which the names of those randomly selected shall be placed. The plan shall fix a minimum number of names to be placed initially in the master jury wheel, which shall be at least one-half of 1 per centum of the total number of persons on the lists used as a source of names for the district or division; but if this number of names is believed to be cumbersome and unnecessary, the plan may fix a smaller number of names to be placed in the master wheel, but in no event less than one thousand. The chief judge of the district court, or such other district court judge as the plan may provide, may order additional names to be placed in the master jury wheel from time to time as necessary. The plan shall provide for periodic emptying and refilling of the master jury wheel at specified times, the interval for which shall not exceed four years.

(5)(A) except as provided in subparagraph (B), specify those groups of persons or occupational classes whose members shall, on individual request therefor, be excused from jury service. Such groups or classes shall be excused only if the district court finds, and the plan states, that jury service by such class or group would entail undue hardship or extreme inconvenience to the members thereof, and excuse of members thereof would not be inconsistent with sections 1861 and 1862 of this title.

(B) specify that volunteer safety personnel, upon individual request, shall be excused from jury service. For purposes of this subparagraph, the term "volunteer safety personnel" means individuals serving a public agency (as defined in section 1203(6) of title I of the Omnibus Crime Control and Safe Streets Act of 1968) in an official capacity, without compensation, as firefighters or members of a rescue squad or ambulance crew.

(6) specify that the following persons are barred from jury service on the ground that they are exempt: (A) members in active service in the Armed Forces of the United States; (B) members of the fire or police departments of any State, the District of Columbia, any territory or possession of the United States, or any subdivision of a State, the District of Columbia, or such territory or possession; (C) public officers

in the executive, legislative, or judicial branches of the Government of the United States, or of any State, the District of Columbia, any territory or possession of the United States, or any subdivision of a State, the District of Columbia, or such territory or possession, who are actively engaged in the performance of official duties.

(7) fix the time when the names drawn from the qualified jury wheel shall be disclosed to parties and to the public. If the plan permits these names to be made public, it may nevertheless permit the chief judge of the district court, or such other district court judge as the plan may provide, to keep these names confidential in any case where the interests of justice so require.

(8) specify the procedures to be followed by the clerk or jury commission in assigning persons whose names have been drawn from the qualified jury wheel to grand and petit jury panels.

(c) The initial plan shall be devised by each district court and transmitted to the reviewing panel specified in subsection (a) of this section within one hundred and twenty days of the date of enactment of the Jury Selection and Service Act of 1968. The panel shall approve or direct the modification of each plan so submitted within sixty days thereafter. Each plan or modification made at the direction of the panel shall become effective after approval at such time thereafter as the panel directs, in no event to exceed ninety days from the date of approval. Modifications made at the instance of the district court under subsection (a) of this section shall be effective at such time thereafter as the panel directs, in no event to exceed ninety days from the date of modification.

(d) State, local, and Federal officials having custody, possession, or control of voter registration lists, lists of actual voters, or other appropriate records shall make such lists and records available to the jury commission or clerks for inspection, reproduction, and copying at all reasonable times as the commission or clerk may deem necessary and proper for the performance of duties under this title. The district courts shall have jurisdiction upon application by the Attorney General of the United States to compel compliance with this subsection by appropriate process.

§ 1865. Qualifications for jury service

(a) The chief judge of the district court, or such other district court judge as the plan may provide, on his initiative or upon recommendation of the clerk or jury commission, or the clerk under supervision of the court if the court's jury selection plan so authorizes, shall determine solely on the basis of information provided on the juror qualification form and other competent evidence whether a person is unqualified for, or exempt, or to be excused from jury service. The clerk shall enter such determination in the space provided on the juror qualification form and in any alphabetical list of names drawn from the master jury wheel. If a person did not appear in response to a summons, such fact shall be noted on said list.

(b) In making such determination the chief judge of the district court, or such other district court judge as the plan may provide, or the clerk if the court's jury selection plan so provides, shall deem any person qualified to serve on grand and petit juries in the district court unless he—

(1) is not a citizen of the United States eighteen years old who has resided for a period of one year within the judicial district;

(2) is unable to read, write, and understand the English language with a degree of proficiency sufficient to fill out satisfactorily the juror qualification form;

(3) is unable to speak the English language;

(4) is incapable, by reason of mental or physical infirmity, to render satisfactory jury service; or

(5) has a charge pending against him for the commission of, or has been convicted in a State or Federal court of record of, a crime punishable by imprisonment for more than one year and his civil rights have not been restored.

§ 1866. Selection and summoning of jury panels

(a) The jury commission, or in the absence thereof the clerk, shall maintain a qualified jury wheel and shall place in such wheel names of all persons drawn from the master jury wheel who are determined to be qualified as jurors and not exempt or excused pursuant to the district court plan. From time to time, the jury commission or the clerk shall publicly draw at random from the qualified jury wheel such number of names of persons as may be required for assignment to grand and petit jury panels. The jury commission or the clerk shall prepare a separate list of names of persons assigned to each grand and petit jury panel.

(b) When the court orders a grand or petit jury to be drawn, the clerk or jury commission or their duly designated deputies shall issue summonses for the required number of jurors.

Each person drawn for jury service may be served personally, or by registered, certified, or first-class mail addressed to such person at his usual residence or business address.

If such service is made personally, the summons shall be delivered by the clerk or the jury commission or their duly designated deputies to the marshal who shall make such service.

If such service is made by mail, the summons may be served by the marshal or by the clerk, the jury commission or their duly designated deputies, who shall make affidavit of service and shall attach thereto any receipt from the addressee for a registered or certified summons.

(c) Except as provided in section 1865 of this title or in any jury selection plan provision adopted pursuant to paragraph (5) or (6) of section 1863(b) of this title, no person or class of persons shall be disqualified, excluded, excused, or exempt from service as jurors: *Provided*, That any person summoned for jury service may be (1) excused by the court, or by the clerk under supervision of the court if the court's jury selection plan so authorizes, upon a showing of undue hardship or extreme inconvenience, for such period as the court deems necessary, at the conclusion of which such person either shall be summoned again for jury service under subsections (b) and (c) of this section or, if the court's jury selection plan so provides, the name of such person shall be reinserted into the qualified jury wheel for selection pursuant to subsection (a) of this section, or (2) excluded by the court on the ground that such person may be unable to render impartial jury service or that his service as a juror would be likely to disrupt the proceedings, or (3) excluded upon peremptory challenge as provided by law, or (4) excluded pursuant to the procedure specified by law upon a challenge by any party for good cause shown, or (5) excluded upon determination by the court that his service as a juror would be likely to threaten the secrecy of the proceedings, or otherwise adversely affect the integrity of jury deliberations. No person shall be excluded under clause (5) of this subsection unless the judge, in open court, determines that such is warranted and that exclusion of the person will not be inconsistent with sections 1861 and 1862 of this title. The number of persons excluded under clause (5) of this subsection shall not exceed one per centum of the number of persons who return executed jury qualification forms during the period, specified in the plan, between two consecutive fillings of the master jury wheel. The names of persons excluded under clause (5) of this subsection, together with detailed explanations for the exclusions, shall be forwarded immediately to the judicial council of the circuit, which shall have the power to make any appropriate order, prospective or retroactive, to redress any misapplication of clause (5) of this subsection, but otherwise exclusions effectuated under such clause shall not be subject to challenge under the provisions of this title. Any person excluded from a particular jury under clause (2), (3), or (4) of this subsection shall be eligible to sit on another jury if the basis for his initial exclusion would not be relevant to his ability to serve on such other jury.

(d) Whenever a person is disqualified, excused, exempt, or excluded from jury service, the jury commission or clerk shall note in the space provided on his juror qualification form or on the juror's card drawn from the qualified jury wheel the specific reason therefor.

(e) In any two-year period, no person shall be required to (1) serve or attend court for prospective service as a petit juror for a total of more than thirty days, except when necessary to complete service in a particular case, or (2) serve on more than one grand jury, or (3) serve as both a grand and petit juror.

(f) When there is an unanticipated shortage of available petit jurors drawn from the qualified jury wheel, the court may require the marshal to summon a sufficient number of petit jurors selected at random from the voter registration lists, lists of actual voters, or other lists specified in the plan, in a manner ordered by the court consistent with sections 1861 and 1862 of this title.

(g) Any person summoned for jury service who fails to appear as directed shall be ordered by the district court to appear forthwith and show cause for his failure to comply with the summons. Any person who fails to show good cause for noncompliance with a summons may be fined not more than $100 or imprisoned not more than three days, or both.

§ 1867. Challenging compliance with selection procedures

(a) In criminal cases, before the voir dire examination begins, or within seven days after the defendant discovered or could have discovered, by the exercise of diligence, the grounds therefor, whichever is earlier, the defendant may move to dismiss the indictment or stay the proceedings against him on the ground of substantial failure to comply with the provisions of this title in selecting the grand or petit jury.

(b) In criminal cases, before the voir dire examination begins, or within seven days after the Attorney General of the United States discovered or could have discovered, by the exercise of diligence, the grounds therefor, whichever is earlier, the Attorney General may move to dismiss the indictment or stay the proceedings on the ground of substantial failure to comply with the provisions of this title in selecting the grand or petit jury.

(c) In civil cases, before the voir dire examination begins, or within seven days after the party discovered or could have discovered, by the exercise of diligence, the grounds therefor, whichever is earlier, any party may move to stay the proceedings on the ground of substantial failure to comply with the provisions of this title in selecting the petit jury.

(d) Upon motion filed under subsection (a), (b), or (c) of this section, containing a sworn statement of facts which, if true, would constitute a substantial failure to comply with the provisions of this title, the moving party shall be entitled to present in support of such motion the testimony of the jury commission or clerk, if available, any relevant records and papers not public or otherwise available used by the jury commissioner or clerk, and any other relevant evidence. If the court determines that there has been a substantial failure to comply with the provisions of this title in selecting the grand jury, the court shall stay the proceedings pending the selection of a grand jury in conformity with this title or dismiss the indictment, whichever is appropriate. If the court determines that there has been a substantial failure to comply with the provisions of this title in selecting the petit jury, the court shall stay the proceedings pending the selection of a petit jury in conformity with this title.

(e) The procedures prescribed by this section shall be the exclusive means by which a person accused of a Federal crime, the Attorney General of the United States or a party in a civil case may challenge any jury on the ground that such jury was not selected in conformity with the provisions of this title. Nothing in this section shall preclude any person or the United States from pursuing any other remedy, civil or criminal, which may be available for the vindication or enforcement of any law prohibiting discrimination on account of race, color, religion, sex, national origin or economic status in the selection of persons for service on grand or petit juries.

(f) The contents of records or papers used by the jury commission or clerk in connection with the jury selection process shall not be disclosed, except pursuant to the district court plan or as may be necessary in the preparation or presentation of a motion under subsection (a), (b), or (c) of this section, until after the master jury wheel has been emptied and refilled pursuant to section 1863(b)(4) of this title and all persons selected to serve as jurors before the master wheel was emptied have completed such service. The parties in a case shall be allowed to inspect, reproduce, and copy such records or papers at all reasonable times during the preparation and pendency of such a motion. Any person who discloses the contents of any record or paper in violation of this subsection may be fined not more than $1,000 or imprisoned not more than one year, or both.

HABEAS CORPUS

(28 U.S.C. §§ 2241–2244, 2253–2255, 2261–2266).

§ 2241. Power to grant writ

(a) Writs of habeas corpus may be granted by the Supreme Court, any justice thereof, the district courts and any circuit judge within their respective jurisdictions. The order of a circuit judge shall be entered in the records of the district court of the district wherein the restraint complained of is had.

(b) The Supreme Court, any justice thereof, and any circuit judge may decline to entertain an application for a writ of habeas corpus and may transfer the application for hearing and determination to the district court having jurisdiction to entertain it.

(c) The writ of habeas corpus shall not extend to a prisoner unless—

(1) He is in custody under or by color of the authority of the United States or is committed for trial before some court thereof; or

(2) He is in custody for an act done or omitted in pursuance of an Act of Congress, or an order, process, judgment or decree of a court or judge of the United States; or

(3) He is in custody in violation of the Constitution or laws or treaties of the United States; or

(4) He, being a citizen of a foreign state and domiciled therein is in custody for an act done or omitted under any alleged right, title, authority, privilege, protection, or exemption claimed under the commission, order or sanction of any foreign state, or under color thereof, the validity and effect of which depend upon the law of nations; or

(5) It is necessary to bring him into court to testify or for trial.

(d) Where an application for a writ of habeas corpus is made by a person in custody under the judgment and sentence of a State court of a State which contains two or more Federal judicial districts, the application may be filed in the district court for the district wherein such person is in custody or in the district court for the district within which the State court was held which convicted and sentenced him and each of such district courts shall have concurrent jurisdiction to entertain the application. The district court for the district wherein such an application is filed in the exercise of its discretion and in furtherance of justice may transfer the application to the other district court for hearing and determination.

§ 2242. Application

Application for a writ of habeas corpus shall be in writing signed and verified by the person for whose relief it is intended or by someone acting in his behalf.

It shall allege the facts concerning the applicant's commitment or detention, the name of the person who has custody over him and by virtue of what claim or authority, if known.

It may be amended or supplemented as provided in the rules of procedure applicable to civil actions.

If addressed to the Supreme Court, a justice thereof or a circuit judge it shall state the reasons for not making application to the district court of the district in which the applicant is held.

§ 2243. Issuance of writ; return; hearing; decision

A court, justice or judge entertaining an application for a writ of habeas corpus shall forthwith award the writ or issue an order directing the respondent to show cause why the writ should not be granted, unless it appears from the application that the applicant or person detained is not entitled thereto.

The writ, or order to show cause shall be directed to the person having custody of the person detained. It shall be returned within three days unless for good cause additional time, not exceeding twenty days, is allowed.

The person to whom the writ or order is directed shall make a return certifying the true cause of the detention.

When the writ or order is returned a day shall be set for hearing, not more than five days after the return unless for good cause additional time is allowed.

Unless the application for the writ and the return present only issues of law the person to whom the writ is directed shall be required to produce at the hearing the body of the person detained.

The applicant or the person detained may, under oath, deny any of the facts set forth in the return or allege any other material facts.

The return and all suggestions made against it may be amended, by leave of court, before or after being filed.

The court shall summarily hear and determine the facts, and dispose of the matter as law and justice require.

§ 2244. Finality of determination

(a) No circuit or district judge shall be required to entertain an application for a writ of habeas corpus to inquire into the detention of a person pursuant to a judgment of a court of the United States if it appears that the legality of such detention has been determined by a judge or court of the United States on a prior application for a writ of habeas corpus, except as provided in section 2255.

(b)(1) A claim presented in a second or successive habeas corpus application under section 2254 that was presented in a prior application shall be dismissed.

(2) A claim presented in a second or successive habeas corpus application under section 2254 that was not presented in a prior application shall be dismissed unless—

(A) the applicant shows that the claim relies on a new rule of constitutional law, made retroactive to cases on collateral review by the Supreme Court, that was previously unavailable; or

(B)(i) the factual predicate for the claim could not have been discovered previously through the exercise of due diligence; and

(ii) the facts underlying the claim, if proven and viewed in light of the evidence as a whole, would be sufficient to establish by clear and convincing evidence that, but for constitutional error, no reasonable factfinder would have found the applicant guilty of the underlying offense.

(3)(A) Before a second or successive application permitted by this section is filed in the district court, the applicant shall move in the appropriate court of appeals for an order authorizing the district court to consider the application.

(B) A motion in the court of appeals for an order authorizing the district court to consider a second or successive application shall be determined by a three-judge panel of the court of appeals.

(C) The court of appeals may authorize the filing of a second or successive application only if it determines that the application makes a prima facie showing that the application satisfies the requirements of this subsection.

(D) The court of appeals shall grant or deny the authorization to file a second or successive application not later than 30 days after the filing of the motion.

(E) The grant or denial of an authorization by a court of appeals to file a second or successive application shall not be appealable and shall not be the subject of a petition for rehearing or for a writ of certiorari.

(4) A district court shall dismiss any claim presented in a second or successive application that the court of appeals has authorized to be filed unless the applicant shows that the claim satisfies the requirements of this section.

(c) In a habeas corpus proceeding brought in behalf of a person in custody pursuant to the judgment of a State court, a prior judgment of the Supreme Court of the United States on an appeal or review by a writ of certiorari at the instance of the prisoner of the decision of such State court, shall be conclusive as to all issues of fact or law with respect to an asserted denial of a Federal right which constitutes ground for discharge in a habeas corpus proceeding, actually adjudicated by the Supreme Court therein, unless the applicant for the writ of habeas corpus shall plead and the court shall find the existence of a material and controlling fact which did not appear in the record of the proceeding in the Supreme Court and the court shall further find that the applicant for the writ of habeas corpus could not have caused such fact to appear in such record by the exercise of reasonable diligence.

(d)(1) A 1-year period of limitation shall apply to an application for a writ of habeas corpus by a person in custody pursuant to the judgment of a State court. The limitation period shall run from the latest of—

(A) the date on which the judgment became final by the conclusion of direct review or the expiration of the time for seeking such review;

(B) the date on which the impediment to filing an application created by State action in violation of the Constitution or laws of the United States is removed, if the applicant was prevented from filing by such State action;

(C) the date on which the constitutional right asserted was initially recognized by the Supreme Court, if the right has been newly recognized by the Supreme Court and made retroactively applicable to cases on collateral review; or

(D) the date on which the factual predicate of the claim or claims presented could have been discovered through the exercise of due diligence.

(2) The time during which a properly filed application for State post-conviction or other collateral review with respect to the pertinent judgment or claim is pending shall not be counted toward any period of limitation under this subsection.

§ 2253.   Appeal

(a) In a habeas corpus proceeding or a proceeding under section 2255 before a district judge, the final order shall be subject to review, on appeal, by the court of appeals for the circuit in which the proceeding is held.

(b) There shall be no right of appeal from a final order in a proceeding to test the validity of a warrant to remove to another district or place for commitment or trial a person charged with a criminal offense against the United States, or to test the validity of such person's detention pending removal proceedings.

(c)(1) Unless a circuit justice or judge issues a certificate of appealability, an appeal may not be taken to the court of appeals from—

(A) the final order in a habeas corpus proceeding in which the detention complained of arises out of process issued by a State court; or

(B) the final order in a proceeding under section 2255.

(2) A certificate of appealability may issue under paragraph (1) only if the applicant has made a substantial showing of the denial of a constitutional right.

(3) The certificate of appealability under paragraph (1) shall indicate which specific issue or issues satisfy the showing required by paragraph (2).

§ 2254.   State custody; remedies in Federal courts

(a) The Supreme Court, a Justice thereof, a circuit judge, or a district court shall entertain an application for a writ of habeas corpus in behalf of a person in custody pursuant to the judgment of a State court only on the ground that he is in custody in violation of the Constitution or laws or treaties of the United States.

(b)(1) An application for a writ of habeas corpus on behalf of a person in custody pursuant to the judgment of a State court shall not be granted unless it appears that—

(A) the applicant has exhausted the remedies available in the courts of the State; or

(B)(i) there is an absence of available State corrective process; or

(ii) circumstances exist that render such process ineffective to protect the rights of the applicant.

(2) An application for a writ of habeas corpus may be denied on the merits, notwithstanding the failure of the applicant to exhaust the remedies available in the courts of the State.

(3) A State shall not be deemed to have waived the exhaustion requirement or be estopped from reliance upon the requirement unless the State, through counsel, expressly waives the requirement.

(c) An applicant shall not be deemed to have exhausted the remedies available in the courts of the State, within the meaning of this section, if he has the right under the law of the State to raise, by any available procedure, the question presented.

(d) An application for a writ of habeas corpus on behalf of a person in custody pursuant to the judgment of a State court shall not be granted with respect to any claim that was adjudicated on the merits in State court proceedings unless the adjudication of the claim—

(1) resulted in a decision that was contrary to, or involved an unreasonable application of, clearly established Federal law, as determined by the Supreme Court of the United States; or

(2) resulted in a decision that was based on an unreasonable determination of the facts in light of the evidence presented in the State court proceeding.

(e)(1) In a proceeding instituted by an application for a writ of habeas corpus by a person in custody pursuant to the judgment of a State court, a determination of a factual issue made by a State court shall be presumed to be correct. The applicant shall have the burden of rebutting the presumption of correctness by clear and convincing evidence.

(2) If the applicant has failed to develop the factual basis of a claim in State court proceedings, the court shall not hold an evidentiary hearing on the claim unless the applicant shows that—

(A) the claim relies on—

(i) a new rule of constitutional law, made retroactive to cases on collateral review by the Supreme Court, that was previously unavailable; or

(ii) a factual predicate that could not have been previously discovered through the exercise of due diligence; and

(B) the facts underlying the claim would be sufficient to establish by clear and convincing evidence that but for constitutional error, no reasonable factfinder would have found the applicant guilty of the underlying offense.

(f) If the applicant challenges the sufficiency of the evidence adduced in such State court proceeding to support the State court's determination of a factual issue made therein, the applicant, if able, shall produce that part of the record pertinent to a determination of the sufficiency of the evidence to support such determination. If the applicant, because of indigency or other reason is unable to produce such part of the record, then the State shall produce such part of the record and the Federal court shall direct the State to do so by order directed to an appropriate State official. If the State cannot provide such pertinent part of the record, then the court shall determine under the existing facts and circumstances what weight shall be given to the State court's factual determination.

(g) A copy of the official records of the State court, duly certified by the clerk of such court to be a true and correct copy of a finding, judicial opinion, or other reliable written indicia showing such a factual determination by the State court shall be admissible in the Federal court proceeding.

(h) Except as provided in section 408 of the Controlled Substances Act, in all proceedings brought under this section, and any subsequent proceedings on review, the court may appoint counsel for an applicant who is or becomes financially unable to afford counsel, except as provided by a rule promulgated by the Supreme Court pursuant to statutory authority. Appointment of counsel under this section shall be governed by section 3006A of title 18.

(i) The ineffectiveness or incompetence of counsel during Federal or State collateral post-conviction proceedings shall not be a ground for relief in a proceeding arising under section 2254.

§ 2255. Federal custody; remedies on motion attacking sentence

A prisoner in custody under sentence of a court established by Act of Congress claiming the right to be released upon the ground that the sentence was imposed in violation of the Constitution or laws of the United States, or that the court was without jurisdiction to impose such sentence, or that the sentence was in excess of the maximum authorized by law, or is otherwise subject to collateral attack, may move the court which imposed the sentence to vacate, set aside or correct the sentence.

Unless the motion and the files and records of the case conclusively show that the prisoner is entitled to no relief, the court shall cause notice thereof to be served upon the United States attorney, grant a prompt hearing thereon, determine the issues and make findings of fact and conclusions of law with respect thereto. If the court finds that the judgment was rendered without jurisdiction, or that the sentence imposed was not authorized by law or otherwise open to collateral attack, or that there has been such a denial or infringement of the constitutional rights of the prisoner as to render the judgment vulnerable to collateral attack, the court shall vacate and set the judgment aside and shall discharge the prisoner or resentence him or grant a new trial or correct the sentence as may appear appropriate.

A court may entertain and determine such motion without requiring the production of the prisoner at the hearing.

An appeal may be taken to the court of appeals from the order entered on the motion as from a final judgment on application for a writ of habeas corpus.

An application for a writ of habeas corpus in behalf of a prisoner who is authorized to apply for relief by motion pursuant to this section, shall not be entertained if it appears that the applicant has failed to apply for relief, by motion, to the court which sentenced him, or that such court has denied him relief, unless it also appears that the remedy by motion is inadequate or ineffective to test the legality of his detention.

A 1-year period of limitation shall apply to a motion under this section. The limitation period shall run from the latest of—

(1) the date on which the judgment of conviction becomes final;

(2) the date on which the impediment to making a motion created by governmental action in violation of the Constitution or laws of the United States is removed, if the movant was prevented from making a motion by such governmental action;

(3) the date on which the right asserted was initially recognized by the Supreme Court, if that right has been newly recognized by the Supreme Court and made retroactively applicable to cases on collateral review; or

(4) the date on which the facts supporting the claim or claims presented could have been discovered through the exercise of due diligence.

Except as provided in section 408 of the Controlled Substances Act, in all proceedings brought under this section, and any subsequent proceedings on review, the court may appoint counsel, except as provided by a rule promulgated by the Supreme Court pursuant to statutory authority. Appointment of counsel under this section shall be governed by section 3006A of title 18.

A second or successive motion must be certified as provided in section 2244 by a panel of the appropriate court of appeals to contain—

(1) newly discovered evidence that, if proven and viewed in light of the evidence as a whole, would be sufficient to establish by clear and convincing evidence that no reasonable factfinder would have found the movant guilty of the offense; or

(2) a new rule of constitutional law, made retroactive to cases on collateral review by the Supreme Court, that was previously unavailable.

§ 2261. Prisoners in State custody subject to capital sentence; appointment of counsel; requirement of rule of court or statute; procedures for appointment

(a) This chapter shall apply to cases arising under section 2254 brought by prisoners in State custody who are subject to a capital sentence. It shall apply only if the provisions of subsections (b) and (c) are satisfied.

(b) This chapter is applicable if a State establishes by statute, rule of its court of last resort, or by another agency authorized by State law, a mechanism for the appointment, compensation, and payment of reasonable litigation expenses of competent counsel in State post-conviction proceedings brought by indigent prisoners whose capital convictions and sentences have been upheld on direct appeal to the court of last resort in the State or have otherwise become final for State law purposes. The rule of court or statute must provide standards of competency for the appointment of such counsel.

(c) Any mechanism for the appointment, compensation, and reimbursement of counsel as provided in subsection (b) must offer counsel to all State prisoners under capital sentence and must provide for the entry of an order by a court of record—

    (1) appointing one or more counsels to represent the prisoner upon a finding that the prisoner is indigent and accepted the offer or is unable competently to decide whether to accept or reject the offer;

    (2) finding, after a hearing if necessary, that the prisoner rejected the offer of counsel and made the decision with an understanding of its legal consequences; or

    (3) denying the appointment of counsel upon a finding that the prisoner is not indigent.

(d) No counsel appointed pursuant to subsections (b) and (c) to represent a State prisoner under capital sentence shall have previously represented the prisoner at trial or on direct appeal in the case for which the appointment is made unless the prisoner and counsel expressly request continued representation.

(e) The ineffectiveness or incompetence of counsel during State or Federal post-conviction proceedings in a capital case shall not be a ground for relief in a proceeding arising under section 2254. This limitation shall not preclude the appointment of different counsel, on the court's own motion or at the request of the prisoner, at any phase of State or Federal post-conviction proceedings on the basis of the ineffectiveness or incompetence of counsel in such proceedings.

§ 2262. Mandatory stay of execution; duration; limits on stays of execution; successive petitions

(a) Upon the entry in the appropriate State court of record of an order under section 2261(c), a warrant or order setting an execution date for a State prisoner shall be stayed upon application to any court that would have jurisdiction over any proceedings filed under section 2254. The application shall recite that the State has invoked the post-conviction review procedures of this chapter and that the scheduled execution is subject to stay.

(b) A stay of execution granted pursuant to subsection (a) shall expire if—

    (1) a State prisoner fails to file a habeas corpus application under section 2254 within the time required in section 2263;

    (2) before a court of competent jurisdiction, in the presence of counsel, unless the prisoner has competently and knowingly waived such counsel, and after having been advised of the consequences, a State prisoner under capital sentence waives the right to pursue habeas corpus review under section 2254; or

    (3) a State prisoner files a habeas corpus petition under section 2254 within the time required by section 2263 and fails to make a

substantial showing of the denial of a Federal right or is denied relief in the district court or at any subsequent stage of review.

(c) If one of the conditions in subsection (b) has occurred, no Federal court thereafter shall have the authority to enter a stay of execution in the case, unless the court of appeals approves the filing of a second or successive application under section 2244(b).

§ 2263. Filing of habeas corpus application; time requirements; tolling rules

(a) Any application under this chapter for habeas corpus relief under section 2254 must be filed in the appropriate district court not later than 180 days after final State court affirmance of the conviction and sentence on direct review or the expiration of the time for seeking such review.

(b) The time requirements established by subsection (a) shall be tolled—

(1) from the date that a petition for certiorari is filed in the Supreme Court until the date of final disposition of the petition if a State prisoner files the petition to secure review by the Supreme Court of the affirmance of a capital sentence on direct review by the court of last resort of the State or other final State court decision on direct review;

(2) from the date on which the first petition for post-conviction review or other collateral relief is filed until the final State court disposition of such petition; and

(3) during an additional period not to exceed 30 days, if—

(A) a motion for an extension of time is filed in the Federal district court that would have jurisdiction over the case upon the filing of a habeas corpus application under section 2254; and

(B) a showing of good cause is made for the failure to file the habeas corpus application within the time period established by this section.

§ 2264. Scope of Federal review; district court adjudications

(a) Whenever a State prisoner under capital sentence files a petition for habeas corpus relief to which this chapter applies, the district court shall only consider a claim or claims that have been raised and decided on the merits in the State courts, unless the failure to raise the claim properly is—

(1) the result of State action in violation of the Constitution or laws of the United States;

(2) the result of the Supreme Court's recognition of a new Federal right that is made retroactively applicable; or

(3) based on a factual predicate that could not have been discovered through the exercise of due diligence in time to present the claim for State or Federal post-conviction review.

(b) Following review subject to subsections (a), (d), and (e) of section 2254, the court shall rule on the claims properly before it.

§ 2265. Application to State unitary review procedure

(a) For purposes of this section, a "unitary review" procedure means a State procedure that authorizes a person under sentence of death to raise, in the course of direct review of the judgment, such claims as could be raised on collateral attack. This chapter shall apply, as provided in this section, in relation to a State unitary review procedure if the State establishes by rule of its court of last resort or by statute a mechanism for the appointment, compensation, and payment of reasonable litigation expenses of competent counsel in the unitary review proceedings, including expenses relating to the litigation of collateral claims in the proceedings. The rule of court or statute must provide standards of competency for the appointment of such counsel.

(b) To qualify under this section, a unitary review procedure must include an offer of counsel following trial for the purpose of representation on unitary review, and entry of an order, as provided in section 2261(c), concerning appointment of counsel or waiver or denial of appointment of counsel for that purpose. No counsel appointed to represent the prisoner in the unitary review proceedings shall have previously represented the prisoner at trial in the case for which the appointment is made unless the prisoner and counsel expressly request continued representation.

(c) Sections 2262, 2263, 2264, and 2266 shall apply in relation to cases involving a sentence of death from any State having a unitary review procedure that qualifies under this section. References to State "post-conviction review" and "direct review" in such sections shall be understood as referring to unitary review under the State procedure. The reference in section 2262(a) to "an order under section 2261(c)" shall be understood as referring to the post-trial order under subsection (b) concerning representation in the unitary review proceedings, but if a transcript of the trial proceedings is unavailable at the time of the filing of such an order in the appropriate State court, then the start of the 180-day limitation period under section 2263 shall be deferred until a transcript is made available to the prisoner or counsel of the prisoner.

§ 2266. Limitation periods for determining applications and motions

(a) The adjudication of any application under section 2254 that is subject to this chapter, and the adjudication of any motion under section 2255 by a person under sentence of death, shall be given priority by the district court and by the court of appeals over all noncapital matters.

(b)(1)(A) A district court shall render a final determination and enter a final judgment on any application for a writ of habeas corpus brought under this chapter in a capital case not later than 180 days after the date on which the application is filed.

(B) A district court shall afford the parties at least 120 days in which to complete all actions, including the preparation of all pleadings and briefs, and if necessary, a hearing, prior to the submission of the case for decision.

(C)(i) A district court may delay for not more than one additional 30–day period beyond the period specified in subparagraph (A), the rendering of a determination of an application for a writ of habeas corpus if the court issues a written order making a finding, and stating the reasons for the finding, that the ends of justice that would be served by allowing the delay outweigh the best interests of the public and the applicant in a speedy disposition of the application.

(ii) The factors, among others, that a court shall consider in determining whether a delay in the disposition of an application is warranted are as follows:

(I) Whether the failure to allow the delay would be likely to result in a miscarriage of justice.

(II) Whether the case is so unusual or so complex, due to the number of defendants, the nature of the prosecution, or the existence of novel questions of fact or law, that it is unreasonable to expect adequate briefing within the time limitations established by subparagraph (A).

(III) Whether the failure to allow a delay in a case that, taken as a whole, is not so unusual or so complex as described in subclause (II), but would otherwise deny the applicant reasonable time to obtain counsel, would unreasonably deny the applicant or the government continuity of counsel, or would deny counsel for the applicant or the government the reasonable time necessary for effective preparation, taking into account the exercise of due diligence.

(iii) No delay in disposition shall be permissible because of general congestion of the court's calendar.

(iv) The court shall transmit a copy of any order issued under clause (i) to the Director of the Administrative Office of the United States Courts for inclusion in the report under paragraph (5).

(2) The time limitations under paragraph (1) shall apply to—

(A) an initial application for a writ of habeas corpus;

(B) any second or successive application for a writ of habeas corpus; and

(C) any redetermination of an application for a writ of habeas corpus following a remand by the court of appeals or the Supreme Court for further proceedings, in which case the limitation period shall run from the date the remand is ordered.

(3)(A) The time limitations under this section shall not be construed to entitle an applicant to a stay of execution, to which the applicant would otherwise not be entitled, for the purpose of litigating any application or appeal.

(B) No amendment to an application for a writ of habeas corpus under this chapter shall be permitted after the filing of the answer to the application, except on the grounds specified in section 2244(b).

(4)(A) The failure of a court to meet or comply with a time limitation under this section shall not be a ground for granting relief from a judgment of conviction or sentence.

(B) The State may enforce a time limitation under this section by petitioning for a writ of mandamus to the court of appeals. The court of appeals shall act on the petition for a writ of mandamus not later than 30 days after the filing of the petition.

(5)(A) The Administrative Office of the United States Courts shall submit to Congress an annual report on the compliance by the district courts with the time limitations under this section.

(B) The report described in subparagraph (A) shall include copies of the orders submitted by the district courts under paragraph (1)(B)(iv).

(c)(1)(A) A court of appeals shall hear and render a final determination of any appeal of an order granting or denying, in whole or in part, an application brought under this chapter in a capital case not later than 120 days after the date on which the reply brief is filed, or if no reply brief is filed, not later than 120 days after the date on which the answering brief is filed.

(B)(i) A court of appeals shall decide whether to grant a petition for rehearing or other request for rehearing en banc not later than 30 days after the date on which the petition for rehearing is filed unless a responsive pleading is required, in which case the court shall decide whether to grant the petition not later than 30 days after the date on which the responsive pleading is filed.

(ii) If a petition for rehearing or rehearing en banc is granted, the court of appeals shall hear and render a final determination of the appeal not later than 120 days after the date on which the order granting rehearing or rehearing en banc is entered.

(2) The time limitations under paragraph (1) shall apply to—

(A) an initial application for a writ of habeas corpus;

(B) any second or successive application for a writ of habeas corpus; and

(C) any redetermination of an application for a writ of habeas corpus or related appeal following a remand by the court of appeals en banc or the Supreme Court for further proceedings, in which case the limitation period shall run from the date the remand is ordered.

(3) The time limitations under this section shall not be construed to entitle an applicant to a stay of execution, to which the applicant would otherwise not be entitled, for the purpose of litigating any application or appeal.

(4)(A) The failure of a court to meet or comply with a time limitation under this section shall not be a ground for granting relief from a judgment of conviction or sentence.

(B) The State may enforce a time limitation under this section by applying for a writ of mandamus to the Supreme Court.

(5) The Administrative Office of the United States Courts shall submit to Congress an annual report on the compliance by the courts of appeals with the time limitations under this section.

PRIVACY PROTECTION ACT OF 1980

(42 U.S.C. §§ 2000aa–2000aa–12); Guidelines (28 C.F.R. § 59.4).

§ 2000aa.   Searches and seizures by government officers and employees in connection with investigation or prosecution of criminal offenses

(a) Work product materials

Notwithstanding any other law, it shall be unlawful for a government officer or employee, in connection with the investigation or prosecution of a criminal offense, to search for or seize any work product materials possessed by a person reasonably believed to have a purpose to disseminate to the public a newspaper, book, broadcast, or other similar form of public communication, in or affecting interstate or foreign commerce; but this provision shall not impair or affect the ability of any government officer or employee, pursuant to otherwise applicable law, to search for or seize such materials, if—

(1) there is probable cause to believe that the person possessing such materials has committed or is committing the criminal offense to which the materials relate: *Provided, however*, That a government officer or employee may not search for or seize such materials under the provisions of this paragraph if the offense to which the materials relate consists of the receipt, possession, communication, or withholding of such materials or the information contained therein (but such a search or seizure may be conducted under the provisions of this paragraph if the offense consists of the receipt, possession, or communication of information relating to the national defense, classified information, or restricted data under the provisions of section 793, 794, 797, or 798 of Title 18, or section 2274, 2275 or 2277 of this title, or section 783 of Title 50, or if the offense involves the production, possession, receipt, mailing, sale, distribution, shipment, or transportation of child pornography, the sexual exploitation of children, or the sale or purchase of children under section 2251, 2251A, 2252, or 2252A of Title 18); or

(2) there is reason to believe that the immediate seizure of such materials is necessary to prevent the death of, or serious bodily injury to, a human being.

(b) Other documents

Notwithstanding any other law, it shall be unlawful for a government officer or employee, in connection with the investigation or prosecution of a criminal offense, to search for or seize documentary materials, other than work product materials, possessed by a person in connection with a purpose to disseminate to the public a newspaper, book, broadcast, or other similar form of public communication, in or affecting interstate or foreign commerce; but this provision shall not impair or affect the ability of any government officer or employee, pursuant to otherwise applicable law, to search for or seize such materials, if—

(1) there is probable cause to believe that the person possessing such materials has committed or is committing the criminal offense to which the materials relate: *Provided, however,* That a government officer or employee may not search for or seize such materials under the provisions of this paragraph if the offense to which the materials relate consists of the receipt, possession, communication, or withholding of such materials or the information contained therein (but such a search or seizure may be conducted under the provisions of this paragraph if the offense consists of the receipt, possession, or communication of information relating to the national defense, classified information, or restricted data under the provisions of section 793, 794, 797, or 798 of Title 18, or section 2274, 2275, or 2277 of this title, or section 783 of Title 50, or if the offense involves the production, possession, receipt, mailing, sale, distribution, shipment, or transportation of child pornography, the sexual exploitation of children, or the sale or purchase of children under section 2251, 2251A, 2252, or 2252A of Title 18);

(2) there is reason to believe that the immediate seizure of such materials is necessary to prevent the death of, or serious bodily injury to, a human being;

(3) there is reason to believe that the giving of notice pursuant to a subpena duces tecum would result in the destruction, alteration, or concealment of such materials; or

(4) such materials have not been produced in response to a court order directing compliance with a subpena duces tecum, and—

(A) all appellate remedies have been exhausted; or

(B) there is reason to believe that the delay in an investigation or trial occasioned by further proceedings relating to the subpena would threaten the interests of justice.

(c) Objections to court ordered subpoenas; affidavits

In the event a search warrant is sought pursuant to paragraph (4)(B) of subsection (b) of this section, the person possessing the materials shall be afforded adequate opportunity to submit an affidavit setting forth the basis for any contention that the materials sought are not subject to seizure.

§ 2000aa–5. Border and customs searches

This chapter shall not impair or affect the ability of a government officer or employee, pursuant to otherwise applicable law, to conduct searches and seizures at the borders of, or at international points of, entry into the United States in order to enforce the customs laws of the United States.

§ 2000aa–6. Civil actions by aggrieved persons

(a) Right of action

A person aggrieved by a search for or seizure of materials in violation of this chapter shall have a civil cause of action for damages for such search or seizure—

(1) against the United States, against a State which has waived its sovereign immunity under the Constitution to a claim for damages

resulting from a violation of this chapter, or against any other governmental unit, all of which shall be liable for violations of this chapter by their officers or employees while acting within the scope or under color of their office or employment; and

(2) against an officer or employee of a State who has violated this chapter while acting within the scope or under color of his office or employment, if such State has not waived its sovereign immunity as provided in paragraph (1).

(b) Good faith defense

It shall be a complete defense to a civil action brought under paragraph (2) of subsection (a) of this section that the officer or employee had a reasonable good faith belief in the lawfulness of his conduct.

(c) Official immunity

The United States, a State, or any other governmental unit liable for violations of this chapter under subsection (a)(1) of this section, may not assert as a defense to a claim arising under this chapter the immunity of the officer or employee whose violation is complained of or his reasonable good faith belief in the lawfulness of his conduct, except that such a defense may be asserted if the violation complained of is that of a judicial officer.

(d) Exclusive nature of remedy

The remedy provided by subsection (a)(1) of this section against the United States, a State, or any other governmental unit is exclusive of any other civil action or proceeding for conduct constituting a violation of this chapter, against the officer or employee whose violation gave rise to the claim, or against the estate of such officer or employee.

(e) Admissibility of evidence

Evidence otherwise admissible in a proceeding shall not be excluded on the basis of a violation of this chapter.

(f) Damages; costs and attorneys' fees

A person having a cause of action under this section shall be entitled to recover actual damages but not less than liquidated damages of $1,000, and such reasonable attorneys' fees and other litigation costs reasonably incurred as the court, in its discretion, may award: *Provided, however*, That the United States, a State, or any other governmental unit shall not be liable for interest prior to judgment.

(g) Attorney General; claims settlement; regulations

The Attorney General may settle a claim for damages brought against the United States under this section, and shall promulgate regulations to provide for the commencement of an administrative inquiry following a determination of a violation of this chapter by an officer or employee of the United States and for the imposition of administrative sanctions against such officer or employee, if warranted.

(h) Jurisdiction

The district courts shall have original jurisdiction of all civil actions arising under this section.

§ 2000aa–7. Definitions

(a) "Documentary materials", as used in this chapter, means materials upon which information is recorded, and includes, but is not limited to, written or printed materials, photographs, motion picture films, negatives, video tapes, audio tapes, and other mechanically, magentically or electronically recorded cards, tapes, or discs, but does not include contraband or the fruits of a crime or things otherwise criminally possessed, or property designed or intended for use, or which is or has been used as, the means of committing a criminal offense.

(b) "Work product materials", as used in this chapter, means materials, other than contraband or the fruits of a crime or things otherwise criminally possessed, or property designed or intended for use, or which is or has been used, as the means of committing a criminal offense, and—

    (1) in anticipation of communicating such materials to the public, are prepared, produced, authored, or created, whether by the person in possession of the materials or by any other person;

    (2) are possessed for the purposes of communicating such materials to the public; and

    (3) include mental impressions, conclusions, opinions, or theories of the person who prepared, produced, authored, or created such material.

(c) "Any other governmental unit", as used in this chapter, includes the District of Columbia, the Commonwealth of Puerto Rico, any territory or possession of the United States, and any local government, unit of local government, or any unit of State government.

§ 2000aa–11. Guidelines for Federal officers and employees

(a) Procedures to obtain documentary evidence; protection of certain privacy interests

The Attorney General shall, within six months of October 13, 1980, issue guidelines for the procedures to be employed by any Federal officer or employee, in connection with the investigation or prosecution of an offense, to obtain documentary materials in the private possession of a person when the person is not reasonably believed to be a suspect in such offense or related by blood or marriage to such a suspect, and when the materials sought are not contraband or the fruits or instrumentalities of an offense. The Attorney General shall incorporate in such guidelines—

    (1) a recognition of the personal privacy interests of the person in possession of such documentary materials;

    (2) a requirement that the least intrusive method or means of obtaining such materials be used which do not substantially jeopardize the availability or usefulness of the materials sought to be obtained;

    (3) a recognition of special concern for privacy interests in cases in which a search or seizure for such documents would intrude upon a known confidential relationship such as that which may exist between clergyman and parishioner; lawyer and client; or doctor and patient; and

(4) a requirement that an application for a warrant to conduct a search governed by this subchapter be approved by an attorney for the government, except that in an emergency situation the application may be approved by another appropriate supervisory official if within 24 hours of such emergency the appropriate United States Attorney is notified.

(b) Use of search warrants; reports to Congress

The Attorney General shall collect and compile information on, and report annually to the Committees on the Judiciary of the Senate and the House of Representatives on the use of search warrants by Federal officers and employees for documentary materials described in subsection (a)(3) of this section.

§ 2000aa–12.   Binding nature of guidelines; disciplinary actions for violations; legal proceedings for non-compliance prohibited

Guidelines issued by the Attorney General under this subchapter shall have the full force and effect of Department of Justice regulations and any violation of these guidelines shall make the employee or officer involved subject to appropriate administrative disciplinary action. However, an issue relating to the compliance, or the failure to comply, with guidelines issued pursuant to this subchapter may not be litigated, and a court may not entertain such an issue as the basis for the suppression or exclusion of evidence.

[EDITOR'S NOTE: These guidelines appear in 28 C.F.R. Pt. 59. The procedural provisions are set out below.]

GUIDELINES

(28 C.F.R. § 59.4).

§ 59.4   Procedures.[1]

(a) Provisions governing the use of search warrants generally.

(1) A search warrant should not be used to obtain documentary materials believed to be in the private possession of a disinterested third party unless it appears that the use of a subpoena, summons, request, or other less intrusive alternative means of obtaining the materials would substantially jeopardize the availability or usefulness of the materials sought, and the application for the warrant has been authorized as provided in paragraph (a)(2) of this section.

(2) No federal officer or employee shall apply for a warrant to search for and seize documentary materials believed to be in the private possession of a disinterested third party unless the application for the warrant has been authorized by an attorney for the government. Provided, however, that in

---

1. Notwithstanding the provisions of this section, any application for a warrant to search for evidence of a criminal tax offense under the jurisdiction of the Tax Division must be specifically approved in advance by the Tax Division pursuant to section 6–2.330 of the U.S. Attorneys' Manual.

an emergency situation in which the immediacy of the need to seize the materials does not permit an opportunity to secure the authorization of an attorney for the government, the application may be authorized by a supervisory law enforcement officer in the applicant's department or agency, if the appropriate U.S. Attorney (or where the case is not being handled by a U.S. Attorney's Office, the appropriate supervisory official of the Department of Justice) is notified of the authorization and the basis for justifying such authorization under this part within 24 hours of the authorization.

(b) Provisions governing the use of search warrants which may intrude upon professional, confidential relationships.

(1) A search warrant should not be used to obtain documentary materials believed to be in the private possession of a disinterested third party physician,[2] lawyer, or clergyman, under circumstances in which the materials sought, or other materials likely to be reviewed during the execution of the warrant, contain confidential information on patients, clients, or parishioners which was furnished or developed for the purposes of professional counseling or treatment, unless—

(i) It appears that the use of a subpoena, summons, request or other less intrusive alternative means of obtaining the materials would substantially jeopardize the availability or usefulness of the materials sought;

(ii) Access to the documentary materials appears to be of substantial importance to the investigation or prosecution for which they are sought; and

(iii) The application for the warrant has been approved as provided in paragraph (b)(2) of this section.

(2) No federal officer or employee shall apply for a warrant to search for and seize documentary materials believed to be in the private possession of a disinterested third party physician, lawyer, or clergyman under the circumstances described in paragraph (b)(1) of this section, unless, upon the recommendation of the U.S. Attorney (or where a case is not being handled by a U.S. Attorney's Office, upon the recommendation of the appropriate supervisory official of the Department of Justice), an appropriate Deputy Assistant Attorney General has authorized the application for the warrant. Provided, however, that in an emergency situation in which the immediacy of the need to seize the materials does not permit an opportunity to secure the authorization of a Deputy Assistant Attorney General, the application may be authorized by the U.S. Attorney (or where the case is not being handled by a U.S. Attorney's Office, by the appropriate supervisory official of the Department of Justice) if an appropriate Deputy Assistant Attorney General is notified of the authorization and the basis for justifying such authorization under this part within 72 hours of the authorization.

(3) Whenever possible, a request for authorization by an appropriate Deputy Assistant Attorney General of a search warrant application pursuant to paragraph (b)(2) of this section shall be made in writing and shall include:

2. Documentary materials created or compiled by a physician, but retained by the physician as a matter of practice at a hospital or clinic shall be deemed to be in the private possession of the physician, unless the clinic or hospital is a suspect in the offense.

(i) The application for the warrant; and

(ii) A brief description of the facts and circumstances advanced as the basis for recommending authorization of the application under this part.

If a request for authorization of the application is made orally or if, in an emergency situation, the application is authorized by the U.S. Attorney or a supervisory official of the Department of Justice as provided in paragraph (b)(2) of this section, a written record of the request including the materials specified in paragraphs (b)(3)(i) and (ii) of this section shall be transmitted to an appropriate Deputy Assistant Attorney General within 7 days. The Deputy Assistant Attorneys General shall keep a record of the disposition of all requests for authorizations of search warrant applications made under paragraph (b) of this section.

(4) A search warrant authorized under paragraph (b)(2) of this section shall be executed in such a manner as to minimize, to the greatest extent practicable, scrutiny of confidential materials.

(5) Although it is impossible to define the full range of additional doctor-like therapeutic relationships which involve the furnishing or development of private information, the U.S. Attorney (or where a case is not being handled by a U.S. Attorney's Office, the appropriate supervisory official of the Department of Justice) should determine whether a search for documentary materials held by other disinterested third party professionals involved in such relationships (e.g. psychologists or psychiatric social workers or nurses) would implicate the special privacy concerns which are addressed in paragraph (b) of this section. If the U.S. Attorney (or other supervisory official of the Department of Justice) determines that such a search would require review of extremely confidential information furnished or developed for the purposes of professional counseling or treatment, the provisions of this subsection should be applied. Otherwise, at a minimum, the requirements of paragraph (a) of this section must be met.

(c) Considerations bearing on choice of methods. In determining whether, as an alternative to the use of a search warrant, the use of a subpoena or other less intrusive means of obtaining documentary materials would substantially jeopardize the availability or usefulness of the materials sought, the following factors, among others, should be considered:

(1) Whether it appears that the use of a subpoena or other alternative which gives advance notice of the government's interest in obtaining the materials would be likely to result in the destruction, alteration, concealment, or transfer of the materials sought; considerations, among others, bearing on this issue may include:

(i) Whether a suspect has access to the materials sought;

(ii) Whether there is a close relationship of friendship, loyalty, or sympathy between the possessor of the materials and a suspect;

(iii) Whether the possessor of the materials is under the domination or control of a suspect;

(iv) Whether the possessor of the materials has an interest in preventing the disclosure of the materials to the government;

(v) Whether the possessor's willingness to comply with a subpoena or request by the government would be likely to subject him to intimidation or threats of reprisal;

(vi) Whether the possessor of the materials has previously acted to obstruct a criminal investigation or judicial proceeding or refused to comply with or acted in defiance of court orders; or

(vii) Whether the possessor has expressed an intent to destroy, conceal, alter, or transfer the materials;

(2) The immediacy of the government's need to obtain the materials; considerations, among others, bearing on this issue may include:

(i) Whether the immediate seizure of the materials is necessary to prevent injury to persons or property;

(ii) Whether the prompt seizure of the materials is necessary to preserve their evidentiary value;

(iii) Whether delay in obtaining the materials would significantly jeopardize an ongoing investigation or prosecution; or

(iv) Whether a legally enforceable form of process, other than a search warrant, is reasonably available as a means of obtaining the materials.

The fact that the disinterested third party possessing the materials may have grounds to challenge a subpoena or other legal process is not in itself a legitimate basis for the use of a search warrant.

FOREIGN INTELLIGENCE SURVEILLANCE ACT

(50 U.S.C.A. § 1861)

§ 1861. Access to certain business records for foreign intelligence and international terrorism investigations

(a)(1) The Director of the Federal Bureau of Investigation or a designee of the Director (whose rank shall be no lower than Assistant Special Agent in Charge) may make an application for an order requiring the production of any tangible things (including books, records, papers, documents, and other items) for an investigation to obtain foreign intelligence information not concerning a United States person or to protect against international terrorism or clandestine intelligence activities, provided that such investigation of a United States person is not conducted solely upon the basis of activities protected by the first amendment to the Constitution.

(2) An investigation conducted under this section shall

(A) be conducted under guidelines approved by the Attorney General under Executive Order 12333 (or a successor order); and

(B) not be conducted of a United States person solely upon the basis of activities protected by the first amendment to the Constitution of the United States.

(b) Each application under this section

(1) shall be made to—

(A) a judge of the court established by section 1803(a) of this title; or

(B) a United States Magistrate Judge under chapter 43 of Title 28, who is publicly designated by the Chief Justice of the United States to have the power to hear applications and grant orders for the production of tangible things under this section on behalf of a judge of that court; and

(2) shall specify that the records concerned are sought for an authorized investigation conducted in accordance with subsection (a)(2) of this section to obtain foreign intelligence information not concerning a United States person or to protect against international terrorism or clandestine intelligence activities.

(c)(1) Upon an application made pursuant to this section, the judge shall enter an ex parte order as requested, or as modified, approving the release of records if the judge finds that the application meets the requirements of this section.

(2) An order under this subsection shall not disclose that it is issued for purposes of an investigation described in subsection (a).

(d) No person shall disclose to any other person (other than those persons necessary to produce the tangible things under this section) that the Federal Bureau of Investigation has sought or obtained tangible things under this section.

(e) A person who, in good faith, produces tangible things under an order pursuant to this section shall not be liable to any other person for such production. Such production shall not be deemed to constitute a waiver of any privilege in any other proceeding or context.

Appendix C

FEDERAL RULES OF CRIMINAL PROCEDURE FOR THE UNITED STATES DISTRICT COURTS

I. SCOPE, PURPOSE AND CONSTRUCTION

Rule 1. Scope; Definitions

(a) Scope.

(1) In General. These rules govern the procedure in all criminal proceedings in the United States district courts, the United States courts of appeals, and the Supreme Court of the United States.

(2) State or Local Judicial Officer. When a rule so states, it applies to a proceeding before a state or local judicial officer.

(3) Territorial Courts. These rules also govern the procedure in all criminal proceedings in the following courts:

(A) the district court of Guam;

(B) the district court for the Northern Mariana Islands, except as otherwise provided by law; and

(C) the district court of the Virgin Islands, except that the prosecution of offenses in that court must be by indictment or information as otherwise provided by law.

(4) Removed Proceedings. Although these rules govern all proceedings after removal from a state court, state law governs a dismissal by the prosecution.

(5) Excluded Proceedings. Proceedings not governed by these rules include:

(A) the extradition and rendition of a fugitive;

(B) a civil property forfeiture for violating a federal statute;

(C) the collection of a fine or penalty;

(D) a proceeding under a statute governing juvenile delinquency to the extent the procedure is inconsistent with the statute, unless Rule 20(d) provides otherwise;

(E) a dispute between seamen under 22 U.S.C. §§ 256–258; and

(F) a proceeding against a witness in a foreign country under 28 U.S.C. § 1784.

(b) Definitions. The following definitions apply to these rules:

(1) "Attorney for the government" means:

    (A) the Attorney General or an authorized assistant;

    (B) a United States attorney or an authorized assistant;

    (C) when applicable to cases arising under Guam law, the Guam Attorney General or other person whom Guam law authorizes to act in the matter; and

    (D) any other attorney authorized by law to conduct proceedings under these rules as a prosecutor.

(2) "Court" means a federal judge performing functions authorized by law.

(3) "Federal judge" means:

    (A) a justice or judge of the United States as these terms are defined in 28 U.S.C. § 451;

    (B) a magistrate judge; and

    (C) a judge confirmed by the United States Senate and empowered by statute in any commonwealth, territory, or possession to perform a function to which a particular rule relates.

(4) "Judge" means a federal judge or a state or local judicial officer.

(5) "Magistrate judge" means a United States magistrate judge as defined in 28 U.S.C. §§ 631–639.

(6) "Oath" includes an affirmation.

(7) "Organization" is defined in 18 U.S.C. § 18.

(8) "Petty offense" is defined in 18 U.S.C. § 19.

(9) "State" includes the District of Columbia, and any commonwealth, territory, or possession of the United States.

(10) "State or local judicial officer" means:

    (A) a state or local officer authorized to act under 18 U.S.C. § 3041; and

    (B) a judicial officer empowered by statute in the District of Columbia or in any commonwealth, territory, or possession to perform a function to which a particular rule relates.

(c) Authority of a Justice or Judge of the United States. When these rules authorize a magistrate judge to act, any other federal judge may also act.

Rule 2. Interpretation

These rules are to be interpreted to provide for the just determination of every criminal proceeding, to secure simplicity in procedure and fairness in administration, and to eliminate unjustifiable expense and delay.

Rule 3.   The Complaint

The complaint is a written statement of the essential facts constituting the offense charged. It must be made under oath before a magistrate judge or, if none is reasonably available, before a state or local judicial officer.

Rule 4.   Arrest Warrant or Summons on a Complaint

(a) Issuance. If the complaint or one or more affidavits filed with the complaint establish probable cause to believe that an offense has been committed and that the defendant committed it, the judge must issue an arrest warrant to an officer authorized to execute it. At the request of an attorney for the government, the judge must issue a summons, instead of a warrant, to a person authorized to serve it. A judge may issue more than one warrant or summons on the same complaint. If a defendant fails to appear in response to a summons, a judge may, and upon request of an attorney for the government must, issue a warrant.

(b) Form.

  (1) Warrant. A warrant must:

    (A) contain the defendant's name or, if it is unknown, a name or description by which the defendant can be identified with reasonable certainty;

    (B) describe the offense charged in the complaint;

    (C) command that the defendant be arrested and brought without unnecessary delay before a magistrate judge or, if none is reasonably available, before a state or local judicial officer; and

    (D) be signed by a judge.

  (2) Summons. A summons must be in the same form as a warrant except that it must require the defendant to appear before a magistrate judge at a stated time and place.

(c) Execution or Service, and Return.

  (1) By Whom. Only a marshal or other authorized officer may execute a warrant. Any person authorized to serve a summons in a federal civil action may serve a summons.

  (2) Location. A warrant may be executed, or a summons served, within the jurisdiction of the United States or anywhere else a federal statute authorizes an arrest.

  (3) Manner.

    (A) A warrant is executed by arresting the defendant. Upon arrest, an officer possessing the warrant must show it to the defendant. If the officer does not possess the warrant, the officer must inform the defendant of the warrant's existence and of the offense charged and, at the defendant's request, must show the warrant to the defendant as soon as possible.

    (B) A summons is served on an individual defendant:

      (i) by delivering a copy to the defendant personally; or

(ii) by leaving a copy at the defendant's residence or usual place of abode with a person of suitable age and discretion residing at that location and by mailing a copy to the defendant's last known address.

(C) A summons is served on an organization by delivering a copy to an officer, to a managing or general agent, or to another agent appointed or legally authorized to receive service of process. A copy must also be mailed to the organization's last known address within the district or to its principal place of business elsewhere in the United States.

(4) Return.

(A) After executing a warrant, the officer must return it to the judge before whom the defendant is brought in accordance with Rule 5. At the request of an attorney for the government, an unexecuted warrant must be brought back to and canceled by a magistrate judge or, if none is reasonably available, by a state or local judicial officer.

(B) The person to whom a summons was delivered for service must return it on or before the return day.

(C) At the request of an attorney for the government, a judge may deliver an unexecuted warrant, an unserved summons, or a copy of the warrant or summons to the marshal or other authorized person for execution or service.

<h3 align="center">Rule 5.   Initial Appearance</h3>

(a) In General.

(1) Appearance Upon an Arrest.

(A) A person making an arrest within the United States must take the defendant without unnecessary delay before a magistrate judge, or before a state or local judicial officer as Rule 5(c) provides, unless a statute provides otherwise.

(B) A person making an arrest outside the United States must take the defendant without unnecessary delay before a magistrate judge, unless a statute provides otherwise.

(2) Exceptions.

(A) An officer making an arrest under a warrant issued upon a complaint charging solely a violation of 18 U.S.C. § 1073 need not comply with this rule if:

(i) the person arrested is transferred without unnecessary delay to the custody of appropriate state or local authorities in the district of arrest; and

(ii) an attorney for the government moves promptly, in the district where the warrant was issued, to dismiss the complaint.

(B) If a defendant is arrested for violating probation or supervised release, Rule 32.1 applies.

(C) If a defendant is arrested for failing to appear in another district, Rule 40 applies.

(3) Appearance Upon a Summons. When a defendant appears in response to a summons under Rule 4, a magistrate judge must proceed under Rule 5(d) or (e), as applicable.

(b) Arrest Without a Warrant. If a defendant is arrested without a warrant, a complaint meeting Rule 4(a)'s requirement of probable cause must be promptly filed in the district where the offense was allegedly committed.

(c) Place of Initial Appearance; Transfer to Another District.

(1) Arrest in the District Where the Offense Was Allegedly Committed. If the defendant is arrested in the district where the offense was allegedly committed:

(A) the initial appearance must be in that district; and

(B) if a magistrate judge is not reasonably available, the initial appearance may be before a state or local judicial officer.

(2) Arrest in a District Other Than Where the Offense Was Allegedly Committed. If the defendant was arrested in a district other than where the offense was allegedly committed, the initial appearance must be:

(A) in the district of arrest; or

(B) in an adjacent district if:

(i) the appearance can occur more promptly there; or

(ii) the offense was allegedly committed there and the initial appearance will occur on the day of arrest.

(3) Procedures in a District Other Than Where the Offense Was Allegedly Committed. If the initial appearance occurs in a district other than where the offense was allegedly committed, the following procedures apply:

(A) the magistrate judge must inform the defendant about the provisions of Rule 20;

(B) if the defendant was arrested without a warrant, the district court where the offense was allegedly committed must first issue a warrant before the magistrate judge transfers the defendant to that district;

(C) the magistrate judge must conduct a preliminary hearing if required by Rule 5.1;

(D) the magistrate judge must transfer the defendant to the district where the offense was allegedly committed if:

(i) the government produces the warrant, a certified copy of the warrant, reliable electronic form of either; and

(ii) the judge finds that the defendant is the same person named in the indictment, information, or warrant; and

(E) when a defendant is transferred and discharged, the clerk must promptly transmit the papers and any bail to the clerk in the district where the offense was allegedly committed.

(d) Procedure in a Felony Case.

(1) Advice. If the defendant is charged with a felony, the judge must inform the defendant of the following:

(A) the complaint against the defendant, and any affidavit filed with it;

(B) the defendant's right to retain counsel or to request that counsel be appointed if the defendant cannot obtain counsel;

(C) the circumstances, if any, under which the defendant may secure pretrial release;

(D) any right to a preliminary hearing; and

(E) the defendant's right not to make a statement, and that any statement made may be used against the defendant.

(2) Consulting with Counsel. The judge must allow the defendant reasonable opportunity to consult with counsel.

(3) Detention or Release. The judge must detain or release the defendant as provided by statute or these rules.

(4) Plea. A defendant may be asked to plead only under Rule 10.

(e) Procedure in a Misdemeanor Case. If the defendant is charged with a misdemeanor only, the judge must inform the defendant in accordance with Rule 58(b)(2).

(f) Video Teleconferencing. Video teleconferencing may be used to conduct an appearance under this rule if the defendant consents.

Rule 5.1.   Preliminary Hearing

(a) In General. If a defendant is charged with an offense other than a petty offense, a magistrate judge must conduct a preliminary hearing unless:

(1) the defendant waives the hearing;

(2) the defendant is indicted;

(3) the government files an information under Rule 7(b) charging the defendant with a felony;

(4) the government files an information charging the defendant with a misdemeanor; or

(5) the defendant is charged with a misdemeanor and consents to trial before a magistrate judge.

(b) Selecting a District. A defendant arrested in a district other than where the offense was allegedly committed may elect to have the preliminary hearing conducted in the district where the prosecution is pending.

(c) Scheduling. The magistrate judge must hold the preliminary hearing within a reasonable time, but no later than 10 days after the initial appearance if the defendant is in custody and no later than 20 days if not in custody.

(d) Extending the Time. With the defendant's consent and upon a showing of good cause—taking into account the public interest in the prompt disposition of criminal cases—a magistrate judge may extend the time limits in Rule 5.1(c) one or more times. If the defendant does not consent, the magistrate judge may extend the time limits only on a showing that extraordinary circumstances exist and justice requires the delay.

(e) Hearing and Finding. At the preliminary hearing, the defendant may cross-examine adverse witnesses and may introduce evidence but may not object to evidence on the ground that it was unlawfully acquired. If the magistrate judge finds probable cause to believe an offense has been committed and the defendant committed it, the magistrate judge must promptly require the defendant to appear for further proceedings.

(f) Discharging the Defendant. If the magistrate judge finds no probable cause to believe an offense has been committed or the defendant committed it, the magistrate judge must dismiss the complaint and discharge the defendant. A discharge does not preclude the government from later prosecuting the defendant for the same offense.

(g) Recording the Proceedings. The preliminary hearing must be recorded by a court reporter or by a suitable recording device. A recording of the proceeding may be made available to any party upon request. A copy of the recording and a transcript may be provided to any party upon request and upon any payment required by applicable Judicial Conference regulations.

(h) Producing a Statement.

　(1) In General. Rule 26.2(a)–(d) and (f) applies at any hearing under this rule, unless the magistrate judge for good cause rules otherwise in a particular case.

　(2) Sanctions for Not Producing a Statement. If a party disobeys a Rule 26.2 order to deliver a statement to the moving party, the magistrate judge must not consider the testimony of a witness whose statement is withheld.

Rule 6.   The Grand Jury

(a) Summoning a Grand Jury.

　(1) In General. When the public interest so requires, the court must order that one or more grand juries be summoned. A grand jury must have 16 to 23 members, and the court must order that enough legally qualified persons be summoned to meet this requirement.

　(2) Alternate Jurors. When a grand jury is selected, the court may also select alternate jurors. Alternate jurors must have the same qualifications and be selected in the same manner as any other juror. Alternate jurors replace jurors in the same sequence in which the alternates were selected. An alternate juror who replaces a juror is subject to the same challenges, takes the same oath, and has the same authority as the other jurors.

(b) Objection to the Grand Jury or to a Grand Juror.

(1) Challenges. Either the government or a defendant may challenge the grand jury on the ground that it was not lawfully drawn, summoned, or selected, and may challenge an individual juror on the ground that the juror is not legally qualified.

(2) Motion to Dismiss an Indictment. A party may move to dismiss the indictment based on an objection to the grand jury or on an individual juror's lack of legal qualification, unless the court has previously ruled on the same objection under Rule 6(b)(1). The motion to dismiss is governed by 28 U.S.C. § 1867(e). The court must not dismiss the indictment on the ground that a grand juror was not legally qualified if the record shows that at least 12 qualified jurors concurred in the indictment.

(c) Foreperson and Deputy Foreperson. The court will appoint one juror as the foreperson and another as the deputy foreperson. In the foreperson's absence, the deputy foreperson will act as the foreperson. The foreperson may administer oaths and affirmations and will sign all indictments. The foreperson—or another juror designated by the foreperson—will record the number of jurors concurring in every indictment and will file the record with the clerk, but the record may not be made public unless the court so orders.

(d) Who May Be Present.

(1) While the Grand Jury Is in Session. The following persons may be present while the grand jury is in session: attorneys for the government, the witness being questioned, interpreters when needed, and a court reporter or an operator of a recording device.

(2) During Deliberations and Voting. No person other than the jurors, and any interpreter needed to assist a hearing-impaired or speech-impaired juror, may be present while the grand jury is deliberating or voting.

(e) Recording and Disclosing the Proceedings.

(1) Recording the Proceedings. Except while the grand jury is deliberating or voting, all proceedings must be recorded by a court reporter or by a suitable recording device. But the validity of a prosecution is not affected by the unintentional failure to make a recording. Unless the court orders otherwise, an attorney for the government will retain control of the recording, the reporter's notes, and any transcript prepared from those notes.

(2) Secrecy.

(A) No obligation of secrecy may be imposed on any person except in accordance with Rule 6(e)(2)(B).

(B) Unless these rules provide otherwise, the following persons must not disclose a matter occurring before the grand jury:

(i) a grand juror;

(ii) an interpreter;

(**iii**) a court reporter;

(**iv**) an operator of a recording device;

(**v**) a person who transcribes recorded testimony;

(**vi**) an attorney for the government; or

(**vii**) a person to whom disclosure is made under Rule 6(e)(3)(A)(ii) or (iii).

(**3**) **Exceptions.**

(**A**) Disclosure of a grand-jury matter—other than the grand jury's deliberations or any grand juror's vote—may be made to:

(**i**) an attorney for the government for use in performing that attorney's duty;

(**ii**) any government personnel—including those of a state, state subdivision, Indian tribe, or foreign government—that an attorney for the government considers necessary to assist in performing that attorney's duty to enforce federal criminal law; or

(**iii**) a person authorized by 18 U.S.C. § 3322.

(**B**) A person to whom information is disclosed under Rule 6(e)(3)(A)(ii) may use that information only to assist an attorney for the government in performing that attorney's duty to enforce federal criminal law. An attorney for the government must promptly provide the court that impaneled the grand jury with the names of all persons to whom a disclosure has been made, and must certify that the attorney has advised those persons of their obligation of secrecy under this rule.

(**C**) An attorney for the government may disclose any grand-jury matter to another federal grand jury.

(**D**) An attorney for the government may disclose any grand-jury matter involving foreign intelligence, counterintelligence (as defined in 50 U.S.C. § 401a), or foreign intelligence information (as defined in Rule 6(e)(3)(D)(iii)) to any federal law enforcement, intelligence, protective, immigration, national defense, or national security official to assist the official receiving the information in the performance of that official's duties. An attorney for the government may also disclose any grand jury matter involving, within the United States or elsewhere, a threat of attack or other grave hostile acts of a foreign power or its agent, a threat of domestic or international sabotage or terrorism, or clandestine intelligence gathering activities by an intelligence service or network of a foreign power or by its agent, to any appropriate federal, state, state subdivision, Indian tribal, or foreign government official, for the purpose of preventing or responding to such threat or activities.

(**i**) Any official who receives information under Rule 6(e)(3)(D) may use the information only as necessary in the conduct of that person's official duties subject to any limitations on the unauthorized disclosure of such information. Any state,

state subdivision, Indian tribal, or foreign government official who receives information under Rule 6(e)(3)(D) may use the information only in a manner consistent with any guidelines issued by the Attorney General and the Director of National Intelligence.

(ii) Within a reasonable time after disclosure is made under Rule 6(e)(3)(D), an attorney for the government must file, under seal, a notice with the court in the district where the grand jury convened stating that such information was disclosed and the departments, agencies, or entities to which the disclosure was made.

(iii) As used in Rule 6(e)(3)(D), the term "foreign intelligence information" means:

(a) information, whether or not it concerns a United States person, that relates to the ability of the United States to protect against—

- actual or potential attack or other grave hostile acts of a foreign power or its agent;

- sabotage or international terrorism by a foreign power or its agent; or

- clandestine intelligence activities by an intelligence service or network of a foreign power or by its agent; or

(b) information, whether or not it concerns a United States person, with respect to a foreign power or foreign territory that relates to—

- the national defense or the security of the United States; or

- the conduct of the foreign affairs of the United States.

(E) The court may authorize disclosure—at a time, in a manner, and subject to any other conditions that it directs—of a grand-jury matter:

(i) preliminarily to or in connection with a judicial proceeding;

(ii) at the request of a defendant who shows that a ground may exist to dismiss the indictment because of a matter that occurred before the grand jury;

(iii) at the request of the government, when sought by a foreign court or prosecutor for use in an official criminal investigation;

(iv) at the request of the government if it shows that the matter may disclose a violation of State, Indian tribal, or foreign criminal law, as long as the disclosure is to an appropriate state, state-subdivision, Indian tribal, or foreign government official for the purpose of enforcing that law; or

(v) at the request of the government if it shows that the matter may disclose a violation of military criminal law under the Uniform Code of Military Justice, as long as the disclosure is to an appropriate military official for the purpose of enforcing that law.

(F) A petition to disclose a grand-jury matter under Rule 6(e)(3)(E)(i) must be filed in the district where the grand jury convened. Unless the hearing is ex parte—as it may be when the government is the petitioner—the petitioner must serve the petition on, and the court must afford a reasonable opportunity to appear and be heard to:

(i) an attorney for the government;

(ii) the parties to the judicial proceeding; and

(iii) any other person whom the court may designate.

(G) If the petition to disclose arises out of a judicial proceeding in another district, the petitioned court must transfer the petition to the other court unless the petitioned court can reasonably determine whether disclosure is proper. If the petitioned court decides to transfer, it must send to the transferee court the material sought to be disclosed, if feasible, and a written evaluation of the need for continued grand-jury secrecy. The transferee court must afford those persons identified in Rule 6(e)(3)(F) a reasonable opportunity to appear and be heard.

(4) Sealed Indictment. The magistrate judge to whom an indictment is returned may direct that the indictment be kept secret until the defendant is in custody or has been released pending trial. The clerk must then seal the indictment, and no person may disclose the indictment's existence except as necessary to issue or execute a warrant or summons.

(5) Closed Hearing. Subject to any right to an open hearing in a contempt proceeding, the court must close any hearing to the extent necessary to prevent disclosure of a matter occurring before a grand jury.

(6) Sealed Records. Records, orders, and subpoenas relating to grand-jury proceedings must be kept under seal to the extent and as long as necessary to prevent the unauthorized disclosure of a matter occurring before a grand jury.

(7) Contempt. A knowing violation of Rule 6, or of guidelines jointly issued by the Attorney General and the Director of National Intelligence pursuant to Rule 6, may be punished as a contempt of court.

(f) Indictment and Return. A grand jury may indict only if at least 12 jurors concur. The grand jury—or its foreperson or deputy foreperson—must return the indictment to a magistrate judge in open court. If a complaint or information is pending against the defendant and 12 jurors do not concur in the indictment, the foreperson must promptly and in writing report the lack of concurrence to the magistrate judge.

(g) Discharging the Grand Jury. A grand jury must serve until the court discharges it, but it may serve more than 18 months only if the court, having determined that an extension is in the public interest, extends the grand jury's service. An extension may be granted for no more than 6 months, except as otherwise provided by statute.

(h) Excusing a Juror. At any time, for good cause, the court may excuse a juror either temporarily or permanently, and if permanently, the court may impanel an alternate juror in place of the excused juror.

(i) "Indian Tribe" Defined. "Indian tribe" means an Indian tribe recognized by the Secretary of the Interior on a list published in the Federal Register under 25 U.S.C. § 479a–1.

Rule 7.   The Indictment and the Information

(a) When Used.

(1) Felony. An offense (other than criminal contempt) must be prosecuted by an indictment if it is punishable:

(A) by death; or

(B) by imprisonment for more than one year.

(2) Misdemeanor. An offense punishable by imprisonment for one year or less may be prosecuted in accordance with Rule 58(b)(1).

(b) Waiving Indictment. An offense punishable by imprisonment for more than one year may be prosecuted by information if the defendant—in open court and after being advised of the nature of the charge and of the defendant's rights—waives prosecution by indictment.

(c) Nature and Contents.

(1) In General. The indictment or information must be a plain, concise, and definite written statement of the essential facts constituting the offense charged and must be signed by an attorney for the government. It need not contain a formal introduction or conclusion. A count may incorporate by reference an allegation made in another count. A count may allege that the means by which the defendant committed the offense are unknown or that the defendant committed it by one or more specified means. For each count, the indictment or information must give the official or customary citation of the statute, rule, regulation, or other provision of law that the defendant is alleged to have violated. For purposes of an indictment referred to in section 3282 of title 18, United States Code, for which the identity of the defendant is unknown, it shall be sufficient for the indictment to describe the defendant as an individual whose name is unknown, but who has a particular DNA profile, as that term is defined in that section 3282.

(2) Criminal Forfeiture. No judgment of forfeiture may be entered in a criminal proceeding unless the indictment or the information provides notice that the defendant has an interest in property that is subject to forfeiture in accordance with the applicable statute.

(3) Citation Error. Unless the defendant was misled and thereby prejudiced, neither an error in a citation nor a citation's omission is a ground to dismiss the indictment or information or to reverse a conviction.

(d) Surplusage. Upon the defendant's motion, the court may strike surplusage from the indictment or information.

(e) Amending an Information. Unless an additional or different offense is charged or a substantial right of the defendant is prejudiced, the court may permit an information to be amended at any time before the verdict or finding.

(f) Bill of Particulars. The court may direct the government to file a bill of particulars. The defendant may move for a bill of particulars before or within 10 days after arraignment or at a later time if the court permits. The government may amend a bill of particulars subject to such conditions as justice requires.

Rule 8. Joinder of Offenses or Defendants

(a) Joinder of Offenses. The indictment or information may charge a defendant in separate counts with 2 or more offenses if the offenses charged—whether felonies or misdemeanors or both—are of the same or similar character, or are based on the same act or transaction, or are connected with or constitute parts of a common scheme or plan.

(b) Joinder of Defendants. The indictment or information may charge 2 or more defendants if they are alleged to have participated in the same act or transaction, or in the same series of acts or transactions, constituting an offense or offenses. The defendants may be charged in one or more counts together or separately. All defendants need not be charged in each count.

Rule 9. Arrest Warrant or Summons on an Indictment or Information

(a) Issuance. The court must issue a warrant—or at the government's request, a summons—for each defendant named in an indictment or named in an information if one or more affidavits accompanying the information establish probable cause to believe that an offense has been committed and that the defendant committed it. The court may issue more than one warrant or summons for the same defendant. If a defendant fails to appear in response to a summons, the court may, and upon request of an attorney for the government must, issue a warrant. The court must issue the arrest warrant to an officer authorized to execute it or the summons to a person authorized to serve it.

(b) Form.

(1) Warrant. The warrant must conform to Rule 4(b)(1) except that it must be signed by the clerk and must describe the offense charged in the indictment or information.

(2) Summons. The summons must be in the same form as a warrant except that it must require the defendant to appear before the court at a stated time and place.

(c) Execution or Service; Return; Initial Appearance.

(1) Execution or Service.

(A) The warrant must be executed or the summons served as provided in Rule 4(c)(1), (2), and (3).

(B) The officer executing the warrant must proceed in accordance with Rule 5(a)(1).

(2) Return. A warrant or summons must be returned in accordance with Rule 4(c)(4).

(3) Initial Appearance. When an arrested or summoned defendant first appears before the court, the judge must proceed under Rule 5.

Rule 10.   Arraignment

(a) In General. An arraignment must be conducted in open court and must consist of:

(1) ensuring that the defendant has a copy of the indictment or information;

(2) reading the indictment or information to the defendant or stating to the defendant the substance of the charge; and then

(3) asking the defendant to plead to the indictment or information.

(b) Waiving Appearance. A defendant need not be present for the arraignment if:

(1) the defendant has been charged by indictment or misdemeanor information;

(2) the defendant, in a written waiver signed by both the defendant and defense counsel, has waived appearance and has affirmed that the defendant received a copy of the indictment or information and that the plea is not guilty; and

(3) the court accepts the waiver.

(c) Video Teleconferencing. Video teleconferencing may be used to arraign a defendant if the defendant consents.

Rule 11.   Pleas

(a) Entering a Plea.

(1) In General. A defendant may plead not guilty, guilty, or (with the court's consent) nolo contendere.

(2) Conditional Plea. With the consent of the court and the government, a defendant may enter a conditional plea of guilty or nolo contendere, reserving in writing the right to have an appellate court review an adverse determination of a specified pretrial motion. A defendant who prevails on appeal may then withdraw the plea.

(3) Nolo Contendere Plea. Before accepting a plea of nolo contendere, the court must consider the parties' views and the public interest in the effective administration of justice.

(4) Failure to Enter a Plea. If a defendant refuses to enter a plea or if a defendant organization fails to appear, the court must enter a plea of not guilty.

(b) Considering and Accepting a Guilty or Nolo Contendere Plea.

(1) Advising and Questioning the Defendant. Before the court accepts a plea of guilty or nolo contendere, the defendant may be placed under oath, and the court must address the defendant personally in open court. During this address, the court must inform the defendant of, and determine that the defendant understands, the following:

(A) the government's right, in a prosecution for perjury or false statement, to use against the defendant any statement that the defendant gives under oath;

(B) the right to plead not guilty, or having already so pleaded, to persist in that plea;

(C) the right to a jury trial;

(D) the right to be represented by counsel—and if necessary have the court appoint counsel—at trial and at every other stage of the proceeding;

(E) the right at trial to confront and cross-examine adverse witnesses, to be protected from compelled self-incrimination, to testify and present evidence, and to compel the attendance of witnesses;

(F) the defendant's waiver of these trial rights if the court accepts a plea of guilty or nolo contendere;

(G) the nature of each charge to which the defendant is pleading;

(H) any maximum possible penalty, including imprisonment, fine, and term of supervised release;

(I) any mandatory minimum penalty;

(J) any applicable forfeiture;

(K) the court's authority to order restitution;

(L) the court's obligation to impose a special assessment;

(M) in determining a sentence, the court's obligation to calculate the applicable sentencing-guideline range and to consider that range, possible departures under the Sentencing Guidelines, and other sentencing factors under 18 U.S.C. § 3553(a); and

(N) the terms of any plea-agreement provision waiving the right to appeal or to collaterally attack the sentence.

(2) Ensuring That a Plea Is Voluntary. Before accepting a plea of guilty or nolo contendere, the court must address the defendant personally in open court and determine that the plea is voluntary and did not result from force, threats, or promises (other than promises in a plea agreement).

(3) Determining the Factual Basis for a Plea. Before entering judgment on a guilty plea, the court must determine that there is a factual basis for the plea.

(c) Plea Agreement Procedure.

(1) In General. An attorney for the government and the defendant's attorney, or the defendant when proceeding pro se, may discuss and reach a plea agreement. The court must not participate in these discussions. If the defendant pleads guilty or nolo contendere to either a charged offense or a lesser or related offense, the plea agreement may specify that an attorney for the government will:

> **(A)** not bring, or will move to dismiss, other charges;

> **(B)** recommend, or agree not to oppose the defendant's request, that a particular sentence or sentencing range is appropriate or that a particular provision of the Sentencing Guidelines, or policy statement, or sentencing factor does or does not apply (such a recommendation or request does not bind the court); or

> **(C)** agree that a specific sentence or sentencing range is the appropriate disposition of the case, or that a particular provision of the Sentencing Guidelines, or policy statement, or sentencing factor does or does not apply (such a recommendation or request binds the court once the court accepts the plea agreement).

(2) Disclosing a Plea Agreement. The parties must disclose the plea agreement in open court when the plea is offered, unless the court for good cause allows the parties to disclose the plea agreement in camera.

(3) Judicial Consideration of a Plea Agreement.

> **(A)** To the extent the plea agreement is of the type specified in Rule 11(c)(1)(A) or (C), the court may accept the agreement, reject it, or defer a decision until the court has reviewed the presentence report.

> **(B)** To the extent the plea agreement is of the type specified in Rule 11(c)(1)(B), the court must advise the defendant that the defendant has no right to withdraw the plea if the court does not follow the recommendation or request.

(4) Accepting a Plea Agreement. If the court accepts the plea agreement, it must inform the defendant that to the extent the plea agreement is of the type specified in Rule 11(c)(1)(A) or (C), the agreed disposition will be included in the judgment.

(5) Rejecting a Plea Agreement. If the court rejects a plea agreement containing provisions of the type specified in Rule 11(c)(1)(A) or (C), the court must do the following on the record and in open court (or, for good cause, in camera):

> **(A)** inform the parties that the court rejects the plea agreement;

(B) advise the defendant personally that the court is not required to follow the plea agreement and give the defendant an opportunity to withdraw the plea; and

(C) advise the defendant personally that if the plea is not withdrawn, the court may dispose of the case less favorably toward the defendant than the plea agreement contemplated.

(d) Withdrawing a Guilty or Nolo Contendere Plea. A defendant may withdraw a plea of guilty or nolo contendere:

(1) before the court accepts the plea, for any reason or no reason; or

(2) after the court accepts the plea, but before it imposes sentence if:

(A) the court rejects a plea agreement under Rule 11(c)(5); or

(B) the defendant can show a fair and just reason for requesting the withdrawal.

(e) Finality of a Guilty or Nolo Contendere Plea. After the court imposes sentence, the defendant may not withdraw a plea of guilty or nolo contendere, and the plea may be set aside only on direct appeal or collateral attack.

(f) Admissibility or Inadmissibility of a Plea, Plea Discussions, and Related Statements. The admissibility or inadmissibility of a plea, a plea discussion, and any related statement is governed by Federal Rule of Evidence 410.

(g) Recording the Proceedings. The proceedings during which the defendant enters a plea must be recorded by a court reporter or by a suitable recording device. If there is a guilty plea or a nolo contendere plea, the record must include the inquiries and advice to the defendant required under Rule 11(b) and (c).

(h) Harmless Error. A variance from the requirements of this rule is harmless error if it does not affect substantial rights.

Rule 12.   Pleadings and Pretrial Motions

(A) Pleadings. The pleadings in a criminal proceeding are the indictment, the information, and the pleas of not guilty, guilty, and nolo contendere.

(b) Pretrial Motions.

(1) In General. Rule 47 applies to a pretrial motion.

(2) Motions That May Be Made Before Trial. A party may raise by pretrial motion any defense, objection, or request that the court can determine without a trial of the general issue.

(3) Motions That Must Be Made Before Trial. The following must be raised before trial:

(A) a motion alleging a defect in instituting the prosecution;

(B) a motion alleging a defect in the indictment or information—but at any time while the case is pending, the court may hear a claim that the indictment or information fails to invoke the court's jurisdiction or to state an offense;

> **(C)** a motion to suppress evidence;
>
> **(D)** a Rule 14 motion to sever charges or defendants; and
>
> **(E)** a Rule 16 motion for discovery.

(4) Notice of the Government's Intent to Use Evidence.

> **(A) At the Government's Discretion.** At the arraignment or as soon afterward as practicable, the government may notify the defendant of its intent to use specified evidence at trial in order to afford the defendant an opportunity to object before trial under Rule 12(b)(3)(C).
>
> **(B) At the Defendant's Request.** At the arraignment or as soon afterward as practicable, the defendant may, in order to have an opportunity to move to suppress evidence under Rule 12(b)(3)(C), request notice of the government's intent to use (in its evidence-in-chief at trial) any evidence that the defendant may be entitled to discover under Rule 16.

(c) Motion Deadline. The court may, at the arraignment or as soon afterward as practicable, set a deadline for the parties to make pretrial motions and may also schedule a motion hearing.

(d) Ruling on a Motion. The court must decide every pretrial motion before trial unless it finds good cause to defer a ruling. The court must not defer ruling on a pretrial motion if the deferral will adversely affect a party's right to appeal. When factual issues are involved in deciding a motion, the court must state its essential findings on the record.

(e) Waiver of a Defense, Objection, or Request. A party waives any Rule 12(b)(3) defense, objection, or request not raised by the deadline the court sets under Rule 12(c) or by any extension the court provides. For good cause, the court may grant relief from the waiver.

(f) Recording the Proceedings. All proceedings at a motion hearing, including any findings of fact and conclusions of law made orally by the court, must be recorded by a court reporter or a suitable recording device.

(g) Defendant's Continued Custody or Release Status. If the court grants a motion to dismiss based on a defect in instituting the prosecution, in the indictment, or in the information, it may order the defendant to be released or detained under 18 U.S.C. § 3142 for a specified time until a new indictment or information is filed. This rule does not affect any federal statutory period of limitations.

(h) Producing Statements at a Suppression Hearing. Rule 26.2 applies at a suppression hearing under Rule 12(b)(3)(C). At a suppression hearing, a law enforcement officer is considered a government witness.

Rule 12.1.   Notice of an Alibi Defense

(a) Government's Request for Notice and Defendant's Response.

(1) Government's Request. An attorney for the government may request in writing that the defendant notify an attorney for the government of any intended alibi defense. The request must state the time, date, and place of the alleged offense.

(2) Defendant's Response. Within 10 days after the request, or at some other time the court sets, the defendant must serve written notice on an attorney for the government of any intended alibi defense. The defendant's notice must state:

    (A) each specific place where the defendant claims to have been at the time of the alleged offense; and

    (B) the name, address, and telephone number of each alibi witness on whom the defendant intends to rely.

(b) Disclosing Government Witnesses.

(1) Disclosure. If the defendant serves a Rule 12.1(a)(2) notice, an attorney for the government must disclose in writing to the defendant or the defendant's attorney:

    (A) the name, address, and telephone number of each witness the government intends to rely on to establish the defendant's presence at the scene of the alleged offense; and

    (B) each government rebuttal witness to the defendant's alibi defense.

(2) Time to Disclose. Unless the court directs otherwise, an attorney for the government must give its Rule 12.1(b)(1) disclosure within 10 days after the defendant serves notice of an intended alibi defense under Rule 12.1(a)(2), but no later than 10 days before trial.

(c) Continuing Duty to Disclose. Both an attorney for the government and the defendant must promptly disclose in writing to the other party the name, address, and telephone number of each additional witness if:

    (1) the disclosing party learns of the witness before or during trial; and

    (2) the witness should have been disclosed under Rule 12.1(a) or (b) if the disclosing party had known of the witness earlier.

(d) Exceptions. For good cause, the court may grant an exception to any requirement of Rule 12.1(a)–(c).

(e) Failure to Comply. If a party fails to comply with this rule, the court may exclude the testimony of any undisclosed witness regarding the defendant's alibi. This rule does not limit the defendant's right to testify.

(f) Inadmissibility of Withdrawn Intention. Evidence of an intention to rely on an alibi defense, later withdrawn, or of a statement made in connection with that intention, is not, in any civil or criminal proceeding, admissible against the person who gave notice of the intention.

Rule 12.2.   Notice of an Insanity Defense; Mental Examination

(a) Notice of an Insanity Defense. A defendant who intends to assert a defense of insanity at the time of the alleged offense must so notify an attorney for the government in writing within the time provided for filing a pretrial motion, or at any later time the court sets, and file a copy of the notice with the clerk. A defendant who fails to do so cannot rely on an insanity defense. The court may, for good cause, allow the defendant to file the notice late, grant additional trial-preparation time, or make other appropriate orders.

(b) Notice of Expert Evidence of a Mental Condition. If a defendant intends to introduce expert evidence relating to a mental disease or defect or any other mental condition of the defendant bearing on either (1) the issue of guilt or (2) the issue of punishment in a capital case, the defendant must—within the time provided for filing a pretrial motion or at any later time the court sets—notify an attorney for the government in writing of this intention and file a copy of the notice with the clerk. The court may, for good cause, allow the defendant to file the notice late, grant the parties additional trial-preparation time, or make other appropriate orders.

(c) Mental Examination.

(1) Authority to Order an Examination; Procedures.

(A) The court may order the defendant to submit to a competency examination under 18 U.S.C. § 4241.

(B) If the defendant provides notice under Rule 12.2(a), the court must, upon the government's motion, order the defendant to be examined under 18 U.S.C. § 4242. If the defendant provides notice under Rule 12.2(b) the court may, upon the government's motion, order the defendant to be examined under procedures ordered by the court.

(2) Disclosing Results and Reports of Capital Sentencing Examination. The results and reports of any examination conducted solely under Rule 12.2(c)(1) after notice under Rule 12.2(b)(2) must be sealed and must not be disclosed to any attorney for the government or the defendant unless the defendant is found guilty of one or more capital crimes and the defendant confirms an intent to offer during sentencing proceedings expert evidence on mental condition.

(3) Disclosing Results and Reports of the Defendant's Expert Examination. After disclosure under Rule 12.2(c)(2) of the results and reports of the government's examination, the defendant must disclose to the government the results and reports of any examination on mental condition conducted by the defendant's expert about which the defendant intends to introduce expert evidence.

(4) Inadmissibility of a Defendant's Statements. No statement made by a defendant in the course of any examination conducted under this rule (whether conducted with or without the defendant's consent), no testimony by the expert based on the statement, and no other fruits of the statement may be admitted into evidence against the defendant in any criminal proceeding except on an issue regarding mental condition on which the defendant:

(A) has introduced evidence of incompetency or evidence requiring notice under Rule 12.2(a) or (b)(1), or

(B) has introduced expert evidence in a capital sentencing proceeding requiring notice under Rule 12.2(b)(2).

(d) Failure to Comply.

(1) Failure to Give Notice or to Submit to Examination. The court may exclude any expert evidence from the defendant on the issue of the defendant's mental disease, mental defect, or any other mental condition bearing on the defendant's guilt or the issue of punishment in a capital case if the defendant fails to:

(A) give notice under Rule 12.2(b); or

(B) submit to an examination when ordered under Rule 12.2(c).

(2) Failure to Disclose. The court may exclude any expert evidence for which the defendant has failed to comply with the disclosure requirement of Rule 12.2(c)(3).

(e) Inadmissibility of Withdrawn Intention. Evidence of an intention as to which notice was given under Rule 12.2(a) or (b), later withdrawn, is not, in any civil or criminal proceeding, admissible against the person who gave notice of the intention.

Rule 12.3. Notice of a Public–Authority Defense

(a) Notice of the Defense and Disclosure of Witnesses.

(1) Notice in General. If a defendant intends to assert a defense of actual or believed exercise of public authority on behalf of a law enforcement agency or federal intelligence agency at the time of the alleged offense, the defendant must so notify an attorney for the government in writing and must file a copy of the notice with the clerk within the time provided for filing a pretrial motion, or at any later time the court sets. The notice filed with the clerk must be under seal if the notice identifies a federal intelligence agency as the source of public authority.

(2) Contents of Notice. The notice must contain the following information:

(A) the law enforcement agency or federal intelligence agency involved;

(B) the agency member on whose behalf the defendant claims to have acted; and

(C) the time during which the defendant claims to have acted with public authority.

(3) Response to the Notice. An attorney for the government must serve a written response on the defendant or the defendant's attorney within 10 days after receiving the defendant's notice, but no later than 20 days before trial. The response must admit or deny that the defendant exercised the public authority identified in the defendant's notice.

(4) Disclosing Witnesses.

(A) Government's Request. An attorney for the government may request in writing that the defendant disclose the name, address, and telephone number of each witness the defendant intends to rely on to establish a public-authority defense. An attorney for the government may serve the request when the government serves its response to the defendant's notice under Rule 12.3(a)(3), or later, but must serve the request no later than 20 days before trial.

(B) Defendant's Response. Within 7 days after receiving the government's request, the defendant must serve on an attorney for the government a written statement of the name, address, and telephone number of each witness.

(C) Government's Reply. Within 7 days after receiving the defendant's statement, an attorney for the government must serve on the defendant or the defendant's attorney a written statement of the name, address, and telephone number of each witness the government intends to rely on to oppose the defendant's public-authority defense.

(5) Additional Time. The court may, for good cause, allow a party additional time to comply with this rule.

(b) Continuing Duty to Disclose. Both an attorney for the government and the defendant must promptly disclose in writing to the other party the name, address, and telephone number of any additional witness if:

(1) the disclosing party learns of the witness before or during trial; and

(2) the witness should have been disclosed under Rule 12.3(a)(4) if the disclosing party had known of the witness earlier.

(c) Failure to Comply. If a party fails to comply with this rule, the court may exclude the testimony of any undisclosed witness regarding the public-authority defense. This rule does not limit the defendant's right to testify.

(d) Protective Procedures Unaffected. This rule does not limit the court's authority to issue appropriate protective orders or to order that any filings be under seal.

(e) Inadmissibility of Withdrawn Intention. Evidence of an intention as to which notice was given under Rule 12.3(a), later withdrawn, is not, in any civil or criminal proceeding, admissible against the person who gave notice of the intention.

Rule 12.4. Disclosure Statement

(a) Who Must File.

(1) Nongovernmental Corporate Party. Any nongovernmental corporate party to a proceeding in a district court must file a statement that identifies any parent corporation and any publicly held corporation that owns 10% or more of its stock or states that there is no such corporation.

(2) Organizational Victim. If an organization is a victim of the alleged criminal activity, the government must file a statement identifying the victim. If the organizational victim is a corporation, the statement must also disclose the information required by Rule 12.4(a)(1) to the extent it can be obtained through due diligence.

(b) Time for Filing; Supplemental Filing. A party must:

(1) file the Rule 12.4(a) statement upon the defendant's initial appearance; and

(2) promptly file a supplemental statement upon any change in the information that the statement requires.

Rule 13.　Joint Trial of Separate Cases

The court may order that separate cases be tried together as though brought in a single indictment or information if all offenses and all defendants could have been joined in a single indictment or information.

Rule 14.　Relief from Prejudicial Joinder

(a) Relief. If the joinder of offenses or defendants in an indictment, an information, or a consolidation for trial appears to prejudice a defendant or the government, the court may order separate trials of counts, sever the defendants' trials, or provide any other relief that justice requires.

(b) Defendant's Statements. Before ruling on a defendant's motion to sever, the court may order an attorney for the government to deliver to the court for in camera inspection any defendant's statement that the government intends to use as evidence.

Rule 15.　Depositions

(a) When Taken.

(1) In General. A party may move that a prospective witness be deposed in order to preserve testimony for trial. The court may grant the motion because of exceptional circumstances and in the interest of justice. If the court orders the deposition to be taken, it may also require the deponent to produce at the deposition any designated material that is not privileged, including any book, paper, document, record, recording, or data.

(2) Detained Material Witness. A witness who is detained under 18 U.S.C. § 3144 may request to be deposed by filing a written motion and giving notice to the parties. The court may then order that the deposition be taken and may discharge the witness after the witness has signed under oath the deposition transcript.

(b) Notice.

(1) In General. A party seeking to take a deposition must give every other party reasonable written notice of the deposition's date and location. The notice must state the name and address of each deponent. If requested by a party receiving the notice, the court may, for good cause, change the deposition's date or location.

(2) To the Custodial Officer. A party seeking to take the deposition must also notify the officer who has custody of the defendant of the scheduled date and location.

(c) Defendant's Presence.

(1) Defendant in Custody. The officer who has custody of the defendant must produce the defendant at the deposition and keep the defendant in the witness's presence during the examination, unless the defendant:

>   **(A)** waives in writing the right to be present; or

>   **(B)** persists in disruptive conduct justifying exclusion after being warned by the court that disruptive conduct will result in the defendant's exclusion.

(2) Defendant Not in Custody. A defendant who is not in custody has the right upon request to be present at the deposition, subject to any conditions imposed by the court. If the government tenders the defendant's expenses as provided in Rule 15(d) but the defendant still fails to appear, the defendant—absent good cause— waives both the right to appear and any objection to the taking and use of the deposition based on that right.

(d) Expenses. If the deposition was requested by the government, the court may—or if the defendant is unable to bear the deposition expenses, the court must—order the government to pay:

>   **(1)** any reasonable travel and subsistence expenses of the defendant and the defendant's attorney to attend the deposition; and

>   **(2)** the costs of the deposition transcript.

(e) Manner of Taking. Unless these rules or a court order provides otherwise, a deposition must be taken and filed in the same manner as a deposition in a civil action, except that:

>   **(1)** A defendant may not be deposed without that defendant's consent.

>   **(2)** The scope and manner of the deposition examination and cross-examination must be the same as would be allowed during trial.

>   **(3)** The government must provide to the defendant or the defendant's attorney, for use at the deposition, any statement of the deponent in the government's possession to which the defendant would be entitled at trial.

(f) Use as Evidence. A party may use all or part of a deposition as provided by the Federal Rules of Evidence.

(g) Objections. A party objecting to deposition testimony or evidence must state the grounds for the objection during the deposition.

(h) Depositions by Agreement Permitted. The parties may by agreement take and use a deposition with the court's consent.

Rule 16. Discovery and Inspection

(a) Government's Disclosure.

(1) Information Subject to Disclosure.

(A) Defendant's Oral Statement. Upon a defendant's request, the government must disclose to the defendant the substance of any relevant oral statement made by the defendant, before or after arrest, in response to interrogation by a person the defendant knew was a government agent if the government intends to use the statement at trial.

(B) Defendant's Written or Recorded Statement. Upon a defendant's request, the government must disclose to the defendant, and make available for inspection, copying, or photographing, all of the following:

(i) any relevant written or recorded statement by the defendant if:

- the statement is within the government's possession, custody, or control; and

- the attorney for the government knows—or through due diligence could know—that the statement exists;

(ii) the portion of any written record containing the substance of any relevant oral statement made before or after arrest if the defendant made the statement in response to interrogation by a person the defendant knew was a government agent; and

(iii) the defendant's recorded testimony before a grand jury relating to the charged offense.

(C) Organizational Defendant. Upon a defendant's request, if the defendant is an organization, the government must disclose to the defendant any statement described in Rule 16(a)(1)(A) and (B) if the government contends that the person making the statement:

(i) was legally able to bind the defendant regarding the subject of the statement because of that person's position as the defendant's director, officer, employee, or agent; or

(ii) was personally involved in the alleged conduct constituting the offense and was legally able to bind the defendant regarding that conduct because of that person's position as the defendant's director, officer, employee, or agent.

(D) Defendant's Prior Record. Upon a defendant's request, the government must furnish the defendant with a copy of the defendant's prior criminal record that is within the government's possession, custody, or control if the attorney for the government knows—or through due diligence could know—that the record exists.

(E) Documents and Objects. Upon a defendant's request, the government must permit the defendant to inspect and to copy or photograph books, papers, documents, data, photographs, tangible objects, buildings or places, or copies or portions of any of these items, if the item is within the government's possession, custody, or control and:

> **(i)** the item is material to preparing the defense;

> **(ii)** the government intends to use the item in its case-in-chief at trial; or

> **(iii)** the item was obtained from or belongs to the defendant.

(F) Reports of Examinations and Tests. Upon a defendant's request, the government must permit a defendant to inspect and to copy or photograph the results or reports of any physical or mental examination and of any scientific test or experiment if:

> **(i)** the item is within the government's possession, custody, or control;

> **(ii)** the attorney for the government knows—or through due diligence could know—that the item exists; and

> **(iii)** the item is material to preparing the defense or the government intends to use the item in its case-in-chief at trial.

(G) Expert witnesses. At the defendant's request, the government must give to the defendant a written summary of any testimony that the government intends to use under Rules 702, 703, or 705 of the Federal Rules of Evidence during its case-in-chief at trial. If the government requests discovery under subdivision (b)(1)(C)(ii) and the defendant complies, the government must, at the defendant's request, give to the defendant a written summary of testimony that the government intends to use under Rules 702, 703, or 705 of the Federal Rules of Evidence as evidence at trial on the issue of the defendant's mental condition. The summary provided under this subparagraph must describe the witness's opinions, the bases and reasons for those opinions, and the witness's qualifications.

(2) Information Not Subject to Disclosure. Except as Rule 16(a)(1) provides otherwise, this rule does not authorize the discovery or inspection of reports, memoranda, or other internal government documents made by an attorney for the government or other government agent in connection with investigating or prosecuting the case. Nor does this rule authorize the discovery or inspection of statements made by prospective government witnesses except as provided in 18 U.S.C. § 3500.*

(3) Grand Jury Transcripts. This rule does not apply to the discovery or inspection of a grand jury's recorded proceedings, except as provided in Rules 6, 12(h), 16(a)(1), and 26.2.

(b) Defendant's Disclosure.

(1) Information Subject to Disclosure.

---

* This provision is set out in Appendix B.

(A) Documents and Objects. If a defendant requests disclosure under Rule 16(a)(1)(E) and the government complies, then the defendant must permit the government, upon request, to inspect and to copy or photograph books, papers, documents, data, photographs, tangible objects, buildings or places, or copies or portions of any of these items if:

(i) the item is within the defendant's possession, custody, or control; and

(ii) the defendant intends to use the item in the defendant's case-in-chief at trial.

(B) Reports of Examinations and Tests. If a defendant requests disclosure under Rule 16(a)(1)(F) and the government complies, the defendant must permit the government, upon request, to inspect and to copy or photograph the results or reports of any physical or mental examination and of any scientific test or experiment if:

(i) the item is within the defendant's possession, custody, or control; and

(ii) the defendant intends to use the item in the defendant's case-in-chief at trial, or intends to call the witness who prepared the report and the report relates to the witness's testimony.

(C) Expert witnesses. The defendant must, at the government's request, give to the government a written summary of any testimony that the defendant intends to use under Rules 702, 703, or 705 of the Federal Rules of Evidence as evidence at trial, if—

(i) the defendant requests disclosure under subdivision (a)(1)(G) and the government complies; or

(ii) the defendant has given notice under Rule 12.2(b) of an intent to present expert testimony on the defendant's mental condition.

This summary must describe the witness's opinions, the bases and reasons for those opinions, and the witness's qualifications.

(2) Information Not Subject to Disclosure. Except for scientific or medical reports, Rule 16(b)(1) does not authorize discovery or inspection of:

(A) reports, memoranda, or other documents made by the defendant, or the defendant's attorney or agent, during the case's investigation or defense; or

(B) a statement made to the defendant, or the defendant's attorney or agent, by:

(i) the defendant;

(ii) a government or defense witness; or

(iii) a prospective government or defense witness.

(c) Continuing Duty to Disclose. A party who discovers additional evidence or material before or during trial must promptly disclose its existence to the other party or the court if:

>   **(1)** the evidence or material is subject to discovery or inspection under this rule; and

>   **(2)** the other party previously requested, or the court ordered, its production.

(d) Regulating Discovery.

>   **(1) Protective and Modifying Orders.** At any time the court may, for good cause, deny, restrict, or defer discovery or inspection, or grant other appropriate relief. The court may permit a party to show good cause by a written statement that the court will inspect ex parte. If relief is granted, the court must preserve the entire text of the party's statement under seal.

>   **(2) Failure to Comply.** If a party fails to comply with this rule, the court may:

>>   **(A)** order that party to permit the discovery or inspection; specify its time, place, and manner; and prescribe other just terms and conditions;

>>   **(B)** grant a continuance;

>>   **(C)** prohibit that party from introducing the undisclosed evidence; or

>>   **(D)** enter any other order that is just under the circumstances.

Rule 17.   Subpoena

(a) Content. A subpoena must state the court's name and the title of the proceeding, include the seal of the court, and command the witness to attend and testify at the time and place the subpoena specifies. The clerk must issue a blank subpoena—signed and sealed—to the party requesting it, and that party must fill in the blanks before the subpoena is served.

(b) Defendant Unable to Pay. Upon a defendant's ex parte application, the court must order that a subpoena be issued for a named witness if the defendant shows an inability to pay the witness's fees and the necessity of the witness's presence for an adequate defense. If the court orders a subpoena to be issued, the process costs and witness fees will be paid in the same manner as those paid for witnesses the government subpoenas.

(c) Producing Documents and Objects.

>   **(1) In General.** A subpoena may order the witness to produce any books, papers, documents, data, or other objects the subpoena designates. The court may direct the witness to produce the designated items in court before trial or before they are to be offered in evidence. When the items arrive, the court may permit the parties and their attorneys to inspect all or part of them.

(2) Quashing or Modifying the Subpoena. On motion made promptly, the court may quash or modify the subpoena if compliance would be unreasonable or oppressive.

(d) Service. A marshal, a deputy marshal, or any nonparty who is at least 18 years old may serve a subpoena. The server must deliver a copy of the subpoena to the witness and must tender to the witness one day's witness-attendance fee and the legal mileage allowance. The server need not tender the attendance fee or mileage allowance when the United States, a federal officer, or a federal agency has requested the subpoena.

(e) Place of Service.

(1) In the United States. A subpoena requiring a witness to attend a hearing or trial may be served at any place within the United States.

(2) In a Foreign Country. If the witness is in a foreign country, 28 U.S.C. § 1783 governs the subpoena's service.

(f) Issuing a Deposition Subpoena.

(1) Issuance. A court order to take a deposition authorizes the clerk in the district where the deposition is to be taken to issue a subpoena for any witness named or described in the order.

(2) Place. After considering the convenience of the witness and the parties, the court may order—and the subpoena may require—the witness to appear anywhere the court designates.

(g) Contempt. The court (other than a magistrate judge) may hold in contempt a witness who, without adequate excuse, disobeys a subpoena issued by a federal court in that district. A magistrate judge may hold in contempt a witness who, without adequate excuse, disobeys a subpoena issued by that magistrate judge as provided in 28 U.S.C. § 636(e).

(h) Information Not Subject to a Subpoena. No party may subpoena a statement of a witness or of a prospective witness under this rule. Rule 26.2 governs the production of the statement.

Rule 18.   Place of Prosecution and Trial

Unless a statute or these rules permit otherwise, the government must prosecute an offense in a district where the offense was committed. The court must set the place of trial within the district with due regard for the convenience of the defendant and the witnesses, and the prompt administration of justice.

Rule 19.   [Reserved]

Rule 20.   Transfer for Plea and Sentence

(a) Consent to Transfer. A prosecution may be transferred from the district where the indictment or information is pending, or from which a warrant on a complaint has been issued, to the district where the defendant is arrested, held, or present if:

(1) the defendant states in writing a wish to plead guilty or nolo contendere and to waive trial in the district where the indictment, information, or complaint is pending, consents in writing to the court's disposing of the case in the transferee district, and files the statement in the transferee district; and

(2) the United States attorneys in both districts approve the transfer in writing.

(b) Clerk's Duties. After receiving the defendant's statement and the required approvals, the clerk where the indictment, information, or complaint is pending must send the file, or a certified copy, to the clerk in the transferee district.

(c) Effect of a Not Guilty Plea. If the defendant pleads not guilty after the case has been transferred under Rule 20(a), the clerk must return the papers to the court where the prosecution began, and that court must restore the proceeding to its docket. The defendant's statement that the defendant wished to plead guilty or nolo contendere is not, in any civil or criminal proceeding, admissible against the defendant.

(d) Juveniles.

(1) Consent to Transfer. A juvenile, as defined in 18 U.S.C. § 5031, may be proceeded against as a juvenile delinquent in the district where the juvenile is arrested, held, or present if:

(A) the alleged offense that occurred in the other district is not punishable by death or life imprisonment;

(B) an attorney has advised the juvenile;

(C) the court has informed the juvenile of the juvenile's rights—including the right to be returned to the district where the offense allegedly occurred—and the consequences of waiving those rights;

(D) the juvenile, after receiving the court's information about rights, consents in writing to be proceeded against in the transferee district, and files the consent in the transferee district;

(E) the United States attorneys for both districts approve the transfer in writing; and

(F) the transferee court approves the transfer.

(2) Clerk's Duties. After receiving the juvenile's written consent and the required approvals, the clerk where the indictment, information, or complaint is pending or where the alleged offense occurred must send the file, or a certified copy, to the clerk in the transferee district.

Rule 21.   Transfer for Trial

(a) For Prejudice. Upon the defendant's motion, the court must transfer the proceeding against that defendant to another district if the court is satisfied that so great a prejudice against the defendant exists in the transferring district that the defendant cannot obtain a fair and impartial trial there.

(b) For Convenience. Upon the defendant's motion, the court may transfer the proceeding, or one or more counts, against that defendant to another district for the convenience of the parties and witnesses and in the interest of justice.

(c) Proceedings on Transfer. When the court orders a transfer, the clerk must send to the transferee district the file, or a certified copy, and any bail taken. The prosecution will then continue in the transferee district.

(d) Time to File a Motion to Transfer. A motion to transfer may be made at or before arraignment or at any other time the court or these rules prescribe.

Rule 22.   [Transferred]

Rule 23.   Jury or Nonjury Trial

(a) Jury Trial. If the defendant is entitled to a jury trial, the trial must be by jury unless:

> **(1)** the defendant waives a jury trial in writing;

> **(2)** the government consents; and

> **(3)** the court approves.

(b) Jury Size.

> **(1) In General.** A jury consists of 12 persons unless this rule provides otherwise.

> **(2) Stipulation for a Smaller Jury.** At any time before the verdict, the parties may, with the court's approval, stipulate in writing that:

>> **(A)** the jury may consist of fewer than 12 persons; or

>> **(B)** a jury of fewer than 12 persons may return a verdict if the court finds it necessary to excuse a juror for good cause after the trial begins.

> **(3) Court Order for a Jury of 11.** After the jury has retired to deliberate, the court may permit a jury of 11 persons to return a verdict, even without a stipulation by the parties, if the court finds good cause to excuse a juror.

(c) Nonjury Trial. In a case tried without a jury, the court must find the defendant guilty or not guilty. If a party requests before the finding of guilty or not guilty, the court must state its specific findings of fact in open court or in a written decision or opinion.

Rule 24.   Trial Jurors

(a) Examination.

> **(1) In General.** The court may examine prospective jurors or may permit the attorneys for the parties to do so.

> **(2) Court Examination.** If the court examines the jurors, it must permit the attorneys for the parties to:

>> **(A)** ask further questions that the court considers proper; or

(B) submit further questions that the court may ask if it considers them proper.

(b) Peremptory Challenges. Each side is entitled to the number of peremptory challenges to prospective jurors specified below. The court may allow additional peremptory challenges to multiple defendants, and may allow the defendants to exercise those challenges separately or jointly.

(1) Capital Case. Each side has 20 peremptory challenges when the government seeks the death penalty.

(2) Other Felony Case. The government has 6 peremptory challenges and the defendant or defendants jointly have 10 peremptory challenges when the defendant is charged with a crime punishable by imprisonment of more than one year.

(3) Misdemeanor Case. Each side has 3 peremptory challenges when the defendant is charged with a crime punishable by fine, imprisonment of one year or less, or both.

(c) Alternate Jurors.

(1) In General. The court may impanel up to 6 alternate jurors to replace any jurors who are unable to perform or who are disqualified from performing their duties.

(2) Procedure.

(A) Alternate jurors must have the same qualifications and be selected and sworn in the same manner as any other juror.

(B) Alternate jurors replace jurors in the same sequence in which the alternates were selected. An alternate juror who replaces a juror has the same authority as the other jurors.

(3) Retaining Alternate Jurors. The court may retain alternate jurors after the jury retires to deliberate. The court must ensure that a retained alternate does not discuss the case with anyone until that alternate replaces a juror or is discharged. If an alternate replaces a juror after deliberations have begun, the court must instruct the jury to begin its deliberations anew.

(4) Peremptory Challenges. Each side is entitled to the number of additional peremptory challenges to prospective alternate jurors specified below. These additional challenges may be used only to remove alternate jurors.

(A) One or Two Alternates. One additional peremptory challenge is permitted when one or two alternates are impaneled.

(B) Three or Four Alternates. Two additional peremptory challenges are permitted when three or four alternates are impaneled.

(C) Five or Six Alternates. Three additional peremptory challenges are permitted when five or six alternates are impaneled.

Rule 25.   Judge's Disability

(a) During Trial. Any judge regularly sitting in or assigned to the court may complete a jury trial if:

(1) the judge before whom the trial began cannot proceed because of death, sickness, or other disability; and

(2) the judge completing the trial certifies familiarity with the trial record.

(b) After a Verdict or Finding of Guilty.

(1) In General. After a verdict or finding of guilty, any judge regularly sitting in or assigned to a court may complete the court's duties if the judge who presided at trial cannot perform those duties because of absence, death, sickness, or other disability.

(2) Granting a New Trial. The successor judge may grant a new trial if satisfied that:

(A) a judge other than the one who presided at the trial cannot perform the post-trial duties; or

(B) a new trial is necessary for some other reason.

Rule 26.   Taking Testimony

In every trial the testimony of witnesses must be taken in open court, unless otherwise provided by a statute or by rules adopted under 28 U.S.C. §§ 2072–2077.

Rule 26.1.   Foreign Law Determination

A party intending to raise an issue of foreign law must provide the court and all parties with reasonable written notice. Issues of foreign law are questions of law, but in deciding such issues a court may consider any relevant material or source—including testimony—without regard to the Federal Rules of Evidence.

Rule 26.2.   Producing a Witness's Statement

(a) Motion to Produce. After a witness other than the defendant has testified on direct examination, the court, on motion of a party who did not call the witness, must order an attorney for the government or the defendant and the defendant's attorney to produce, for the examination and use of the moving party, any statement of the witness that is in their possession and that relates to the subject matter of the witness's testimony.

(b) Producing the Entire Statement. If the entire statement relates to the subject matter of the witness's testimony, the court must order that the statement be delivered to the moving party.

(c) Producing a Redacted Statement. If the party who called the witness claims that the statement contains information that is privileged or does not relate to the subject matter of the witness's testimony, the court must inspect the statement in camera. After excising any privileged or unrelated portions, the court must order delivery of the redacted statement to the moving party. If the defendant objects to an excision, the court must preserve the entire statement with the excised portion indicated, under seal, as part of the record.

(d) Recess to Examine a Statement. The court may recess the proceedings to allow time for a party to examine the statement and prepare for its use.

(e) Sanction for Failure to Produce or Deliver a Statement. If the party who called the witness disobeys an order to produce or deliver a statement, the court must strike the witness's testimony from the record. If an attorney for the government disobeys the order, the court must declare a mistrial if justice so requires.

(f) "Statement" Defined. As used in this rule, a witness's "statement" means:

> **(1)** a written statement that the witness makes and signs, or otherwise adopts or approves;

> **(2)** a substantially verbatim, contemporaneously recorded recital of the witness's oral statement that is contained in any recording or any transcription of a recording; or

> **(3)** the witness's statement to a grand jury, however taken or recorded, or a transcription of such a statement.

(g) Scope. This rule applies at trial, at a suppression hearing under Rule 12, and to the extent specified in the following rules:

> **(1)** Rule 5.1(h) (preliminary hearing);

> **(2)** Rule 32(i)(2) (sentencing);

> **(3)** Rule 32.1(e) (hearing to revoke or modify probation or supervised release);

> **(4)** Rule 46(j) (detention hearing); and

> **(5)** Rule 8 of the Rules Governing Proceedings under 28 U.S.C. § 2255.

Rule 26.3.   Mistrial

Before ordering a mistrial, the court must give each defendant and the government an opportunity to comment on the propriety of the order, to state whether that party consents or objects, and to suggest alternatives.

Rule 27.   Proving an Official Record

A party may prove an official record, an entry in such a record, or the lack of a record or entry in the same manner as in a civil action.

Rule 28.   Interpreters

The court may select, appoint, and set the reasonable compensation for an interpreter. The compensation must be paid from funds provided by law or by the government, as the court may direct.

Rule 29.   Motion for a Judgment of Acquittal

(a) Before Submission to the Jury. After the government closes its evidence or after the close of all the evidence, the court on the defendant's motion must enter a judgment of acquittal of any offense for which the evidence is insufficient to sustain a conviction. The court may on its own consider whether the evidence is insufficient to sustain a conviction. If the court denies a motion for a judgment of acquittal at the close of the government's evidence, the defendant may offer evidence without having reserved the right to do so.

(b) Reserving Decision. The court may reserve decision on the motion, proceed with the trial (where the motion is made before the close of all the evidence), submit the case to the jury, and decide the motion either before the jury returns a verdict or after it returns a verdict of guilty or is discharged without having returned a verdict. If the court reserves decision, it must decide the motion on the basis of the evidence at the time the ruling was reserved.

(c) After Jury Verdict or Discharge.

(1) Time for a Motion. A defendant may move for a judgment of acquittal, or renew such a motion, within 7 days after a guilty verdict or after the court discharges the jury, whichever is later.

(2) Ruling on the Motion. If the jury has returned a guilty verdict, the court may set aside the verdict and enter an acquittal. If the jury has failed to return a verdict, the court may enter a judgment of acquittal.

(3) No Prior Motion Required. A defendant is not required to move for a judgment of acquittal before the court submits the case to the jury as a prerequisite for making such a motion after jury discharge.

(d) Conditional Ruling on a Motion for a New Trial.

(1) Motion for a New Trial. If the court enters a judgment of acquittal after a guilty verdict, the court must also conditionally determine whether any motion for a new trial should be granted if the judgment of acquittal is later vacated or reversed. The court must specify the reasons for that determination.

(2) Finality. The court's order conditionally granting a motion for a new trial does not affect the finality of the judgment of acquittal.

(3) Appeal.

(A) Grant of a Motion for a New Trial. If the court conditionally grants a motion for a new trial and an appellate court later reverses the judgment of acquittal, the trial court must proceed with the new trial unless the appellate court orders otherwise.

(B) Denial of a Motion for a New Trial. If the court conditionally denies a motion for a new trial, an appellee may assert that the denial was erroneous. If the appellate court later reverses the judgment of acquittal, the trial court must proceed as the appellate court directs.

Rule 29.1.   Closing Argument

Closing arguments proceed in the following order:

(a) the government argues;

(b) the defense argues; and

(c) the government rebuts.

Rule 30.   Jury Instructions

(a) In General. Any party may request in writing that the court instruct the jury on the law as specified in the request. The request must be made at the close of the evidence or at any earlier time that the court reasonably sets. When the request is made, the requesting party must furnish a copy to every other party.

(b) Ruling on a Request. The court must inform the parties before closing arguments how it intends to rule on the requested instructions.

(c) Time for Giving Instructions. The court may instruct the jury before or after the arguments are completed, or at both times.

(d) Objections to Instructions. A party who objects to any portion of the instructions or to a failure to give a requested instruction must inform the court of the specific objection and the grounds for the objection before the jury retires to deliberate. An opportunity must be given to object out of the jury's hearing and, on request, out of the jury's presence. Failure to object in accordance with this rule precludes appellate review, except as permitted under Rule 52(b).

Rule 31.   Jury Verdict

(a) Return. The jury must return its verdict to a judge in open court. The verdict must be unanimous.

(b) Partial Verdicts, Mistrial, and Retrial.

(1) Multiple Defendants. If there are multiple defendants, the jury may return a verdict at any time during its deliberations as to any defendant about whom it has agreed.

(2) Multiple Counts. If the jury cannot agree on all counts as to any defendant, the jury may return a verdict on those counts on which it has agreed.

(3) Mistrial and Retrial. If the jury cannot agree on a verdict on one or more counts, the court may declare a mistrial on those counts. The government may retry any defendant on any count on which the jury could not agree.

(c) Lesser Offense or Attempt. A defendant may be found guilty of any of the following:

(1) an offense necessarily included in the offense charged;

(2) an attempt to commit the offense charged; or

(3) an attempt to commit an offense necessarily included in the offense charged, if the attempt is an offense in its own right.

(d) Jury Poll. After a verdict is returned but before the jury is discharged, the court must on a party's request, or may on its own, poll the jurors individually. If the poll reveals a lack of unanimity, the court may direct the jury to deliberate further or may declare a mistrial and discharge the jury.

Rule 32.   Sentencing and Judgment

(a) Definitions. The following definitions apply under this rule:

(1) "Crime of violence or sexual abuse" means:

(A) a crime that involves the use, attempted use, or threatened use of physical force against another's person or property; or

(B) a crime under 18 U.S.C. §§ 2241–2248 or §§ 2251–2257.

(2) "Victim" means an individual against whom the defendant committed an offense for which the court will impose sentence.

(b) Time of Sentencing.

(1) In General. The court must impose sentence without unnecessary delay.

(2) Changing Time Limits. The court may, for good cause, change any time limits prescribed in this rule.

(c) Presentence Investigation.

(1) Required Investigation.

(A) In General. The probation officer must conduct a presentence investigation and submit a report to the court before it imposes sentence unless:

(i) 18 U.S.C. § 3593(c) or another statute requires otherwise; or

(ii) the court finds that the information in the record enables it to meaningfully exercise its sentencing authority under 18 U.S.C. § 3553, and the court explains its finding on the record.

(B) Restitution. If the law requires restitution, the probation officer must conduct an investigation and submit a report that contains sufficient information for the court to order restitution.

(2) Interviewing the Defendant. The probation officer who interviews a defendant as part of a presentence investigation must, on request, give the defendant's attorney notice and a reasonable opportunity to attend the interview.

(d) Presentence Report.

(1) Applying the Sentencing Guidelines. The presentence report must:

(A) identify all applicable guidelines and policy statements of the Sentencing Commission;

(B) calculate the defendant's offense level and criminal history category;

(C) state the resulting sentencing range and kinds of sentences available;

(D) identify any factor relevant to:

(i) the appropriate kind of sentence, or

(ii) the appropriate sentence within the applicable sentencing range; and

(E) identify any basis for departing from the applicable sentencing range.

(2) Additional Information. The presentence report must also contain the following information:

(A) the defendant's history and characteristics, including:

(i) any prior criminal record;

(ii) the defendant's financial condition; and

(iii) any circumstances affecting the defendant's behavior that may be helpful in imposing sentence or in correctional treatment;

(B) verified information, stated in a nonargumentative style, that assesses the financial, social, psychological, and medical impact on any individual against whom the offense has been committed;

(C) when appropriate, the nature and extent of nonprison programs and resources available to the defendant;

(D) when the law provides for restitution, information sufficient for a restitution order;

(E) if the court orders a study under 18 U.S.C. § 3552(b), any resulting report and recommendation; and

(F) any other information that the court requires, including information relevant to the factors under 18 U.S.C. § 3553(a).

(3) Exclusions. The presentence report must exclude the following:

(A) any diagnoses that, if disclosed, might seriously disrupt a rehabilitation program;

(B) any sources of information obtained upon a promise of confidentiality; and

(C) any other information that, if disclosed, might result in physical or other harm to the defendant or others.

(e) Disclosing the Report and Recommendation.

(1) Time to Disclose. Unless the defendant has consented in writing, the probation officer must not submit a presentence report to the court or disclose its contents to anyone until the defendant has pleaded guilty or nolo contendere, or has been found guilty.

(2) Minimum Required Notice. The probation officer must give the presentence report to the defendant, the defendant's attorney, and an attorney for the government at least 35 days before sentencing unless the defendant waives this minimum period.

(3) Sentence Recommendation. By local rule or by order in a case, the court may direct the probation officer not to disclose to anyone other than the court the officer's recommendation on the sentence.

(f) Objecting to the Report.

(1) Time to Object. Within 14 days after receiving the presentence report, the parties must state in writing any objections, including objections to material information, sentencing guideline ranges, and policy statements contained in or omitted from the report.

(2) Serving Objections. An objecting party must provide a copy of its objections to the opposing party and to the probation officer.

(3) Action on Objections. After receiving objections, the probation officer may meet with the parties to discuss the objections. The probation officer may then investigate further and revise the presentence report as appropriate.

(g) Submitting the Report. At least 7 days before sentencing, the probation officer must submit to the court and to the parties the presentence report and an addendum containing any unresolved objections, the grounds for those objections, and the probation officer's comments on them.

(h) Notice of Possible Departure from Sentencing Guidelines. Before the court may depart from the applicable sentencing range on a ground not identified for departure either in the presentence report or in a party's prehearing submission, the court must give the parties reasonable notice that it is contemplating such a departure. The notice must specify any ground on which the court is contemplating a departure.

(i) Sentencing.

(1) In General. At sentencing, the court:

(A) must verify that the defendant and the defendant's attorney have read and discussed the presentence report and any addendum to the report;

(B) must give to the defendant and an attorney for the government a written summary of—or summarize in camera—any information excluded from the presentence report under Rule 32(d)(3) on which the court will rely in sentencing, and give them a reasonable opportunity to comment on that information;

(C) must allow the parties' attorneys to comment on the probation officer's determinations and other matters relating to an appropriate sentence; and

(D) may, for good cause, allow a party to make a new objection at any time before sentence is imposed.

(2) Introducing Evidence; Producing a Statement. The court may permit the parties to introduce evidence on the objections. If a witness testifies at sentencing, Rule 26.2(a)–(d) and (f) applies. If a party fails to comply with a Rule 26.2 order to produce a witness's statement, the court must not consider that witness's testimony.

(3) Court Determinations. At sentencing, the court:

(A) may accept any undisputed portion of the presentence report as a finding of fact;

(B) must—for any disputed portion of the presentence report or other controverted matter—rule on the dispute or determine that a ruling is unnecessary either because the matter will not affect sentencing, or because the court will not consider the matter in sentencing; and

(C) must append a copy of the court's determinations under this rule to any copy of the presentence report made available to the Bureau of Prisons.

(4) Opportunity to Speak.

(A) By a Party. Before imposing sentence, the court must:

(i) provide the defendant's attorney an opportunity to speak on the defendant's behalf;

(ii) address the defendant personally in order to permit the defendant to speak or present any information to mitigate the sentence; and

(iii) provide an attorney for the government an opportunity to speak equivalent to that of the defendant's attorney.

(B) By a Victim. Before imposing sentence, the court must address any victim of a crime of violence or sexual abuse who is present at sentencing and must permit the victim to speak or submit any information about the sentence. Whether or not the victim is present, a victim's right to address the court may be exercised by the following persons if present:

(i) a parent or legal guardian, if the victim is younger than 18 years or is incompetent; or

(ii) one or more family members or relatives the court designates, if the victim is deceased or incapacitated.

(C) In Camera Proceedings. Upon a party's motion and for good cause, the court may hear in camera any statement made under Rule 32(i)(4).

(j) Defendant's Right to Appeal.

(1) Advice of a Right to Appeal.

(A) Appealing a Conviction. If the defendant pleaded not guilty and was convicted, after sentencing the court must advise the defendant of the right to appeal the conviction.

(B) Appealing a Sentence. After sentencing—regardless of the defendant's plea—the court must advise the defendant of any right to appeal the sentence.

(C) Appeal Costs. The court must advise a defendant who is unable to pay appeal costs of the right to ask for permission to appeal in forma pauperis.

(2) Clerk's Filing of Notice. If the defendant so requests, the clerk must immediately prepare and file a notice of appeal on the defendant's behalf.

(k) Judgment.

(1) In General. In the judgment of conviction, the court must set forth the plea, the jury verdict or the court's findings, the adjudication, and the sentence. If the defendant is found not guilty or is otherwise entitled to be discharged, the court must so order. The judge must sign the judgment, and the clerk must enter it.

(2) Criminal Forfeiture. Forfeiture procedures are governed by Rule 32.2.

Rule 32.1.   Revoking or Modifying Probation or Supervised Release

(a) Initial Appearance.

(1) Person In Custody. A person held in custody for violating probation or supervised release must be taken without unnecessary delay before a magistrate judge.

(A) If the person is held in custody in the district where an alleged violation occurred, the initial appearance must be in that district.

(B) If the person is held in custody in a district other than where an alleged violation occurred, the initial appearance must be in that district, or in an adjacent district if the appearance can occur more promptly there.

(2) Upon a Summons. When a person appears in response to a summons for violating probation or supervised release, a magistrate judge must proceed under this rule.

(3) Advice. The judge must inform the person of the following:

(A) the alleged violation of probation or supervised release;

(B) the person's right to retain counsel or to request that counsel be appointed if the person cannot obtain counsel; and

(C) the person's right, if held in custody, to a preliminary hearing under Rule 32.1(b)(1).

(4) Appearance in the District With Jurisdiction. If the person is arrested or appears in the district that has jurisdiction to conduct a revocation hearing—either originally or by transfer of jurisdiction—the court must proceed under Rule 32.1(b)–(e).

(5) Appearance in a District Lacking Jurisdiction. If the person is arrested or appears in a district that does not have jurisdiction to conduct a revocation hearing, the magistrate judge must:

(A) if the alleged violation occurred in the district of arrest, conduct a preliminary hearing under Rule 32.1(b) and either:

(i) transfer the person to the district that has jurisdiction, if the judge finds probable cause to believe that a violation occurred; or

(ii) dismiss the proceedings and so notify the court that has jurisdiction, if the judge finds no probable cause to believe that a violation occurred; or

(B) if the alleged violation did not occur in the district of arrest, transfer the person to the district that has jurisdiction if:

(i) the government produces certified copies of the judgment, warrant, and warrant application or produces copies of those certified documents by reliable electronic means; and

(ii) the judge finds that the person is the same person named in the warrant.

(6) Release or Detention. The magistrate judge may release or detain the person under 18 U.S.C. § 3143(a) pending further proceedings. The burden of establishing that the person will not flee or pose a danger to any other person or to the community rests with the person.

(b) Revocation.

(1) Preliminary Hearing.

(A) In General. If a person is in custody for violating a condition of probation or supervised release, a magistrate judge must promptly conduct a hearing to determine whether there is probable cause to believe that a violation occurred. The person may waive the hearing.

(B) Requirements. The hearing must be recorded by a court reporter or by a suitable recording device. The judge must give the person:

(i) notice of the hearing and its purpose, the alleged violation, and the person's right to retain counsel or to request that counsel be appointed if the person cannot obtain counsel;

(ii) an opportunity to appear at the hearing and present evidence; and

(iii) upon request, an opportunity to question any adverse witness, unless the judge determines that the interest of justice does not require the witness to appear.

(C) Referral. If the judge finds probable cause, the judge must conduct a revocation hearing. If the judge does not find probable cause, the judge must dismiss the proceeding.

(2) Revocation Hearing. Unless waived by the person, the court must hold the revocation hearing within a reasonable time in the district having jurisdiction. The person is entitled to:

(A) written notice of the alleged violation;

(B) disclosure of the evidence against the person;

(C) an opportunity to appear, present evidence, and question any adverse witness unless the court determines that the interest of justice does not require the witness to appear;

(D) notice of the person's right to retain counsel or to request that counsel be appointed if the person cannot obtain counsel; and

(E) an opportunity to make a statement and present any information in mitigation.

(c) Modification.

(1) In General. Before modifying the conditions of probation or supervised release, the court must hold a hearing, at which the person has the right to counsel and an opportunity to make a statement and present any information in mitigation.

(2) Exceptions. A hearing is not required if:

(A) the person waives the hearing; or

(B) the relief sought is favorable to the person and does not extend the term of probation or of supervised release; and

(C) an attorney for the government has received notice of the relief sought, has had a reasonable opportunity to object, and has not done so.

(d) Disposition of the Case. The court's disposition of the case is governed by 18 U.S.C. § 3563 and § 3565 (probation) and § 3583 (supervised release).

(e) Producing a Statement. Rule 26.2(a)–(d) and (f) applies at a hearing under this rule. If a party fails to comply with a Rule 26.2 order to produce a witness's statement, the court must not consider that witness's testimony.

Rule 32.2. Criminal Forfeiture

(a) Notice to the Defendant. A court must not enter a judgment of forfeiture in a criminal proceeding unless the indictment or information contains notice to the defendant that the government will seek the forfeiture of property as part of any sentence in accordance with the applicable statute.

(b) Entering a Preliminary Order of Forfeiture.

(1) In General. As soon as practicable after a verdict or finding of guilty, or after a plea of guilty or nolo contendere is accepted, on any count in an indictment or information regarding which criminal forfeiture is sought, the court must determine what property is subject to forfeiture under the applicable statute. If the government seeks forfeiture of specific property, the court must determine whether the government has established the requisite nexus between the property and the offense. If the government seeks a personal money judgment, the court must determine the amount of money that the defendant will be ordered to pay. The court's determination may be based on evidence already in the record, including any written plea agreement or, if the forfeiture is contested, on evidence or information presented by the parties at a hearing after the verdict or finding of guilt.

(2) Preliminary Order. If the court finds that property is subject to forfeiture, it must promptly enter a preliminary order of forfeiture setting forth the amount of any money judgment or directing the forfeiture of specific property without regard to any third party's interest in all or part of it. Determining whether a third party has such an interest must be deferred until any third party files a claim in an ancillary proceeding under Rule 32.2(c).

(3) Seizing Property. The entry of a preliminary order of forfeiture authorizes the Attorney General (or a designee) to seize the specific property subject to forfeiture; to conduct any discovery the court considers proper in identifying, locating, or disposing of the property; and to commence proceedings that comply with any statutes governing third-party rights. At sentencing—or at any time before sentencing if the defendant consents—the order of forfeiture becomes final as to the defendant and must be made a part of the sentence and be included in the judgment. The court may include in the order of forfeiture conditions reasonably necessary to preserve the property's value pending any appeal.

(4) Jury Determination. Upon a party's request in a case in which a jury returns a verdict of guilty, the jury must determine whether the government has established the requisite nexus between the property and the offense committed by the defendant.

(c) Ancillary Proceeding; Entering a Final Order of Forfeiture.

(1) In General. If, as prescribed by statute, a third party files a petition asserting an interest in the property to be forfeited, the court must conduct an ancillary proceeding, but no ancillary proceeding is required to the extent that the forfeiture consists of a money judgment.

 (A) In the ancillary proceeding, the court may, on motion, dismiss the petition for lack of standing, for failure to state a claim, or for any other lawful reason. For purposes of the motion, the facts set forth in the petition are assumed to be true.

 (B) After disposing of any motion filed under Rule 32.2(c)(1)(A) and before conducting a hearing on the petition, the court may permit the parties to conduct discovery in accordance with the Federal Rules of Civil Procedure if the court determines that discovery is necessary or desirable to resolve factual issues. When discovery ends, a party may move for summary judgment under Federal Rule of Civil Procedure 56.

(2) Entering a Final Order. When the ancillary proceeding ends, the court must enter a final order of forfeiture by amending the preliminary order as necessary to account for any third-party rights. If no third party files a timely petition, the preliminary order becomes the final order of forfeiture if the court finds that the defendant (or any combination of defendants convicted in the case) had an interest in the property that is forfeitable under the applicable statute. The defendant may not object to the entry of the final order on the ground that the property belongs, in whole or in part, to a codefendant or third party; nor may a third party object to the final order on the ground that the third party had an interest in the property.

(3) Multiple Petitions. If multiple third-party petitions are filed in the same case, an order dismissing or granting one petition is not appealable until rulings are made on all the petitions, unless the court determines that there is no just reason for delay.

(4) Ancillary Proceeding Not Part of Sentencing. An ancillary proceeding is not part of sentencing.

(d) Stay Pending Appeal. If a defendant appeals from a conviction or an order of forfeiture, the court may stay the order of forfeiture on terms appropriate to ensure that the property remains available pending appellate review. A stay does not delay the ancillary proceeding or the determination of a third party's rights or interests. If the court rules in favor of any third party while an appeal is pending, the court may amend the order of forfeiture but must not transfer any property interest to a third party until the decision on appeal becomes final, unless the defendant consents in writing or on the record.

(e) Subsequently Located Property; Substitute Property.

(1) In General. On the government's motion, the court may at any time enter an order of forfeiture or amend an existing order of forfeiture to include property that:

(A) is subject to forfeiture under an existing order of forfeiture but was located and identified after that order was entered; or

(B) is substitute property that qualifies for forfeiture under an applicable statute.

(2) Procedure. If the government shows that the property is subject to forfeiture under Rule 32.2(e)(1), the court must:

(A) enter an order forfeiting that property, or amend an existing preliminary or final order to include it; and

(B) if a third party files a petition claiming an interest in the property, conduct an ancillary proceeding under Rule 32.2(c).

(3) Jury Trial Limited. There is no right to a jury trial under Rule 32.2(e).

Rule 33. New Trial

(a) Defendant's Motion. Upon the defendant's motion, the court may vacate any judgment and grant a new trial if the interest of justice so requires. If the case was tried without a jury, the court may take additional testimony and enter a new judgment.

(b) Time to File.

(1) Newly Discovered Evidence. Any motion for a new trial grounded on newly discovered evidence must be filed within 3 years after the verdict or finding of guilty. If an appeal is pending, the court may not grant a motion for a new trial until the appellate court remands the case.

(2) Other Grounds. Any motion for a new trial grounded on any reason other than newly discovered evidence must be filed within 7 days after the verdict or finding of guilty.

Rule 34. Arresting Judgment

(a) In General. Upon the defendant's motion or on its own, the court must arrest judgment if:

(1) the indictment or information does not charge an offense; or

(2) the court does not have jurisdiction of the charged offense.

(b) Time to File. The defendant must move to arrest judgment within 7 days after the court accepts a verdict or finding of guilty, or after a plea of guilty or nolo contendere.

Rule 35. Correcting or Reducing a Sentence

(a) Correcting Clear Error. Within 7 days after sentencing, the court may correct a sentence that resulted from arithmetical, technical, or other clear error.

(b) Reducing a Sentence for Substantial Assistance.

(1) In General. Upon the government's motion made within one year of sentencing, the court may reduce a sentence if the defendant, after sentencing, provided substantial assistance in investigating or prosecuting another person.

(2) Later Motion. Upon the government's motion made more than one year after sentencing, the court may reduce a sentence if the defendant's substantial assistance involved:

(A) information not known to the defendant until one year or more after sentencing;

(B) information provided by the defendant to the government within one year of sentencing, but which did not become useful to the government until more than one year after sentencing; or

(C) information the usefulness of which could not reasonably have been anticipated by the defendant until more than one year after sentencing and which was promptly provided to the government after its usefulness was reasonably apparent to the defendant.

(3) Evaluating Substantial Assistance. In evaluating whether the defendant has provided substantial assistance, the court may consider the defendant's presentence assistance.

(4) Below Statutory Minimum. When acting under Rule 35(b), the court may reduce the sentence to a level below the minimum sentence established by statute.

(c) "Sentencing" Defined. As used in this rule, "sentencing" means the oral announcement of the sentence.

Rule 36. Clerical Error

After giving any notice it considers appropriate, the court may at any time correct a clerical error in a judgment, order, or other part of the record, or correct an error in the record arising from oversight or omission.

Rule 37. [Reserved]

Rule 38. Staying a Sentence or a Disability

(a) Death Sentence. The court must stay a death sentence if the defendant appeals the conviction or sentence.

(b) Imprisonment.

(1) Stay Granted. If the defendant is released pending appeal, the court must stay a sentence of imprisonment.

(2) Stay Denied; Place of Confinement. If the defendant is not released pending appeal, the court may recommend to the Attorney General that the defendant be confined near the place of the trial or appeal for a period reasonably necessary to permit the defendant to assist in preparing the appeal.

(c) Fine. If the defendant appeals, the district court, or the court of appeals under Federal Rule of Appellate Procedure 8, may stay a sentence to pay a fine or a fine and costs. The court may stay the sentence on any terms considered appropriate and may require the defendant to:

(1) deposit all or part of the fine and costs into the district court's registry pending appeal;

(2) post a bond to pay the fine and costs; or

(3) submit to an examination concerning the defendant's assets and, if appropriate, order the defendant to refrain from dissipating assets.

(d) Probation. If the defendant appeals, the court may stay a sentence of probation. The court must set the terms of any stay.

(e) Restitution and Notice to Victims.

(1) In General. If the defendant appeals, the district court, or the court of appeals under Federal Rule of Appellate Procedure 8, may stay—on any terms considered appropriate—any sentence providing for restitution under 18 U.S.C. § 3556 or notice under 18 U.S.C. § 3555.

(2) Ensuring Compliance. The court may issue any order reasonably necessary to ensure compliance with a restitution order or a notice order after disposition of an appeal, including:

(A) a restraining order;

(B) an injunction;

(C) an order requiring the defendant to deposit all or part of any monetary restitution into the district court's registry; or

(D) an order requiring the defendant to post a bond.

(f) Forfeiture. A stay of a forfeiture order is governed by Rule 32.2(d).

(g) Disability. If the defendant's conviction or sentence creates a civil or employment disability under federal law, the district court, or the court of appeals under Federal Rule of Appellate Procedure 8, may stay the disability pending appeal on any terms considered appropriate. The court may issue any order reasonably necessary to protect the interest represented by the disability pending appeal, including a restraining order or an injunction.

Rule 39. [Reserved]

Rule 40. Arrest for Failing to Appear in Another District

(a) In General. A person must be taken without unnecessary delay before a magistrate judge in the district of arrest if the person has been arrested under a warrant issued in another district for:

(i) failing to appear as required by the terms of that person's release under 18 U.S.C. §§ 3141–3156 or by a subpoena; or

(ii) violating conditions of release set in another district.

(b) Proceedings. The judge must proceed under Rule 5(c)(3) as applicable.

(c) Release or Detention Order. The judge may modify any previous release or detention order issued in another district, but must state in writing the reasons for doing so.

Rule 41. Search and Seizure

(a) Scope and Definitions.

(1) Scope. This rule does not modify any statute regulating search or seizure, or the issuance and execution of a search warrant in special circumstances.

(2) Definitions. The following definitions apply under this rule:

(A) "Property" includes documents, books, papers, any other tangible objects, and information.

(B) "Daytime" means the hours between 6:00 a.m. and 10:00 p.m. according to local time.

(C) "Federal law enforcement officer" means a government agent (other than an attorney for the government) who is engaged in enforcing the criminal laws and is within any category of officers authorized by the Attorney General to request a search warrant.

(D) "Domestic terrorism" and "international terrorism" have the meanings set out in 18 U.S.C. § 2331.

(E) "Tracking device" has the meaning set out in 18 U.S.C. § 3117(b).

(b) Authority to Issue a Warrant. At the request of a federal law enforcement officer or an attorney for the government:

(1) a magistrate judge with authority in the district—or if none is reasonably available, a judge of a state court of record in the district—has authority to issue a warrant to search for and seize a person or property located within the district;

(2) a magistrate judge with authority in the district has authority to issue a warrant for a person or property outside the district if the person or property is located within the district when the warrant is issued but might move or be moved outside the district before the warrant is executed; and

(3) a magistrate judge—in an investigation of domestic terrorism or international terrorism—with authority in any district in which activities related to the terrorism may have occurred has authority to issue a warrant for a person or property within or outside that district; and

(4) a magistrate judge with authority in the district has authority to issue a warrant to install within the district a tracking device; the warrant may authorize use of the device to track the movement of a person or property located within the district, outside the district, or both.

(c) Persons or Property Subject to Search or Seizure. A warrant may be issued for any of the following:

(1) evidence of a crime;

(2) contraband, fruits of crime, or other items illegally possessed;

(3) property designed for use, intended for use, or used in committing a crime; or

(4) a person to be arrested or a person who is unlawfully restrained.

(d) Obtaining a Warrant.

(1) In General. After receiving an affidavit or other information, a magistrate judge—or if authorized by Rule 41(b), a judge of a state court of record—must issue the warrant if there is probable cause to search for and seize a person or property or to install and use a tracking device.

(2) Requesting a Warrant in the Presence of a Judge.

(A) Warrant on an Affidavit. When a federal law enforcement officer or an attorney for the government presents an affidavit in support of a warrant, the judge may require the affiant to appear personally and may examine under oath the affiant and any witness the affiant produces.

(B) Warrant on Sworn Testimony. The judge may wholly or partially dispense with a written affidavit and base a warrant on sworn testimony if doing so is reasonable under the circumstances.

(C) Recording Testimony. Testimony taken in support of a warrant must be recorded by a court reporter or by a suitable recording device, and the judge must file the transcript or recording with the clerk, along with any affidavit.

(3) Requesting a Warrant by Telephonic or Other Means.

(A) In General. A magistrate judge may issue a warrant based on information communicated by telephone or other reliable electronic means.

(B) Recording Testimony. Upon learning that an applicant is requesting a warrant under Rule 41(d)(3)(A), a magistrate judge must:

> **(i)** place under oath the applicant and any person on whose testimony the application is based; and

> **(ii)** make a verbatim record of the conversation with a suitable recording device, if available, or by a court reporter, or in writing.

(C) Certifying Testimony. The magistrate judge must have any recording or court reporter's notes transcribed, certify the transcription's accuracy, and file a copy of the record and the transcription with the clerk. Any written verbatim record must be signed by the magistrate judge and filed with the clerk.

(D) Suppression Limited. Absent a finding of bad faith, evidence obtained from a warrant issued under Rule 41(d)(3)(A) is not subject to suppression on the ground that issuing the warrant in that manner was unreasonable under the circumstances.

(e) Issuing the Warrant.

(1) In General. The magistrate judge or a judge of a state court of record must issue the warrant to an officer authorized to execute it.

(2) Contents of the Warrant.

(A) Warrant to Search for and Seize a Person or Property. Except for a tracking-device warrant, the warrant must identify the person or property to be searched, identify any person or property to be seized, and designate the magistrate judge to whom it must be returned. The warrant must command the officer to:

> **(i)** execute the warrant within a specified time no longer than 10 days;

> **(ii)** execute the warrant during the daytime, unless the judge for good cause expressly authorizes execution at another time; and

> **(iii)** return the warrant to the magistrate judge designated in the warrant.

(B) Warrant for a Tracking Device. A tracking-device warrant must identify the person or property to be tracked, designate the magistrate judge to whom it must be returned, and specify a reasonable length of time that the device may be used. The time must not exceed 45 days from the date the warrant was issued. The court may, for good cause, grant one or more extensions for a reasonable period not to exceed 45 days each. The warrant must command the officer to:

> **(i)** complete any installation authorized by the warrant within a specified time no longer than 10 calendar days;

(ii) perform any installation authorized by the warrant during the daytime, unless the judge for good cause expressly authorizes installation at another time; and

(iii) return the warrant to the judge designated in the warrant.

(3) Warrant by Telephonic or Other Means. If a magistrate judge decides to proceed under Rule 41(d)(3)**(A)**, the following additional procedures apply:

(A) Preparing a Proposed Duplicate Original Warrant. The applicant must prepare a "proposed duplicate original warrant" and must read or otherwise transmit the contents of that document verbatim to the magistrate judge.

(B) Preparing an Original Warrant. If the applicant reads the contents of the proposed duplicate original warrant, the magistrate judge must enter those contents into an original warrant. If the applicant transmits the contents by reliable electronic means, that transmission may serve as the original warrant.

(C) Modification. The magistrate judge may modify the original warrant. The judge must transmit any modified warrant to the applicant by reliable electronic means under Rule 41(e)(3)(D) or direct the applicant to modify the proposed duplicate original warrant accordingly.

(D) Signing the Warrant. Upon determining to issue the warrant, the magistrate judge must immediately sign the original warrant, enter on its face the exact date and time it is issued, and transmit it by reliable electronic means to the applicant or direct the applicant to sign the judge's name on the duplicate original warrant.

(f) Executing and Returning the Warrant.

(1) Warrant to Search for and Seize a Person or Property.

(A) Noting the Time. The officer executing the warrant must enter on it the exact date and time it was executed.

(B) Inventory. An officer present during the execution of the warrant must prepare and verify an inventory of any property seized. The officer must do so in the presence of another officer and the person from whom, or from whose premises, the property was taken. If either one is not present, the officer must prepare and verify the inventory in the presence of at least one other credible person.

(C) Receipt. The officer executing the warrant must give a copy of the warrant and a receipt for the property taken to the person from whom, or from whose premises, the property was taken or leave a copy of the warrant and receipt at the place where the officer took the property.

(D) Return. The officer executing the warrant must promptly return it—together with a copy of the inventory—to the magistrate judge designated on the warrant. The judge must, on request, give a copy of the inventory to the person from whom, or from whose premises, the property was taken and to the applicant for the warrant.

(2) Warrant for a Tracking Device.

(A) Noting the Time. The officer executing a tracking-device warrant must enter on it the exact date and time the device was installed and the period during which it was used.

(B) Return. Within 10 calendar days after the use of the tracking device has ended, the officer executing the warrant must return it to the judge designated in the warrant.

(C) Service. Within 10 calendar days after the use of the tracking device has ended, the officer executing a tracking-device warrant must serve a copy of the warrant on the person who was tracked or whose property was tracked. Service may be accomplished by delivering a copy to the person who, or whose property, was tracked; or by leaving a copy at the person's residence or usual place of abode with an individual of suitable age and discretion who resides at that location and by mailing a copy to the person's last known address. Upon request of the government, the judge may delay notice as provided in Rule 41(f)(3).

(3) Delayed Notice. Upon the government's request, a magistrate judge—or if authorized by Rule 41(b), a judge of a state court of record—may delay any notice required by this rule if the delay is authorized by statute.

(g) Motion to Return Property. A person aggrieved by an unlawful search and seizure of property or by the deprivation of property may move for the property's return. The motion must be filed in the district where the property was seized. The court must receive evidence on any factual issue necessary to decide the motion. If it grants the motion, the court must return the property to the movant, but may impose reasonable conditions to protect access to the property and its use in later proceedings.

(h) Motion to Suppress. A defendant may move to suppress evidence in the court where the trial will occur, as Rule 12 provides.

(i) Forwarding Papers to the Clerk. The magistrate judge to whom the warrant is returned must attach to the warrant a copy of the return, of the inventory, and of all other related papers and must deliver them to the clerk in the district where the property was seized.

Rule 42. Criminal Contempt

(a) Disposition After Notice. Any person who commits criminal contempt may be punished for that contempt after prosecution on notice.

(1) Notice. The court must give the person notice in open court, in an order to show cause, or in an arrest order. The notice must:

(A) state the time and place of the trial;

(B) allow the defendant a reasonable time to prepare a defense; and

(C) state the essential facts constituting the charged criminal contempt and describe it as such.

(2) Appointing a Prosecutor. The court must request that the contempt be prosecuted by an attorney for the government, unless the interest of justice requires the appointment of another attorney. If the government declines the request, the court must appoint another attorney to prosecute the contempt.

(3) Trial and Disposition. A person being prosecuted for criminal contempt is entitled to a jury trial in any case in which federal law so provides and must be released or detained as Rule 46 provides. If the criminal contempt involves disrespect toward or criticism of a judge, that judge is disqualified from presiding at the contempt trial or hearing unless the defendant consents. Upon a finding or verdict of guilty, the court must impose the punishment.

(b) Summary Disposition. Notwithstanding any other provision of these rules, the court (other than a magistrate judge) may summarily punish a person who commits criminal contempt in its presence if the judge saw or heard the contemptuous conduct and so certifies; a magistrate judge may summarily punish a person as provided in 28 U.S.C. § 636(e). The contempt order must recite the facts, be signed by the judge, and be filed with the clerk.

Rule 43.   Defendant's Presence

(a) When Required. Unless this rule, Rule 5, or Rule 10 provides otherwise, the defendant must be present at:

(1) the initial appearance, the initial arraignment, and the plea;

(2) every trial stage, including jury impanelment and the return of the verdict; and

(3) sentencing.

(b) When Not Required. A defendant need not be present under any of the following circumstances:

(1) Organizational Defendant. The defendant is an organization represented by counsel who is present.

(2) Misdemeanor Offense. The offense is punishable by fine or by imprisonment for not more than one year, or both, and with the defendant's written consent, the court permits arraignment, plea, trial, and sentencing to occur in the defendant's absence.

(3) Conference or Hearing on a Legal Question. The proceeding involves only a conference or hearing on a question of law.

(4) Sentence Correction. The proceeding involves the correction or reduction of sentence under Rule 35 or 18 U.S.C. § 3582(c).

(c) Waiving Continued Presence.

(1) In General. A defendant who was initially present at trial, or who had pleaded guilty or nolo contendere, waives the right to be present under the following circumstances:

(A) when the defendant is voluntarily absent after the trial has begun, regardless of whether the court informed the defendant of an obligation to remain during trial;

(B) in a noncapital case, when the defendant is voluntarily absent during sentencing; or

(C) when the court warns the defendant that it will remove the defendant from the courtroom for disruptive behavior, but the defendant persists in conduct that justifies removal from the courtroom.

(2) Waiver's Effect. If the defendant waives the right to be present, the trial may proceed to completion, including the verdict's return and sentencing, during the defendant's absence.

Rule 44.   Right to and Appointment of Counsel

(a) Right to Appointed Counsel. A defendant who is unable to obtain counsel is entitled to have counsel appointed to represent the defendant at every stage of the proceeding from initial appearance through appeal, unless the defendant waives this right.

(b) Appointment Procedure. Federal law and local court rules govern the procedure for implementing the right to counsel.

(c) Inquiry Into Joint Representation.

(1) Joint Representation. Joint representation occurs when:

(A) two or more defendants have been charged jointly under Rule 8(b) or have been joined for trial under Rule 13; and

(B) the defendants are represented by the same counsel, or counsel who are associated in law practice.

(2) Court's Responsibilities in Cases of Joint Representation. The court must promptly inquire about the propriety of joint representation and must personally advise each defendant of the right to the effective assistance of counsel, including separate representation. Unless there is good cause to believe that no conflict of interest is likely to arise, the court must take appropriate measures to protect each defendant's right to counsel.

Rule 45.   Computing and Extending Time

(a) Computing Time. The following rules apply in computing any period of time specified in these rules, any local rule, or any court order:

(1) Day of the Event Excluded. Exclude the day of the act, event, or default that begins the period.

(2) Exclusion from Brief Periods. Exclude intermediate Saturdays, Sundays, and legal holidays when the period is less than 11 days.

(3) Last Day. Include the last day of the period unless it is a Saturday, Sunday, legal holiday, or day on which weather or other conditions make the clerk's office inaccessible. When the last day is excluded, the period runs until the end of the next day that is not a

Saturday, Sunday, legal holiday, or day when the clerk's office is inaccessible.

(4) "Legal Holiday" Defined. As used in this rule, "legal holiday" means:

(A) the day set aside by statute for observing:

(i) New Year's Day;

(ii) Martin Luther King, Jr.'s Birthday;

(iii) Washington's Birthday;

(iv) Memorial Day;

(v) Independence Day;

(vi) Labor Day;

(vii) Columbus Day;

(viii) Veterans' Day;

(ix) Thanksgiving Day;

(x) Christmas Day; and

(B) any other day declared a holiday by the President, the Congress, or the state where the district court is held.

(b) Extending Time.

(1) In General. When an act must or may be done within a specified period, the court on its own may extend the time, or for good cause may do so on a party's motion made:

(A) before the originally prescribed or previously extended time expires; or

(B) after the time expires if the party failed to act because of excusable neglect.

(2) Exception. The court may not extend the time to take any action under Rule 35, except as stated in that rule.

(c) Additional Time After Certain Kinds of Service. Whenever a party must or may act within a specified period after service and service is made in the manner provided under Federal Rule of Civil Procedure 5(b)(2)(B), (C), or (D), 3 days are added after the period would otherwise expire under subdivision (a).

Rule 46.   Release from Custody; Supervising Detention

(a) Before Trial. The provisions of 18 U.S.C. §§ 3142 and 3144 govern pretrial release.

(b) During Trial. A person released before trial continues on release during trial under the same terms and conditions. But the court may order different terms and conditions or terminate the release if necessary to ensure that the person will be present during trial or that the person's conduct will not obstruct the orderly and expeditious progress of the trial.

(c) Pending Sentencing or Appeal. The provisions of 18 U.S.C. § 3143 govern release pending sentencing or appeal. The burden of establishing that the defendant will not flee or pose a danger to any other person or to the community rests with the defendant.

(d) Pending Hearing on a Violation of Probation or Supervised Release. Rule 32.1(a)(6) governs release pending a hearing on a violation of probation or supervised release.

(e) Surety. The court must not approve a bond unless any surety appears to be qualified. Every surety, except a legally approved corporate surety, must demonstrate by affidavit that its assets are adequate. The court may require the affidavit to describe the following:

>   **(1)** the property that the surety proposes to use as security;

>   **(2)** any encumbrance on that property;

>   **(3)** the number and amount of any other undischarged bonds and bail undertakings the surety has issued; and

>   **(4)** any other liability of the surety.

(f) Bail Forfeiture.

>   **(1) Declaration.** The court must declare the bail forfeited if a condition of the bond is breached.

>   **(2) Setting Aside.** The court may set aside in whole or in part a bail forfeiture upon any condition the court may impose if:

>>   **(A)** the surety later surrenders into custody the person released on the surety's appearance bond; or

>>   **(B)** it appears that justice does not require bail forfeiture.

>   **(3) Enforcement.**

>>   **(A) Default Judgment and Execution.** If it does not set aside a bail forfeiture, the court must, upon the government's motion, enter a default judgment.

>>   **(B) Jurisdiction and Service.** By entering into a bond, each surety submits to the district court's jurisdiction and irrevocably appoints the district clerk as its agent to receive service of any filings affecting its liability.

>>   **(C) Motion to Enforce.** The court may, upon the government's motion, enforce the surety's liability without an independent action. The government must serve any motion, and notice as the court prescribes, on the district clerk. If so served, the clerk must promptly mail a copy to the surety at its last known address.

>   **(4) Remission.** After entering a judgment under Rule 46(f)(3), the court may remit in whole or in part the judgment under the same conditions specified in Rule 46(f)(2).

(g) Exoneration. The court must exonerate the surety and release any bail when a bond condition has been satisfied or when the court has set aside or remitted the forfeiture. The court must exonerate a surety who deposits cash in the amount of the bond or timely surrenders the defendant into custody.

(h) Supervising Detention Pending Trial.

(1) In General. To eliminate unnecessary detention, the court must supervise the detention within the district of any defendants awaiting trial and of any persons held as material witnesses.

(2) Reports. An attorney for the government must report biweekly to the court, listing each material witness held in custody for more than 10 days pending indictment, arraignment, or trial. For each material witness listed in the report, an attorney for the government must state why the witness should not be released with or without a deposition being taken under Rule 15(a).

(i) Forfeiture of Property. The court may dispose of a charged offense by ordering the forfeiture of 18 U.S.C. § 3142(c)(1)(B)(xi) property under 18 U.S.C. § 3146(d), if a fine in the amount of the property's value would be an appropriate sentence for the charged offense.

(j) Producing a Statement.

(1) In General. Rule 26.2(a)–(d) and (f) applies at a detention hearing under 18 U.S.C. § 3142, unless the court for good cause rules otherwise.

(2) Sanctions for Not Producing a Statement. If a party disobeys a Rule 26.2 order to produce a witness's statement, the court must not consider that witness's testimony at the detention hearing.

Rule 47.   Motions and Supporting Affidavits

(a) In General. A party applying to the court for an order must do so by motion.

(b) Form and Content of a Motion. A motion—except when made during a trial or hearing—must be in writing, unless the court permits the party to make the motion by other means. A motion must state the grounds on which it is based and the relief or order sought. A motion may be supported by affidavit.

(c) Timing of a Motion. A party must serve a written motion—other than one that the court may hear ex parte—and any hearing notice at least 5 days before the hearing date, unless a rule or court order sets a different period. For good cause, the court may set a different period upon ex parte application.

(d) Affidavit Supporting a Motion. The moving party must serve any supporting affidavit with the motion. A responding party must serve any opposing affidavit at least one day before the hearing, unless the court permits later service.

Rule 48.   Dismissal

(a) By the Government. The government may, with leave of court, dismiss an indictment, information, or complaint. The government may not dismiss the prosecution during trial without the defendant's consent.

(b) By the Court. The court may dismiss an indictment, information, or complaint if unnecessary delay occurs in:

(1) presenting a charge to a grand jury;

(2) filing an information against a defendant; or

(3) bringing a defendant to trial.

Rule 49.   Serving and Filing Papers

(a) When Required. A party must serve on every other party any written motion (other than one to be heard ex parte), written notice, designation of the record on appeal, or similar paper.

(b) How Made. Service must be made in the manner provided for a civil action. When these rules or a court order requires or permits service on a party represented by an attorney, service must be made on the attorney instead of the party, unless the court orders otherwise.

(c) Notice of a Court Order. When the court issues an order on any post-arraignment motion, the clerk must provide notice in a manner provided for in a civil action. Except as Federal Rule of Appellate Procedure 4(b) provides otherwise, the clerk's failure to give notice does not affect the time to appeal, or relieve—or authorize the court to relieve—a party's failure to appeal within the allowed time.

(d) Filing. A party must file with the court a copy of any paper the party is required to serve. A paper must be filed in a manner provided for in a civil action.

Rule 49.1.   Privacy Protection for Filings Made with the Court

(a) Redacted Filings. Unless the court orders otherwise, in an electronic or paper filing with the court that contains an individual's social-security number, taxpayer-identification number, or birth date, the name of an individual known to be a minor, a financial-account number, or the home address of an individual, a party or nonparty making the filing may include only:

(1) the last four digits of the social-security number and taxpayer-identification number;

(2) the year of the individual's birth;

(3) the minor's initials;

(4) the last four digits of the financial-account number; and

(5) the city and state of the home address.

(b) Exemptions from the Redaction Requirement. The redaction requirement does not apply to the following:

(1) a financial-account number or real property address that identifies the property allegedly subject to forfeiture in a forfeiture proceeding;

(2) the record of an administrative or agency proceeding;

(3) the official record of a state-court proceeding;

(4) the record of a court or tribunal, if that record was not subject to the redaction requirement when originally filed;

(5) a filing covered by Rule 49.1(d);

(6) a pro se filing in an action brought under 28 U.S.C. §§ 2241, 2254, or 2255;

(7) a court filing that is related to a criminal matter or investigation and that is prepared before the filing of a criminal charge or is not filed as part of any docketed criminal case;

(8) an arrest or search warrant; and

(9) a charging document and an affidavit filed in support of any charging document.

(c) Immigration Cases. A filing in an action brought under 28 U.S.C. § 2241 that relates to the petitioner's immigration rights is governed by Federal Rule of Civil Procedure 5.2.

(d) Filings Made Under Seal. The court may order that a filing be made under seal without redaction. The court may later unseal the filing or order the person who made the filing to file a redacted version for the public record.

(e) Protective Orders. For good cause, the court may by order in a case:

(1) require redaction of additional information; or

(2) limit or prohibit a nonparty's remote electronic access to a document filed with the court.

(f) Option for Additional Unredacted Filing Under Seal. A person making a redacted filing may also file an unredacted copy under seal. The court must retain the unredacted copy as part of the record.

(g) Option for Filing a Reference List. A filing that contains redacted information may be filed together with a reference list that identifies each item of redacted information and specifies an appropriate identifier that uniquely corresponds to each item listed. The list must be filed under seal and may be amended as of right. Any reference in the case to a listed identifier will be construed to refer to the corresponding item of information.

(h) Waiver of Protection of Identifiers. A person waives the protection of Rule 49.1(a) as to the person's own information by filing it without redaction and not under seal.

Rule 50.   Prompt Disposition

Scheduling preference must be given to criminal proceedings as far as practicable.

Rule 51.   Preserving Claimed Error

(a) Exceptions Unnecessary. Exceptions to rulings or orders of the court are unnecessary.

(b) Preserving a Claim of Error. A party may preserve a claim of error by informing the court—when the court ruling or order is made or sought—of the action the party wishes the court to take, or the party's objection to the court's action and the grounds for that objection. If a party does not have an opportunity to object to a ruling or order, the absence of an objection does not later prejudice that party. A ruling or order that admits or excludes evidence is governed by Federal Rule of Evidence 103.

Rule 52. Harmless and Plain Error

(a) Harmless Error. Any error, defect, irregularity, or variance that does not affect substantial rights must be disregarded.

(b) Plain Error. A plain error that affects substantial rights may be considered even though it was not brought to the court's attention.

Rule 53. Courtroom Photographing and Broadcasting Prohibited

Except as otherwise provided by a statute or these rules, the court must not permit the taking of photographs in the courtroom during judicial proceedings or the broadcasting of judicial proceedings from the courtroom.

Rule 54. [Transferred [1]]

Rule 55. Records

The clerk of the district court must keep records of criminal proceedings in the form prescribed by the Director of the Administrative Office of the United States courts. The clerk must enter in the records every court order or judgment and the date of entry.

Rule 56. When Court Is Open

(a) In General. A district court is considered always open for any filing, and for issuing and returning process, making a motion, or entering an order.

(b) Office Hours. The clerk's office—with the clerk or a deputy in attendance—must be open during business hours on all days except Saturdays, Sundays, and legal holidays.

(c) Special Hours. A court may provide by local rule or order that its clerk's office will be open for specified hours on Saturdays or legal holidays other than those set aside by statute for observing New Year's Day, Martin Luther King, Jr.'s Birthday, Washington's Birthday, Memorial Day, Independence Day, Labor Day, Columbus Day, Veterans' Day, Thanksgiving Day, and Christmas Day.

Rule 57. District Court Rules

(a) In General.

(1) Adopting Local Rules. Each district court acting by a majority of its district judges may, after giving appropriate public notice and an opportunity to comment, make and amend rules governing its practice. A local rule must be consistent with—but not duplicative of—federal statutes and rules adopted under 28 U.S.C. § 2072 and must conform to any uniform numbering system prescribed by the Judicial Conference of the United States.

(2) Limiting Enforcement. A local rule imposing a requirement of form must not be enforced in a manner that causes a party to lose

---

1. All of Rule 54 was moved to Rule 1.

rights because of an unintentional failure to comply with the requirement.

(b) Procedure When There Is No Controlling Law. A judge may regulate practice in any manner consistent with federal law, these rules, and the local rules of the district. No sanction or other disadvantage may be imposed for noncompliance with any requirement not in federal law, federal rules, or the local district rules unless the alleged violator was furnished with actual notice of the requirement before the noncompliance.

(c) Effective Date and Notice. A local rule adopted under this rule takes effect on the date specified by the district court and remains in effect unless amended by the district court or abrogated by the judicial council of the circuit in which the district is located. Copies of local rules and their amendments, when promulgated, must be furnished to the judicial council and the Administrative Office of the United States Courts and must be made available to the public.

Rule 58.   Petty Offenses and Other Misdemeanors

(a) Scope.

(1) In General. These rules apply in petty offense and other misdemeanor cases and on appeal to a district judge in a case tried by a magistrate judge, unless this rule provides otherwise.

(2) Petty Offense Case Without Imprisonment. In a case involving a petty offense for which no sentence of imprisonment will be imposed, the court may follow any provision of these rules that is not inconsistent with this rule and that the court considers appropriate.

(3) Definition. As used in this rule, the term "petty offense for which no sentence of imprisonment will be imposed" means a petty offense for which the court determines that, in the event of conviction, no sentence of imprisonment will be imposed.

(b) Pretrial Procedure.

(1) Charging Document. The trial of a misdemeanor may proceed on an indictment, information, or complaint. The trial of a petty offense may also proceed on a citation or violation notice.

(2) Initial Appearance. At the defendant's initial appearance on a petty offense or other misdemeanor charge, the magistrate judge must inform the defendant of the following:

(A) the charge, and the minimum and maximum penalties, including imprisonment, fines, any special assessment under 18 U.S.C. § 3013, and restitution under 18 U.S.C. § 3556;

(B) the right to retain counsel;

(C) the right to request the appointment of counsel if the defendant is unable to retain counsel—unless the charge is a petty offense for which the appointment of counsel is not required;

(D) the defendant's right not to make a statement, and that any statement made may be used against the defendant;

(E) the right to trial, judgment, and sentencing before a district judge—unless:

(i) the charge is a petty offense; or

(ii) the defendant consents to trial, judgment, and sentencing before a magistrate judge;

(F) the right to a jury trial before either a magistrate judge or a district judge—unless the charge is a petty offense; and

(G) any right to a preliminary hearing under Rule 5.1, and the general circumstances, if any, under which the defendant may secure pretrial release.

(3) Arraignment.

(A) Plea Before a Magistrate Judge. A magistrate judge may take the defendant's plea in a petty offense case. In every other misdemeanor case, a magistrate judge may take the plea only if the defendant consents either in writing or on the record to be tried before a magistrate judge and specifically waives trial before a district judge. The defendant may plead not guilty, guilty, or (with the consent of the magistrate judge) nolo contendere.

(B) Failure to Consent. Except in a petty offense case, the magistrate judge must order a defendant who does not consent to trial before a magistrate judge to appear before a district judge for further proceedings.

(c) Additional Procedures in Certain Petty Offense Cases. The following procedures also apply in a case involving a petty offense for which no sentence of imprisonment will be imposed:

(1) Guilty or Nolo Contendere Plea. The court must not accept a guilty or nolo contendere plea unless satisfied that the defendant understands the nature of the charge and the maximum possible penalty.

(2) Waiving Venue.

(A) Conditions of Waiving Venue. If a defendant is arrested, held, or present in a district different from the one where the indictment, information, complaint, citation, or violation notice is pending, the defendant may state in writing a desire to plead guilty or nolo contendere; to waive venue and trial in the district where the proceeding is pending; and to consent to the court's disposing of the case in the district where the defendant was arrested, is held, or is present.

(B) Effect of Waiving Venue. Unless the defendant later pleads not guilty, the prosecution will proceed in the district where the defendant was arrested, is held, or is present. The district clerk must notify the clerk in the original district of the defendant's waiver of venue. The defendant's statement of a desire to plead guilty or nolo contendere is not admissible against the defendant.

(3) Sentencing. The court must give the defendant an opportunity to be heard in mitigation and then proceed immediately to sentencing.

The court may, however, postpone sentencing to allow the probation service to investigate or to permit either party to submit additional information.

(4) Notice of a Right to Appeal. After imposing sentence in a case tried on a not-guilty plea, the court must advise the defendant of a right to appeal the conviction and of any right to appeal the sentence. If the defendant was convicted on a plea of guilty or nolo contendere, the court must advise the defendant of any right to appeal the sentence.

(d) Paying a Fixed Sum in Lieu of Appearance.

(1) In General. If the court has a local rule governing forfeiture of collateral, the court may accept a fixed-sum payment in lieu of the defendant's appearance and end the case, but the fixed sum may not exceed the maximum fine allowed by law.

(2) Notice to Appear. If the defendant fails to pay a fixed sum, request a hearing, or appear in response to a citation or violation notice, the district clerk or a magistrate judge may issue a notice for the defendant to appear before the court on a date certain. The notice may give the defendant an additional opportunity to pay a fixed sum in lieu of appearance. The district clerk must serve the notice on the defendant by mailing a copy to the defendant's last known address.

(3) Summons or Warrant. Upon an indictment, or upon a showing by one of the other charging documents specified in Rule 58(b)(1) of probable cause to believe that an offense has been committed and that the defendant has committed it, the court may issue an arrest warrant or, if no warrant is requested by an attorney for the government, a summons. The showing of probable cause must be made under oath or under penalty of perjury, but the affiant need not appear before the court. If the defendant fails to appear before the court in response to a summons, the court may summarily issue a warrant for the defendant's arrest.

(e) Recording the Proceedings. The court must record any proceedings under this rule by using a court reporter or a suitable recording device.

(f) New Trial. Rule 33 applies to a motion for a new trial.

(g) Appeal.

(1) From a District Judge's Order or Judgment. The Federal Rules of Appellate Procedure govern an appeal from a district judge's order or a judgment of conviction or sentence.

(2) From a Magistrate Judge's Order or Judgment.

(A) Interlocutory Appeal. Either party may appeal an order of a magistrate judge to a district judge within 10 days of its entry if a district judge's order could similarly be appealed. The party appealing must file a notice with the clerk specifying the order being appealed and must serve a copy on the adverse party.

(B) Appeal from a Conviction or Sentence. A defendant may appeal a magistrate judge's judgment of conviction or sentence to a district judge within 10 days of its entry. To appeal, the defendant must file a notice with the clerk specifying the judgment being appealed and must serve a copy on an attorney for the government.

(C) Record. The record consists of the original papers and exhibits in the case; any transcript, tape, or other recording of the proceedings; and a certified copy of the docket entries. For purposes of the appeal, a copy of the record of the proceedings must be made available to a defendant who establishes by affidavit an inability to pay or give security for the record. The Director of the Administrative Office of the United States Courts must pay for those copies.

(D) Scope of Appeal. The defendant is not entitled to a trial de novo by a district judge. The scope of the appeal is the same as in an appeal to the court of appeals from a judgment entered by a district judge.

(3) Stay of Execution and Release Pending Appeal. Rule 38 applies to a stay of a judgment of conviction or sentence. The court may release the defendant pending appeal under the law relating to release pending appeal from a district court to a court of appeals.

Rule 59.   Matters Before a Magistrate Judge

(a) Nondispositive Matters. A district judge may refer to a magistrate judge for determination any matter that does not dispose of a charge or defense. The magistrate judge must promptly conduct the required proceedings and, when appropriate, enter on the record an oral or written order stating the determination. A party may serve and file objections to the order within 10 days after being served with a copy of a written order or after the oral order is stated on the record, or at some other time the court sets. The district judge must consider timely objections and modify or set aside any part of the order that is contrary to law or clearly erroneous. Failure to object in accordance with this rule waives a party's right to review.

(b) Dispositive Matters.

(1) Referral to Magistrate Judge. A district judge may refer to a magistrate judge for recommendation a defendant's motion to dismiss or quash an indictment or information, a motion to suppress evidence, or any matter that may dispose of a charge or defense. The magistrate judge must promptly conduct the required proceedings. A record must be made of any evidentiary proceeding and of any other proceeding if the magistrate judge considers it necessary. The magistrate judge must enter on the record a recommendation for disposing of the matter, including any proposed findings of fact. The clerk must immediately serve copies on all parties.

(2) Objections to Findings and Recommendations. Within 10 days after being served with a copy of the recommended disposition, or at some other time the court sets, a party may serve and file specific written objections to the proposed findings and recommendations. Unless the district judge directs otherwise, the objecting party must promptly arrange for transcribing the record, or whatever portions of it the parties agree to or the magistrate judge considers sufficient. Failure to object in accordance with this rule waives a party's right to review.

(3) De Novo Review of Recommendations. The district judge must consider de novo any objection to the magistrate judge's recommendation. The district judge may accept, reject, or modify the recommendation, receive further evidence, or resubmit the matter to the magistrate judge with instructions.

Rule 60. Title

These rules may be known and cited as the Federal Rules of Criminal Procedure.

Appendix D

PENDING AMENDMENTS TO FEDERAL RULES OF CRIMINAL PROCEDURE

[These amendments to Rules 1, 12.1, 17, 18, 32, 40, 45 and 60 and new Rule 61 were approved by the Supreme Court April 23, 2008, and were forwarded to Congress. They will take effect on December 1, 2008 unless Congress enacts legislation to reject, modify or defer them.]

Rule 1. Scope; Definitions

* * *

(b) Definitions. The following definitions apply to these rules:

* * *

(11) "Victim" means a "crime victim" as defined in 18 U.S.C. § 3771(e).

* * *

Rule 12.1. Notice of an Alibi Defense

* * *

(b) Disclosing Government Witnesses.

(1) Disclosure.

(A) In General. If the defendant serves a Rule 12.1(a)(2) notice, an attorney for the government must disclose in writing to the defendant or the defendant's attorney:

(i) the name of each witness—and the address and telephone number of each witness other than a victim—that the government intends to rely on to establish that the defendant was present at the scene of the alleged offense; and

(ii) each government rebuttal witness to the defendant's alibi defense.

(B) Victim's Address and Telephone Number. If the government intends to rely on a victim's testimony to establish that the defendant was present at the scene of the alleged offense and the defendant establishes a need for the victim's address and telephone number, the court may:

(i) order the government to provide the information in writing to the defendant or the defendant's attorney; or

(ii) fashion a reasonable procedure that allows preparation of the defense and also protects the victim's interests.

(2) Time to Disclose. Unless the court directs otherwise, an attorney for the government must give its Rule 12.1(b)(1) disclosure within 10 days after the defendant serves notice of an intended alibi defense under Rule 12.1(a)(2), but no later than 10 days before trial.

(c) Continuing Duty to Disclose.

(1) In General. Both an attorney for the government and the defendant must promptly disclose in writing to the other party the name of each additional witness—and the address and telephone number of each additional witness other than a victim—if:

(A) the disclosing party learns of the witness before or during trial; and

(B) the witness should have been disclosed under Rule 12.1(a) or (b) if the disclosing party had known of the witness earlier.

(2) Address and Telephone Number of an Additional Victim Witness. The address and telephone number of an additional victim witness must not be disclosed except as provided in Rule 12.1 (b)(1)(B).

* * *

Rule 17. Subpoena

* * *

(c) Producing Documents and Objects.

* * *

(3) Subpoena for Personal or Confidential Information About a Victim. After a complaint, indictment, or information is filed, a subpoena requiring the production of personal or confidential information about a victim may be served on a third party only by court order. Before entering the order and unless there are exceptional circumstances, the court must require giving notice to the victim so that the victim can move to quash or modify the subpoena or otherwise object.

* * *

Rule 18. Place of Prosecution and Trial

Unless a statute or these rules permit otherwise, the government must prosecute an offense in a district where the offense was committed. The court must set the place of trial within the district with due regard for the convenience of the defendant, any victim, and the witnesses, and the prompt administration of justice.

Rule 32. Sentencing and Judgment

(a) [Reserved.]

* * *

(c) Presentence Investigation.

(1) Required Investigation.

* * *

(B) Restitution. If the law permits restitution, the probation officer must conduct an investigation and submit a report that contains sufficient information for the court to order restitution.

* * *

(d) Presentence Report.

* * *

(2) Additional Information. The presentence report must also contain the following:

(A) the defendant's history and characteristics, including:

(i) any prior criminal record;

(ii) the defendant's financial condition; and

(iii) any circumstances affecting the defendant's behavior that may be helpful in imposing sentence or in correctional treatment;

(B) information that assesses any financial, social, psychological, and medical impact on any victim;

* * *

(i) Sentencing.

* * *

(4) Opportunity to Speak.

(A) By a Party. Before imposing sentence, the court must:

(i) provide the defendant's attorney an opportunity to speak on the defendant's behalf;

(ii) address the defendant personally in order to permit the defendant to speak or present any information to mitigate the sentence; and

(iii) provide an attorney for the government an opportunity to speak equivalent to that of the defendant's attorney.

(B) By a Victim. Before imposing sentence, the court must address any victim of the crime who is present at sentencing and must permit the victim to be reasonably heard.

* * *

Rule 41.   Search and Seizure

* * *

(b) Authority to Issue a Warrant. At the request of a federal law enforcement officer or an attorney for the government:

* * *

(3) a magistrate judge—in an investigation of domestic terrorism or international terrorism—with authority in any district in which activities related to the terrorism may have occurred has authority to issue a warrant for a person or property within or outside that district;

(4) a magistrate judge with authority in the district has authority to issue a warrant to install within the district a tracking device; the warrant may authorize use of the device to track the movement of a person or property located within the district, outside the district, or both; and

(5) a magistrate judge having authority in any district where activities related to the crime may have occurred, or in the District of Columbia, may issue a warrant for property that is located outside the jurisdiction of any state or district, but within any of the following:

(A) a United States territory, possession, or commonwealth;

(B) the premises—no matter who owns them—of a United States diplomatic or consular mission in a foreign state, including any appurtenant building, part of a building, or land used for the mission's purposes; or

(C) a residence and any appurtenant land owned or leased by the United States and used by United States personnel assigned to a United States diplomatic or consular mission in a foreign state.

* * *

Rule 45. Computing and Extending Time

* * *

(c) Additional Time After Certain Kinds of Service. Whenever a party must or may act within a specified period after service and service is made in the manner provided under Federal Rule of Civil Procedure 5(b)(2)(C), (D), (E), or (F), 3 days are added after the period would otherwise expire under subdivision (a).

Rule 60. Victim's Rights

(a) In General.

(1) Notice of a Proceeding. The government must use its best efforts to give the victim reasonable, accurate, and timely notice of any public court proceeding involving the crime.

(2) Attending the Proceeding. The court must not exclude a victim from a public court proceeding involving the crime, unless the court determines by clear and convincing evidence that the victim's testimony would be materially altered if the victim heard other testimony at that proceeding. In determining whether to exclude a victim, the court must make every effort to permit the fullest attendance possible by the victim and must consider reasonable alternatives to exclusion. The reasons for any exclusion must be clearly stated on the record.

(3) Right to Be Heard on Release, a Plea, or Sentencing. The court must permit a victim to be reasonably heard at any public proceeding in the district court concerning release, plea, or sentencing involving the crime.

(b) Enforcement and Limitations.

(1) Time for Deciding a Motion. The court must promptly decide any motion asserting a victim's rights described in these rules.

(2) Who May Assert the Rights. A victim's rights described in these rules may be asserted by the victim, the victim's lawful representative, the attorney for the government, or any other person as authorized by 18 U.S.C. § 3771(d) and (e).

(3) Multiple Victims. If the court finds that the number of victims makes it impracticable to accord all of them their rights described in these rules, the court must fashion a reasonable procedure that gives effect to these rights without unduly complicating or prolonging the proceedings.

(4) Where Rights May Be Asserted. A victim's rights described in these rules must be asserted in the district where a defendant is being prosecuted for the crime.

(5) Limitations on Relief. A victim may move to reopen a plea or sentence only if:

    (A) the victim asked to be heard before or during the proceeding at issue, and the request was denied;

    (B) the victim petitions the court of appeals for a writ of mandamus within 10 days after the denial, and the writ is granted; and

    (C) in the case of a plea, the accused has not pleaded to the highest offense charged.

(6) No New Trial. A failure to afford a victim any right described in these rules is not grounds for a new trial.

Rule 61. Title

These rules may be known and cited as the Federal Rules of Criminal Procedure.

Appendix E

PROPOSED AMENDMENTS TO THE FEDERAL RULES OF CRIMINAL PROCEDURE

[These proposed amendments to Rules 7, 32, 32.2 and 41 have been circulated to bench and bar for comment. If all further approvals occur, they would probably take effect in December 2009. New material is underlined; matter to be omitted is lined through.]

Rule 7.   The Indictment and the Information

* * *

(c) Nature and Contents.

* * *

(2) *Criminal Forfeiture.* No judgment of forfeiture may be entered in a criminal proceeding unless the indictment or the information provides notice that the defendant has an interest in property that is subject to forfeiture in accordance with the applicable statute.

(3)(2) *Citation Error.* Unless the defendant was misled and thereby prejudiced, neither an error in a citation nor a citation's omission is a ground to dismiss the indictment or information or to reverse a conviction.

Rule 32.   Sentence and Judgment

* * *

(d) Presentence Report.

* * *

(2) *Additional Information.* The presentence report must also contain the following information:

(A) the defendant's history and characteristics, including:

(i) any prior criminal record;

(ii) the defendant's financial condition; and

(iii) any circumstances affecting the defendant's behavior that may be helpful in imposing sentence or in correctional treatment;

(B) verified information, stated in a nonargumentative style, that assesses the financial, social, psychological, and medical impact on any individual against whom the offense has been committed;

(C) when appropriate, the nature and extent of nonprison programs and resources available to the defendant;

(D) when the law provides for restitution, information sufficient for a restitution order;

(E) if the court orders a study under 18 U.S.C. § 3552(b), any resulting report and recommendation; ~~and~~

(F) any other information that the court requires, including information relevant to the factors under 18 U.S.C. § 3553(a); and

(G) whether the Government seeks forfeiture under Rule 32.2.

* * *

Rule 32.2. Criminal Forfeiture

(a) Notice to the Defendant. A court must not enter a judgment of forfeiture in a criminal proceeding unless the indictment or information contains notice to the defendant that the government will seek the forfeiture of property as part of any sentence in accordance with the applicable statute. The notice should not be designated as a count of the indictment or information. The indictment or information need not identify the property subject to forfeiture or specify the amount of any forfeiture money judgment that the government seeks.

(b) Entering a Preliminary Order of Forfeiture

(1) ~~*In General.*~~ *Forfeiture Phase of the Trial.*

(A) *Forfeiture Determinations.* As soon as practical after a verdict or finding of guilty,—or after a plea of guilty or nolo contendere is accepted,—on any count in an indictment or information on ~~regarding~~ which criminal forfeiture is sought, the court must determine what property is subject to forfeiture under the applicable statute. If the government seeks forfeiture of specific property, the court must determine whether the government has established the requisite nexus between the property and the offense. If the government seeks a personal money judgment, the court must determine the amount of money that the defendant will be ordered to pay.

(B) *Evidence and Hearing.* The court's determination may be based on evidence already in the record, including any written plea agreement, ~~or;~~ and on any additional evidence or information submitted by the parties and accepted by the court as relevant and reliable. If ~~if~~ the forfeiture is contested, on either party's request the court must conduct a hearing ~~on evidence or information presented by the parties at a hearing~~ after the verdict or finding of guilt.

(2) *Preliminary Order.*

(A) *Contents.* If the court finds that property is subject to forfeiture, it must promptly enter a preliminary order of forfeiture setting forth the amount of any money judgment, ~~or~~ directing the forfeiture of specific property, and directing the forfeiture of any substitute assets if the government has met the statutory criteria, ~~without regard to any third party's interest in all or part of it.~~ The order must be entered without regard to any third party's interest in the property. Determining whether a third party has such an interest must be deferred until any third party files a claim in an ancillary proceeding under Rule 32.2(c).

(B) *Timing.* Unless doing so is impractical, the court must enter the preliminary order of forfeiture sufficiently in advance of sentencing to allow the parties to suggest revisions or modifications before the order becomes final as to the defendant under Rule 32.2(b)(4).

(C) *General Order.* If, before sentencing, the court cannot identify all the specific property subject to forfeiture or calculate the total amount of the money judgment, the court may enter a forfeiture order listing any identified property, describing other property in general terms, and stating that the order will be amended under Rule 32.2(e)(1) when additional specific property is identified or the amount of the money judgment has been calculated.

(3) *Seizing Property.* The entry of a preliminary order of forfeiture authorizes the Attorney General (or a designee) to seize the specific property subject to forfeiture; to conduct any discovery the court considers proper in identifying, locating, or disposing of the property; and to commence proceedings that comply with any statutes governing third party rights. ~~At sentencing—or at any time before sentencing if the defendant consents—the order of forfeiture becomes final as to the defendant and must be made a part of the sentence and be included in the judgment.~~ The court may include in the order of forfeiture conditions reasonably necessary to preserve the property's value pending any appeal.

(4) *Sentence and Judgment.*

(A) *When Final.* At sentencing—or at any time before sentencing if the defendant consents—the preliminary order of forfeiture becomes final as to the defendant. If the order directs the defendant to forfeit specific assets, it remains preliminary as to third parties until the ancillary proceeding is concluded under Rule 32.2 (c).

(B) *Notice and Inclusion in Judgment.* The district court must include the forfeiture when orally announcing the sentence or otherwise ensure that the defendant knows of the forfeiture at sentencing. The court must also include the order of forfeiture, directly or by reference, in the judgment, but the court's failure to do so may be corrected at any time under Rule 36.

(C) *Time for Appeal.* The time for a party to file an appeal from the order of forfeiture, or from the district court's failure to enter an order, begins to run when judgment is entered. If the court later amends or declines to amend an order of forfeiture to include an additional asset under Rule 32.2(e), a party may file an appeal regarding that asset under Federal Rule of Appellate Procedure 4(b). The time for that appeal runs from the date when the order granting or denying the amendment becomes final.

(~~4~~ 5) *Jury Determination.*

(A) *Retaining Jury.* ~~Upon a party's request in a case in which a jury returns a verdict of guilty, the jury must~~ In any case tried before a jury, if the indictment or information states that the government is seeking forfeiture, the court must determine before the jury begins deliberating whether either party requests that the jury be retained to determine the forfeitability of specific property if it returns a guilty verdict.

(B) *Special Verdict Form.* If a timely request to have the jury determine the forfeiture is made, the government must submit a proposed Special Verdict Form listing each asset subject to forfeiture and asking the jury to determine whether the government has established the requisite nexus between the property and the offense committed by the defendant.

(6) *Notice of the Order of Forfeiture.*

(A) *Publishing and Sending Notice.* If the court orders the forfeiture of specific property, the government must publish notice of the order and send notice to any person who reasonably appears to be a potential claimant with standing to contest the forfeiture in the ancillary proceeding.

(B) *Content of Notice.* The notice must describe the forfeited property, state the times under the applicable statute when a petition contesting the forfeiture must be filed, and state the name and contact information for the attorney for the government to be served with the petition.

(C) *Means of Publication.* Publication must take place as described in Supplemental Rule G(4)(a)(iii) of the Federal Rules of Civil Procedure, and may be by any means described in Supplemental Rule G(4)(a)(iv). Publication is unnecessary if any exception in Supplemental Rule G(4)(a)(i) applies.

(D) *Means of Sending Notice.* The notice may be sent in accordance with Supplemental Rule G(4)(b)(iii)-(v) of the Federal Rules of Civil Procedure.

(7) *Interlocutory Sale.* At any time before entry of a final order of forfeiture, the court may, in accordance with Supplemental Rule G(7) of the Federal Rules of Civil Procedure, order the interlocutory sale of property alleged to be forfeitable.

* * *

Rule 41. Search and Seizure

* * *

(e) Issuing the Warrant.

* * *

(2) *Contents of the Warrant.*

* * *

(B) *Warrant to Search for Electronically Stored Information.* A warrant may authorize the seizure of electronic storage media or the seizure or copying of electronically stored information. Unless otherwise specified, the warrant authorizes later review of the storage media or electronically stored information consistent with the warrant. The time for the executing the warrant in Rule 41(e) and (f) refers to the seizing or on-site copying of the storage media or electronically stored information, and not to any later review.

(BC) *Warrant for a Tracking Device.* A tracking-device warrant must identify the person or property to be tracked, designate the magistrate judge to whom it must be returned, and specify a reasonable length of time that the device may be used. The time must not exceed 45 days from the date the warrant was issued. The court may, for good cause, grant one or more extensions for a reasonable period not to exceed 45 days each. The warrant must command the officer to:

* * *

(f) Executing and Returning the Warrant.

(1) *Warrant to Search for and Seize a Person or Property.*

* * *

(B) *Inventory.* An officer present during the execution of the warrant must prepare and verify an inventory of any property seized. The officer must do so in the presence of another officer and the person from whom, or from whose premises, the property was taken. If either one is not present, the officer must prepare and verify the inventory in the presence of at least one other credible person. In a case involving the seizure of electronic storage media or the seizure or copying of electronically stored information, the inventory may be limited to a description of the physical storage media that was seized or copied. The officer may maintain a copy of the electronically stored information that was seized or copied.

* * *

†